BEST O

Who the Hell . . .?

BEST OF Q
Who the Hell . . .?

Tom Hibbert

For Lionel. For Prim.
For Alex 'Skip' Spence.

First published in Great Britain in 1994 by
Virgin Books
an imprint of Virgin Publishing Ltd
332 Ladbroke Grove
London W10 5AH

A catalogue record for this book is available from the
British Library

ISBN 0 86369 878 6

Phototypeset by Intype, London
Printed and bound in Great Britain by
Cox & Wyman Ltd, Reading, Berks

Contents

Contents

Illustrations

Except where otherwise indicated, all pictures are by Hugo Dixon

David Icke
Screamin' Lord Sutch
Sir Jimmy Savile
Status Quo
The Chippendales
Paul Gascoigne
Benny Hill
David Mellor
Mr Blobby
Rolf Harris
Ringo Starr
William Roache
Jeffrey Archer (*Ken Sharpe*)
Dennis Potter (*Paul Rider*)
Freddie Starr
Cliff Richard

Foreword

What unites them, the celebrities collected in this book? Are they universally adored? Are they recommended role models for all our children? Are they selfless pillars of the community deserving of our unswerving respect and admiration?

No, they are not. They are a monstrous regiment of pseuds, dullards and self-loving goons and any sane person should approach them only with extreme caution.

When the rock bible *Q* Magazine launched in the mid-'80s, its world view was fairly straightforward: irreverent affection and slack-cutting for the musical fraternity; rigorous scepticism towards their cousins in the wider media. The former were innocent until proved guilty, the latter guilty unless proven innocent.

This second category come from all points of the entertainment compass, from broadcasting, politics, sport, cinema, comedy, gastronomy, grand larceny and, just occasionally, rock'n'roll – deluded pop musicians who've drifted too far into the demeaning arena of Showbiz. Anyone lumbering into range with a slightly inflated view of their own worth, who's poked the old noddle a touch too high above the parapet, is considered ripe for a few rounds with Tom Hibbert. A prime editorial site is set aside and, once a month, some unsuspecting juggins is gently shepherded towards it, their PR having been advised, not untruthfully, that they are 'something of a cult figure with the readers', and that they are to be the focus of 'a three-page general profile'. Mr Hibbert limbers up with a fag and a light ale in the *Q* corner and there is an ominous tolling of the bell.

On rare occasions, the cornered victim will give a good account of themselves, always the most anarchic and truculent types in whom the author detects some sort of kindred spirit, and he will admit to rather liking them after all and advising us to do the same. But normally their fate is as good as sealed: an hour later – often mere minutes – his luckless sparring partner re-emerges, public image in severe disarray, career, one fondly imagines, in tatters.

The legendary 'Who The Hell ...?' series – so titled as each episode is headlined 'Who The Hell Does (Ringo Starr or whoever) Think He Is? – has now clocked up its first century, exactly 100 episodes, the most entertaining of which appear in the lavish compendium you hold before you. Together they paint an extraordinary picture of celebrity – ill-gotten, ill-used or simply gone-to-seed – from the absurd idiosyncrasies of the eternally famous (such as Chuck Berry or Jimmy Savile), the plaintive bleating of the briefly notorious (Edwina Currie, David Mellor), souls frozen forever in the controversy that suddenly shoved them centre stage, or simply the one-hit wonders (Mr Blobby or Eddie 'The Eagle' Edwards, buffoon of the ski slopes), creatures who rose without trace, somehow snagged the public imagination sufficiently to have their own agent, dominated the popular prints, and were just as swiftly buried forever in the stampede to find their sales-generating replacement.

But what of the author himself, a figure still nobly upholding the scuffed romantic traditions of green-visor journalism, hunched over a battered word-processor, cigarette clamped between teeth, a tumbler of electric soup conveniently to hand? He is careful to reveal very little of himself in his writing, though the serious 'Who The Hell ...?' student will by now have constructed some sort of composite portrait of the man. Compared to The Chippendales, for example, Hibbert is 'pallid, unshaven, shrivelled, eight stone' and the proud possessor of 'crumby teeth'. In the view of then-Health Minister Edwina Currie, his colossal smoking habit guarantees 'a low sperm count'.

As for his interviewing technique, the bedside manner that can turn even the most circumspect of subjects tearfully confessional, we can but hazard a guess. I can only offer one insight, via a member of that regretful assembly of souls, People Who Have Been Interviewed By Him. Ten years ago Tom worked at *Smash Hits* magazine alongside Neil Tennant, now of the vastly successful Pet

Shop Boys. It was an almost supernaturally chipper Tennant who dropped by the office mere weeks after quitting the job and mere minutes after hearing he'd just achieved a life-long ambition: his single 'West End Girls' had rocketed to the top of the UK singles chart. His confidence was armour-plated, his *joie de vivre* could be measured in gallons.

And then the interview began. Tom employed what must be one of an entire arsenal of interrogatory devices, The Siege Tactic (he is utterly unembarrassed by silence, which his wrong-footed interviewee will then inadvisedly fill). 'So, Neil . . .' he began. 'Number 1 . . .' He gave a hollow laugh and arched a quizzical eyebrow, clearly suggestive of pathetic underachievement. Neil flinched, quickly downplayed his success, panicked a little, *apologised* in fact, embarked upon a monologue about the essentially facile nature of pop music as a medium, said 'disposable' and 'ephemeral' a lot, panicked some more, promised to get a proper job, blushed, muttered something about charity work, began sweating profusely, ventured that perhaps it was all a desperate bid for attention triggered by some childhood trauma, mumbled, dithered, more mumbling, sense of invincibility shattered, depression, self-hatred, despair . . .

Tom sat silently in the corner sucking on a Marlboro, a delighted eye upon his ever-rolling tape machine.

Beyond that, and despite having been his editor on the first 50 of these outings, I have no idea how he does it. His fearless investigative journalism revealed, for example, that Rolf Harris's Stylophone recordings were the result of some sinister payola scandal. And it requires extraordinary confidence to remind Jeffrey Archer of his alleged encounter with a call girl, or inform Jeremy Beadle that his television programme is 'appalling rubbish', or tell Dennis Potter to 'fuck off', or call David Icke 'a loony', or wonder aloud how it's funny Cliff Richard never married. And it's almost unimaginable to ask Jimmy Savile if he has a fascination with dead bodies.

But he is that rare breed of writer who has no interest in befriending his subjects. His loyalty has always remained with his readers. He refuses to comply with the publicity machine, opting instead to tell you everything you always wanted to know about the person in question but were afraid to ask, or simply supply enough rope for a public self-execution.

The appeal of his 'Who The Hell . . .?' series is eternal and, perhaps, quaintly British. Unlike the Americans, we are famously impatient with our celebrities and have firm views as to the boundaries of decent human behaviour. These people have let us down, we gripe, but just wait till Judgement Day.

There is a delicious thrill in reading this book. We take up our seats, like Parisian fishwives knitting at the foot of the guillotine, and we await the arrival of another hapless clot fairly tried for their crimes against humanity. And we note, beside them, the spectral figure of Hibbert, lever in hand. And we hoot with glee as their head thuds into the basket. And we delight loudly in the notion of Justice Being Done. And we hear, somewhere deep inside of us, the sound of a giddy cabaret lurching ever onward, and a cackling voice barking a one-word refrain. Next, it cries, NEEEEEXT!

'Who The Hell . . .?' is a fine tradition. Here's to the second century.

Mark Ellen, founding editor of Q Magazine

Introduction

had flown to Paris's Charles de Gaulle airport, clambered upon a coach transferring me to Orly, taken another flight to Avignon and attempted, in my wonky schoolboy French, to explain to a taxi driver what my mission was. 'Je dois suivre les éléphants.' The driver looked at me with disdain. I showed him money. Off we went, fleet-wheeled down the roads in pursuit of a Great English Sportsperson engaged upon a Great Charity Trek featuring pachyderms in imitation of Hannibal. Said sportsperson's agent had already 'okayed' an interview, so everything would be alright, wouldn't it?

Of course it bloody wouldn't. The driver – who thought me quite bonkers ('Les Anglais, ooh-la-la, fou,' or something) – caught up with the parade of Mr B— (fill in name of Great English Sportsperson, for it was he); I leapt out and scuttled up, puffing past the elephants, to the one in question. 'Excuse me Mr B—,' I wheezed, 'my name is Tom Hibbert from Q Magazine. You have agreed to an interview.' The burly one did not so much as cast a glance in my direction. His arms swung causing static electrical storms in his man-made-fibre tracksuit as he strode sturdily down the highway surrounded by his sycophantic minions. 'From the press, are you?' he grunted, as I trotted along, pathetically trying to keep up the pace. 'Yes, Q magazine, pant, pant,' went I. 'You're all the same, aren't you, you fucking journalists?' he gruffed. 'You can fuck off.'

And so I did.

No, it was never a piece of cake doing a 'Who The Hell . . .?'

interview. From the start, it was a jungle out there. In 1986 Britain was awash with celebrities like never before, under threat from the famous only famous for being famous, the famously awful, turning the soul of a once-brave country to mush. My eight-year mission? To confront, to take them down a peg if possible, armed only with a packet of cigarettes and a tape recorder. Quite miserably, of course, I failed. There's a lot of tosh talked about the 'power' of the press. The printed word, in a modest circulation magazine, can hope to do little more than entertain. Whereas gits on the telly, before gawping millions, can wreak havoc, and it's not really fair.

Many of the media-craving scamps taken to task in this collection would go on to even greater success. Look at Jeffrey Archer. Shortly after the interview contained here, he won his libel case, was awarded massive damages (the judge, you remember, simply could not believe that the esteemed novelist would ever require 'rubber-insulated sex' when he had such a 'fragrant' wife). Archer was elevated later to the peerage. 'Lord Archer'. Jolly good show. Or look at Julie Burchill (sorry, Jules, couldn't fit you in), now the greatest shopping'n'fucking novelist in the business and possibly the richest woman on earth if you don't count Jackie O, who's dead anyway . . . (Actually, when I met Julie Burchill I could have fallen in love with her, she seemed so sound and sensible. This happens sometimes – you enter the interview zone with marked prejudice, you come out converted – but not very often . . . These people usually made me feel bloody sick. Dennis Potter didn't. Yoko Ono certainly did. And as for Chuck Berry, I don't *care* if he once wrote quite a good song or two, the man is a cad and a rotter.)

Sometimes a 'Who The Hell . . .?' interview would go horribly wrong. There was Robert Maxwell – the piece is not included here (and neither, naturally, is the Mr B— one) because the piece was never written. For three hours I waited in the outer sanctum for an audience with the gargantuan crook (an audience he had agreed to some weeks earlier) and then, summoned into his expansive office at the *Daily Mirror*, he threw me out within 90 seconds, booming 'I'm far too busy to talk to you! I am at WAR!!!' (At war with whom? At war with what? With his conscience?) More often, these meetings went horribly right, public figure blurting nonsense and revealing themselves to be even more absurd than one had previously imagined.

Sometimes, in my cups or elsewhere, I try to fool myself into believing that I played some small part in the downfall of the interviewees whose careers hit the buffers, who went a-slithering down the dumper quicker than you can say 'tra-la-la' or 'ha-ha', or something. I congratulate myself on the death of Maxwell – the curse of 'Who The Hell . . .?' – knowing full well that the demise of the bellowing tree frog had nothing at all to do with me. Benny Hill, presumed 'funny' man, died shortly after our meeting; he was found in his Teddington flat amongst piles of bank notes and uncashed cheques, apparently. Albert Goldman, 'shock' biographer, passed away on an aeroplane in 1994; he was cremated in England and his ashes sent back to America by Federal Express. A fitting end for the maestro of 'Gothic'-styled character-assassination, when you think of it. The curse of 'Who The Hell . . .?' I fear not. It was the spectre of Jim Morrison (the latest dead pop star that Goldman was about to be horrible about for pots of money) that did for Albert, if you ask me. Probably. As for Dennis Potter, one of the other deceased talkers featured here, well, anyone who can christen the cancer that polished him off 'Rupert', after Rupert Murdoch, is alright by me.

No attempt has been made here to rework these pieces, to bring them up to date. They appear in their original form, as trivial little bits-on-sticks of history. You will peruse them, perhaps, and think to yourself Whatever The Hell Happened To . . .?

Edwina Currie? She 'resigned' from Mrs Thatcher's government just *days* after the interview included here, having told everyone in Britain that eating eggs was a guarantee of instant death. But she is still among us, more's the pity, writing terrible 'blockbuster' novels about MPs having sex, and popping up on the telly as an amusing prop ever so often. God bless her.

Samantha Fox? She no longer appears 'unplugged' in our super soaraway 'news'papers but she continues to have silly bosoms and is a huge 'singing' phenomenon in the less discerning countries of Europe, i.e. Japan. I don't know what happened to her monkey.

Jeremy Beadle? Went from strength to strength in the 'aren't-common-little-people-a-treat-when-they're-on-the-telly?' stakes with *You've Been Framed*, a telly show featuring home videos of persons who fall off bicycles and bump their heads on lumps of concrete, which is always very amusing.

Bros? Broke up. Hurrah!

Nigel Kennedy? Went mad. Decided he was Jimi Hendrix.

Eddie 'The Eagle' Edwards? Went bankrupt. Decided he was David Mellor.

Tony Blackburn? Gary Glitter? Michael Winner? No change.

The Chippendales? Do you know, 'ladies'? Who bloody cares?

We used to have much sport in the Q office deciding upon who would be the next target for a 'Who The Hell . . .?' feature. Who The Hell Does KLAUS BARBIE Think He Is? That was one suggestion. Who The Hell Does THE POPE Think He Is?, another, Who The Hell Does TED BUNDY Think He Is? Who The Hell Does MOTHER TERESA Think She Is? Or Prince Johnson of Liberia? Dan Quayle, General Noriega, Bush, Ronald 'Mad Dog McDonald' Reagan, Saddam Hussein, Bastards, Robert Maxwell . . . oh, sorry, we did him but it was less than satisfactory . . .

We never got to these people. We never tried, but it doesn't matter one jot because – allow me to be a trifle pompous for a moment – it's the second division players included here, your snooker players, your TV nonentity, your guys'n'gals of the fatuous 'sound-bites', that tell us most about Britain during the period these interviews cover. I'm burying a copy of this book in a time capsule thingie (as seen on *Blue Peter*) in my back garden (except I haven't got a back garden, so the local park will have to do), and 100 years from now some person will dig it up and . . . that person will be Lord Cliff Richard. 'Crumbs!' he will say, 'I always thought Jerry Lee Lewis was rather a suspicious character. If only he had learned to "swing" like me!' . . .

There we have it.

This is an *English* book. God save Postman Pat, vaudeville and variety . . .

I hope you get more pleasure in reading these things than I had in writing them. It really was *hell* . . .

Tom Hibbert
Fulham, June 1994

Acknowledgements

Bloody boring Oscar-styled speech and nobody will read this bit but . . . thankyou: Mark Ellen, Paul Du Noyer, Danny so-called Kelly, Mal Peachey, David Hepworth, Phil Webb, Adrian Deevoy, all the little people who made this possible and my wife and Malcolm Marshall, Juggins, Doug, Tony. Anne? Anne? Can you get a fix on Tony? . . . I think that's enough 'acknowledgements', don't you?

Jeffrey Archer

Rich men in the corridors of power. Women of great beauty. Race tracks and gaming tables. Cricket, politics, the suggestion of sex. Never mind the quality, look at the sales figures. Never mind the scandals, the Parliamentary disgrace, the wrath of the righteous – when he takes to the streets, his public wave, they clap, they ask for his autograph.

J EFFREY ARCHER leans back in his comfortable contemporary armchair, toys with a brass button on his double-breasted blazer – the dark blue jacket of the yachting club rake – and gazes through the glass walls of his tenth floor Thameside luxury apartment; across the water, the Houses of Parliament. 'I love politics,' he says. 'I don't know what *you* love, but politics is like a drug. Oh, of course I could be on my own island in the West Indies with lots of Pina Coladas. I have more money than I need. But politics, I just love it. *Love* it . . .'

Twice the Conservative adventurer has fallen from political grace but still he returns for another hit of his chosen drug. 'I've bounced back before and I'll do it again,' he says in a hard staccato voice that makes the statement sound like some awesome threat.

In 1974, ill-considered investments left Jeffrey Archer steeped in debt and promoted his resignation from the House. It was the honourable thing to do. He bounced back. By the '80s he had paid back his creditors and made a fortune for himself through his 'gift' for 'storytelling'. Archer, herald of free enterprise, had become a moneyed popular novelist. In March 1985 he was appointed Deputy Chairman of the Conservative Party. In October 1986 the News Of The World splashed the famous Archer And The Call Girl scandal. Once more he resigned. It was the honourable thing to do.

But Jeffrey Archer will not go away; still he hangs on as a 'private supporter', rallying the Tory troops with jaunty sloganeering in vulgarian 'Kiss Me Quick' hats in marginal seats, on breakfast TV sofas, oozing cheap talk of booming economies and shares for all. He's not being paid, so he must be doing it from the heart – with hopes, presumably, of higher office.

He doesn't *need* paying; one glance around this lofty town flat – opulent, spacious, bright and charmless, conservatively dotted with thoughtfully-placed executive-style objets d'art, forbiddingly polished, fanatically neat – will tell you that. But express any surprise at his disinclination to take the best-selling novelist's shilling and run to tax exile and the life of Reilly, and Archer will fix you with his quizzical 'it's-a-matter-of-honour' glare and say: 'After I resigned as Deputy Chairman, I had on the books 130 invitations to speak between January and October, and you either write and say, Well, look, I'm off to a desert island and I'm going to have a good time and sit in the sun with Pina Coladas and call it a day, or you say, I'll be there, I won't let you down. Now cynics would not understand that but that's the way I am.' And then he'll lean back once more and smile a smile that cynics might describe as 'smug'; his eyes will half-close, his substantial cheeks will puff out and he will resemble a mischievous, almost malevolent, chipmunk.

Jeffrey Archer was *born* a Conservative. His father was a soldier, his mother a housewife and sometime local councillor in Weston Super Mare. Asked to speak of his childhood, Archer rattles out an abrupt, shorthand account as if keen to hasten on to wider debate: 'Upbringing? Nothing special. Very middle class. Went to a little school in Somerset. Wellington. Nice middle class school. Went to Oxford. Brasenose. Read Education. Wanted to teach. Oxford sort of widened my horizons. Made me more interested in other things. Got interested in politics. Fascinated by it.'

After Oxford, Archer settled in London, founded a successful public relations firm and stood for the GLC, to which he was duly elected. Three years later, in 1969, he entered Parliament as the Rt. Hon. Member for Louth. At 29 he was the youngest member in the House. 'My maiden speech was about finance, the economy and my belief in free market enterprise. I didn't make much of an impression but everybody who enters the House of Commons as its youngest member wants to be Prime Minister. But the chances of being Prime Minister are one in 650 and many outstanding men who are worthy of being Prime Minister don't make it.'

Jeffrey Archer didn't make it (yet?) because he invested 'very foolishly' in a Canadian company which crashed in 1974 and 'I lost overnight about £427,000. So I was in debt. It certainly wasn't going to do the party any good to have someone who was in debt to the tune of £427,000 trying to conduct the normal life of a Member of Parliament, so the honourable thing to do was to go and go quickly and try and pay my debts off.'

He sold the PR firm and, whilst looking for 'what my wife called a real job that earned money on a weekly basis', began to write a novel, Not A Penny More, Not A Penny Less. He'd never written a word in his life before, had no idea that he *could* write, but nonetheless popped down to W. H. Smith, bought some paper and some Tempo pens and wrote. Why?

'Why? Because I was on the *ground*.' Archer thrusts his arms out, palms turned upwards in a gesture of helplessness. '*Flat* on the ground.' It's all so obvious, he seems to be saying: if you're on your uppers, write a popular novel. 'I felt that the story was not a bad story and perhaps it would succeed. It took nine months and it was a nightmare. I've yet to meet a writer who enjoys the process. It is . . . agony! It's very, very hard work. I hand write every word and I do ten drafts, and when you do ten drafts of every book hand written . . .? *Hard* work. Water torture. *Ag-on-y!*'

Agony, however, would turn to ecstasy. '*Jorg, expect $7 million from Credit Parisien in the No. 2 account by 6 pm tonight, Central European Time, and place it with first-class banks and triple "A" commercial names. Otherwise, invest it in the overnight Euro-dollar market. Understood*?' must surely rank as one of the less absorbing opening paragraphs of a novel of our time, but Not A Penny More, Not A Penny Less sold healthily enough for Archer to embark on another. And another. Shall We Tell The President? and A Quiver Full Of Arrows (a collection of short stories). Kane and Abel, published in 1980, saw an end to his debts and 'I remember the day that I got rid of the Mini and bought a BMW. I remember that day vividly. And it was seven years and three months almost to the day of my resignation. I felt a vivid triumph. I had become extremely successful – by accident, not by design.'

Rich men and richer men in the corridors of corporate power. Women of great beauty. Race tracks and gaming tables. Money piled upon money. Smatterings of cricket and ample portions of politics. Sex beckoning from the sidelines but never smearing the page (à la Jackie Collins). Such are the ingredients of the Jeffrey Archer novel – fare for travellers and a 'jolly good read'. The high literary world may scorn these soapy narratives but it's Archer – hearing the latest sales figures over his cordless telephone – who will have the last laughs.

'I don't *pretend* to be a great writer. I'm not going to get the Nobel Prize and when the list comes out each year I don't rush to the papers to see if I've been considered. I know my limitations and I want to be read. That's the *point* of writing. I think that's a very honourable thing and not many people do it.'

Archer has little regard for those whose writings do not sell.

'I hate stories where I hear authors who've sold 50,000 copies then 40,000, then 30,000 and then they don't even get in the bestsellers list. And then they have to talk about the book they wrote ten years ago. It's tragic when you meet an author who says, I wrote Gone With The Wind. It's *tragic*. My stories are *dreadfully* simple. You can tell them all in three sentences. You can say Kane and Abel is the story of two men both born on the same day, one with nothing, one with everything. They meet once. That's the story. Not A Penny More, Not A Penny Less is the story of four men who between them lose a fortune. They find out who stole it from them and they steal it back. That's it. Prodigal Daughter . . .'

Archer proceeds to encapsulate the plot of each of his novels at a rattling pace. This, one takes it, is a form of modesty, though one could say, for example, that Hamlet is the story of a man who's a bit upset about his father's death and frets a bit or that Moby Dick is the story of a man who tries to kill a whale and drowns.

All stories are simple. Archer is happy to keep them that way without turning them into high literature. He doesn't pretend to be a great writer, he says, nor does he seem to be much of a reader. Though the shelves of his penthouse are filled with books, the rows of spines are flush – and almost every volume is an Archer: Jeffrey Archer first editions. Jeffrey Archer foreign editions. Jeffrey Archer gift editions in lovingly-tooled leather. On the expansive glass-topped coffee-table before us there are more books – art books, ceramics books, historical print books, 'over-sized' books (as the libraries call them), coffee-table books (as we do) – piled high but trimly stacked, unthumbed, seemingly unread. I ask him. Do you read?

'I'm a *big* reader. But I wouldn't say necessarily of novels. I read every national newspaper every day. I'm a great reader of the newspapers. And I'll read things like the Turner book which has just been given to me.' He picks up from the table the Turner book – a book with colour plates, Turner the painter. 'I've already read that and I've only had it two days. That sort of book fascinates me.'

Jeffrey Archer, squatting amongst his riches, appears proud to remain a low-brow individual. Ask him if he has pretensions to higher artistic achievement and he will snap 'No', as if the very suggestion were an insult, a slap in the face.

But is Jeffrey Archer satisfied with what he is? If he were, would he not have dozed on his laurels, continuing to feed the public with what he is pleased to call his 'yarns' rather than choosing to re-enter the political fray, for no financial reward, as Deputy Chairman of the Conservative Party?

'You say, What on earth induced you to return to politics? Well, I'll tell you. Nutcases return. I'd be off tomorrow if I didn't love this country, but I do. I'm basically a Somerset nutter. A British nutter. There's no need for me to stay here but I *am* a nutter. God, I love it.

Jeffrey Archer, as you will have gathered, is a 'nutter'. But his Deputy Chairmanship of the party – during which he managed to put his foot in it with ill-advised utterances about unemployment which made even Norman Tebbit's on-yer-bike statements seem benign – was short-lived. The News Of The World saw to that with its call girl story and Archer hit mud once again.

'That was very interesting,' he says with no signs of embarrassment. Just a spent sigh of resignation. 'I always knew I hadn't met the girl. That wasn't the problem. The problem was sending the money to get rid of her. That was stupidity. If I had met the girl, of course, I'd have been in real trouble, but everybody knows that I didn't meet the girl. When I say everybody knows that I didn't meet the girl, I think *most* people know now that I wasn't there that night or anywhere near there that night. And I'm not sure you can print that, by the way. Because it could get you into court. I wouldn't like to see you in court.'

So if Jeffrey Archer was so innocent of sexual misdemeanour, as he evidently was, why did he feel bound to resign?

'There are two sides to that. One is you say, Look, I'm totally innocent and I'm going to stay, to which the next day's headline is, Is Norman Tebbit Avoiding Him In The Corridors? and this goes on until finally you say, Oh, Christ, I'm going to go. The best thing, though, is to resign quickly, clear your name and return. That's the most honourable thing. People who hang on harm the party and the party must come first.'

The Party must come first, and on the lawn of their Cambridge country house, the Archers, Jeffrey and wife Mary, did their utmost in the aftermath of the scandal – Mary serving tea on trays to the Fleet Street hordes trampling her herbaceous borders whilst Jeffrey was pleased to emerge from the French windows with a courteous 'no comment'.

'I think what's sad about journalists is, I remember when they were stuck outside my house after my resignation from Deputy Chairman, and I said to my wife, You know, they look rather a nice lot. And it's so unfair that two or three evil people can bring down a whole profession. It's ridiculous. But, in fact, the amount of letters I received from journalists apologising for their profession was staggering.'

So journalism is, in the main, according to Jeffrey Archer, an honourable profession. But the Wapping sharks had not quite finished with Jeffrey Archer yet. Once the call girl libel suit has been delivered comes another allegation – that Jeffrey Archer, What's My Line? panellist, is a cheat – a man 'who likes to look clever' and so wants the answers to this cheap, philistine game show in advance. Is this true?

'It's not worth discussing,' says Archer with glowering brow. 'I wouldn't be willing to say anything and I'd hate to have to sue you, Tom.'

And so we move swiftly on. To why, precisely, Jeffrey Archer, best-selling novelist and carrier of the Conservative baton, feels the need to slink into the public eye with appearances on game shows, chat shows, public affairs shows and any other shows that are going. Why? Duty.

'It's my duty, as I see it. And I think that's part of the deal. If you sell two and a half million copies of each book you're not exactly public property, but if you go into politics you are. And if you dare to combine the both, it becomes part of the deal. I've never had any abuse in my life. You just come walking around the streets and see the reaction I get. Spend the day with me. You'll find out. They wave and they clap and they come up for my autograph . . .'

No abuse *ever*?

'Never. *Never.* You can get very depressed about what the press writes about you but the public are marvellous. And when I get depressed about the press, well, you should see what the Prime Minister goes through in any one week. You can have a Falklands, you can have a Westland, you can have an American raid on Libya. In each case the Prime Minister will go through six weeks of vitriol on the front page of every paper. But let me tell you this. Has Gaddafi retaliated for the raid on Libya? Has he? No! He has *not* retaliated. Gaddafi's reputation has gone down. Gaddafi's power has gone down as well. So Margaret Thatcher made the right decision. It was a brave decision. And it was the *right* decision.'

We're leading up to an election (though the election's all over as you read this) so Jeffrey Archer wants to talk politics. In his 1984 book First Among Equals, a quasi-fictional account of 30 years of parliamentary politics in which, despite the obligatory novel rider 'the characters and situations in this book are entirely imaginary and bear no relation to any real person or actual happening', Margaret Thatcher, Neil Kinnock, Roy Hattersley, Cecil Parkinson, Michael Meacher and other non-imaginary characters rub shoulders with those of Archer fabrication (and in which – oh towering irony – '. . . Mrs Thatcher was not helped in her cause by the election of Gary Hart to the White House in November 1988 . . .'), Jeffrey Archer predicted a June 1987 election and a victory for the Conservative party under the leadership of Thatcher. Pre-election fervour has him drumming the tub: 'I don't believe the Labour Party can win again,' he says, throwing back his eyebrows as if it were a crying matter. 'I think they are finished. The very word Labour is a disadvantage. It's not a modern word. SDP, funnily enough, *is* a modern word and Liberal is acceptable. It is a *dictionary* word and thus acceptable. Conservative? Well, that's what we are. We always have been and we always will be. But Labour has a ring of the 1930s, Jarrow marches, people dying in the streets because they're underfed. And that's just not convincing these days.'

He wants to continue but I interrupt by asking him if – outside politics and writing – he has any achievement yet to fulfil. He shrugs and turns it into a joke. Jeffrey Archer, athlete of yesteryear ('He represented Oxford, Somerset and Great Britain in the 100 metres', the potted biographies in his novels proclaim) wants to captain the Somerset cricket team, the England cricket team and beat the Australians at Lord's. 'But the chances are not high. At my age and with my average which last year was 2,486, I think, or 2,487, I think my chances are not high. I went to see Mr Cowdrey at the MCC but he'd never heard of me, which is a minor disadvantage. But I know I'm a rabbit and I love it. Love the game. Love it. I'm a nutter for the game. And though I joke about it, you know, I *love* to win.'

At cricket?

'At cricket. At cricket and everything. I don't feel like a loser. I am *not* a loser.'

Samantha Fox

She's top of the heap in the bosom business, the Forces' Favourite on a lucrative mission to 'cheer up' the oppressed occupants of the public bars of Britain. She's got her standards, mind – 'I don't do no porn.' And when you've gone professional, with a singing career propelled by a father what's creative, you don't take kindly to righteous inquisition about your moral code from people.

SAMANTHA FOX squats on a chair in the reception area of her record company's offices and prepares to pose for the Q magazine photographer.

'Ooh, it's David Bailey over there, innit?' she coos, putting on her cheery public face. She says 'cheese' for the camera and she says 'sex' for the camera and when she says 'sex' she giggles the giggle of a playground tot saying 'knickers'. And then she turns on me. 'Ere, I've seen you before, ain't I? You've interviewed me before, ain't yer?' I have. 'You said I was four foot eleven and I'm five foot one.' She seems somewhat aggrieved at this gross piece of misrepresentation.

The previous interview took place just over a year ago. Back then Samantha Fox had yet to make the transformation from Page 3 'bird' to pop star. She was about to release her single, Touch Me (I Want Your Body), and the business of singing was a diversion, a skylark, nothing more. But today, cast a glance around the walls of the record company and you'll see row upon row of framed golden copies of Touch Me – the 3-million-selling album and 1.5-million single – awarded for sales in Norway, in Australia, in Sweden, in Canada . . .

'I've got about sixteen gold and five platinum so far,' pipes Samantha, 'and I just gone gold in America. I got a gay following in America; they wear T-shirts with me on their T-shirts and they go really mad. It's nice to appeal to everyone, innit?'

We are here at Jive Records in the heart of Willesden, Samantha Fox and me, to talk about her new LP, Sam Fox. Ostensibly. If we were *not* here to talk about her new LP, if this were not a Fox promotion, Q magazine would have to *pay* for the privilege of talking to her. Pat Fox, the topless-model-cum-singer's father/manager charges the media a tidy sum for an audience with his cheerful daughter. And more often than not the media are happy to pay. The Fox face is an easy selling point. But the Q interview is for free – 'Oh, yeah, I seen Q in the office. It's like a ... it's got everything in it sort of thing, ain't it? Oh, I get all the magazines 'cos of the job I'm in and my favourite is Q but I'm only joking ain't I, 'cos God I like all them teenage magazines like Smash Hits and Mizz and Just Seventeen the best but at the moment I'm really into interior design books 'cos I bought a house . . .'

And so we start off by talking about the new LP. When Samantha Fox talks, she *talks*. The cheery Cockney banter – distinguished by sentences they seldom end, riddled with squeaks and *non sequiturs* – flows, pauseless and confident. If Samantha's comfortable with the question, the answer pops out of a chatterbox . . .

'It was great with this album 'cos with the first one it was alright and everything but this one's I learnt a lot about my voice more than I ever did 'cos I didn't think I had the range like I did have and there was notes I was getting what I could never before like on the cover of Satisfaction it goes down really low and in the choruses it goes really high so it's quite a weird song to sing. It was my dad's idea to do Satisfaction, well, because he was a big Stones fan and I was more or less brought up with the Stones in me earholes 'cos all through me childhood there used to be the Stones playing and Sergeant Pepper's albums and that was all me dad was into and he suggested doing Satisfaction so I listened to the original and I thought we can't really do it the same 'cos it's Mick Jagger's baby and he probably won't like it 'cos the original was always going to be the classic wasn't it and it's really good so I thought it's got to be totally different so we do it in a very Eighties way.'

By 'Eighties' she refers to the ubiquitous drum crash and text-book guitar and synthesiser treatments which have come to characterise that most translatable of modern musical phenomena, the Euro-Rock act. We move on to her influences and Samantha never draws breath . . .

'My musical upbringing was Seventies really, wasn't it? It was

Gary Glitter and everybody and Suzi Quatro and The Osmonds and Cat Stevens and that and I can remember buying January by them Pilot whatsit and I remember buying Donna Summer stuff a lot and I buyed Puppy Love when I was about five I think and I used to go roller-skating on a Sunday and it was always playing up Ally Pally and it was like going to the country 'cos I used to live in the Holloway Road and we used to take a flask of sandwiches and it was like going on this big day trip and it was like Puppy Love used to be playing and we used to skate around going oooh, Donny Osmond, hahaha, and oooh Bay City Rollers, of course. God, I used to have tartan trousers and everything and a pair of white plimsolls with Bay City Rollers written on them and tartan socks and when I got older I went to UK Subs and Stranglers I can remember and Three Degrees once with me mum and I loved the UK Subs and I used to like The Clash because I had a punk boyfriend and I suppose I didn't have much choice 'cos every time I went round his house he'd play Sham 69 and he used to take me to all them concerts with people pogoing and gobbing everywhere and I used to stand there dodging the gobs 'cos it was disgusting and it wasn't really me, I don't think.'

Samantha Fox, tiny, blonde, naive and artless, was born in 1966, brought up in London and educated at a Catholic school. She was just 16 when, encouraged by her parents, she entered the Sunday People's 'Face and Shape of '83' glamour girl contest and so got her figure on the People cover and then a two year 'modelling' contract with the Sun.

'I didn't even think about it 'cos at the time all me girlfriends were leaving school and me two best girlfriends got pregnant and *had* to leave school and it was a pretty sad case and lots of kids wasn't getting jobs and that and I just saw a great opportunity and just took it really and went into it very professionally 'cos it's the sort of thing you dream about as a kid and when it happens to you it's quite a weird feeling not only for you but for your nan and grandad and your mum and dad and me little sister Nessie and everyone. It was quite a big change in my family 'cos it had never happened before but I think I was really made to do it 'cos I wasn't put on this earth to sit on a typewriter doing letters and stuff and me mum and dad knew I could handle it 'cos a lot of people used to say to them don't you think she's a bit young and me mum always she'd say I was a lot older than I really was.'

As 'our' Sam, 'sizzling' Sam, saucy Sam, hugging Twingo Bingo cards to her chest, beaming in frillies from Page 3, Samantha Fox became famous. Never was a girl so well-known just for taking her clothes off (and not even *all* her clothes – just her top: 'I don't do no porn'). She was the sweetheart of the factory floor, a working-class girl whose pertly smiling face and ample bosoms winked down from calendars in canteens and garage backrooms across a nation. She replaced Dolly Parton (who had replaced Raquel Welch) as the subject of unfunny big melon jokes cracked by populist comics in working clubs and on vulgar game shows. She was cheap celebrity, caught in casual embrace with the almost famous in flitsy nightclubs and Stringfellows. The amount of cash being generated by her personal and tabloid appearances was sufficient for her to consider buying a house next door to the Prime Minster in Dulwich. She had her reasons for backing out, of course. 'The garden was too small. It weren't worth the money.'

And she did more to sell Rupert Murdoch's newspaper than the bumper Bingo wars ever did. The Sun would use their bright and trite Fox ammunition at every opportunity. On one notorious occasion, when the printers were still laying siege to fortress Wapping, she was driven in a tank through the picket lines for a cheeky front page splash. An affront, some might say, but Samantha puts it down to just 'a bit of fun'.

'I did that thing at Wapping going in the tank thing for a bit of fun 'cos they were all standing out there and freezing cold these pickets and I signed them all autographs to cheer them up and it was great. I ain't got regrets. I don't care about that. I've always been a freelancer, as they say, but I suppose they all got their point of views.'

The Sun as ideologically unsound organ draws little comment from Samantha.

'I don't want to get involved,' she says almost snappily. 'I know what the press are like, see, and the best thing to do is win them over so I got out there and put a smile on me face so I've got a great rapport with them. I don't do a Madonna and walk away and say no photographs 'cos they'd hate me for that and try and get sneaky pictures but they're alright really and I do a lot of the Sun commercials these days and things like that. I did one for the Bingo and they had the Hunchback of Notre Dame I think it was and I was Esmerelda which was quite fun. That's all it is with the newspapers – it's just a bit of fun.'

But the tabloids can go a little too far on occasion even for Samantha Fox's hard-nosed tastes:

'Yeah, sometimes it's a bit much what they say in them papers like I was in Montreux when there was all that thing about The Beastie Boys and the children and it was rubbish that story. It was in the Mirror that rubbish story so I phoned the Sun up and said it was a load of rubbish and they were going to do something the next day about what a lot of rubbish it was and they didn't. It's really sad. I wish they did. 'Cos a lot of kids didn't even know they'd got leukaemia and they read them newspapers and it's just shoved in their face. It's not very nice at all. But it don't do no harm usually and The Beastie Boys don't mind 'cos they're the next Frankie Goes To Hollywood, ain't they, 'cos they spit beer on people and in this day and age you got to be careful who you spit on, ain't yer? I think that's disgusting, I really do. But they were complaining about them using a 25 foot plastic penis in their stage act and Jonathan King said now what harm can a 25 foot rubber penis do anyone dear, he said.' Miss Fox wrinkles her nose and emits one of her naughty 'knickers' giggles. 'It's true, innit?' and there's our newspapers-and-morality 'debate' at an end.

I try Samantha on the subject of politics and she has some perceptive points to make about tomorrow's General Election (it's June 10).

'It's so boring innit seeing all these politicians with little kids trying to pretend they're really like nice people pretending they do it every day of the week wiping babies' snotty noses and stuff and there's Maggie in Venice with Reagan . . .'

Are you voting?

'Yeah. It's me first year of voting and don't you ask me as well what I'm voting 'cos I've had enough of it with every paper in the land asking me even in Norway and I won't tell anybody 'cos I think it's private. Politics should be kept to yourself if you're not a politician. I'm not telling yer. I'm not telling. I support me legs because my legs support me. There you go. I ain't telling. It's secret . . .'

We move swiftly on to talk of feminism, but before I've even completed the fourth syllable, Miss Fox's face turns stern and cold. 'I don't want to talk about that because I think it's really boring,' she says. She snatches a Silk Cut from the packet in her lap, lights up and exhales crossly. This topic, one feels, is closed. But she must have *some* thoughts about it, I press. Does it not get her goat when feminists accuse her of degrading her sex, or aiding and abetting rape, etc, etc?

Samantha Fox casts me a darting look. 'I don't think about feminists unless an interviewer asks me.' Well, an interviewer *has* asked you. 'Well I don't react to them feminists. I don't really bother. I don't really care about other people, what their views are. As long as I'm happy and my family are happy. I'm a girl next door done well, so to speak, and I keep my views to myself else I'd get in deep waters. I've got a lot of views what they got but I don't shout them out 'cos they're right in a lot of things they believe in but obviously I don't believe in banning Page 3 'cos I did it and I worked hard and I'm proud of it although I like a lot of their views . . .'

Samantha Fox is chatting forty to the dozen once more, clasping the issue in hand and meandering wildly as she does so . . .

'It's like people knock me saying I've used Page 3 to get records but I never 'cos a lot of people have used topless pictures to get the money to get into a career but whatever you're tops in people is trying to bring you down and that's my philosophy 'cos some singers have been plumbers before so what's the difference? And there are girls in modelling who have been *exploited* as your feminists would say but that's because they haven't got a brain and that's where this whole thing comes from, dumb blondes and everything. You got to be clear. You haven't got to have millions of O levels but you've got to be streetwise and got loads of common sense and know when someone's ripping you off. And if you do it proper you got to take care of your fans 'cos all the fans from my Page 3 days are still there and they love the music because it's another thing what they can do and it's just grown and I get all sorts of fans and it's not just the men as you might say because I've got a computer which just files everything and I've had five years of the modelling to gain experience and to become worldly and mature to cope with the music business in itself and I been very careful 'cos me dad's managed me and I'm his daughter and he loves me . . .'

Dad – Patrick Fox – is the power behind 'our' Sammy's phenomenon; some might call him a pimp, peddling his daughter's flesh for the public gaze, others would call him an astute product of Thatcherism. Samantha just called him 'dad' and 'lovely'.

'He's great with me look, you know. He prefers me hair straight and he hates it wavy like that and he keeps saying to me I'm a man and I should know what men like. It's nice to have a dad like that what's creative.'

Even now Patrick Fox waits upstairs; in five minutes there is a video meeting – 'the last video for Nothin's Gonna Stop Me Now was all me dad's idea, the car and the speedboat and everything. I love all that speed and so does me dad. He bought me a monkey for my 21st and he's called Norman . . .' – and time is pressing. One last question. Does Samantha Fox have a strict moral code?

Samantha, tussling with another Silk Cut is distracted: 'Who, me? Sorry, I can't concentrate and think like do two things at the same time with a fag in me mouth and all that. Sorry, what do you want to ask me?'

Do you live by a strict moral code?

'I don't think it's anybody's business.' There's that stern look again. The diminutive frame goes rigid in the seat and the eyes turn to the wall. She exhales. She turns back to face me with a grin. She resumes the patter . . .

'I'd like to get married in five years and I'll be, what is it?, 26, and I don't really want to be a singing housewife. But I've been with me boyfriend Peter a year and he's me boyfriend and he's the only man in my life 'cos I'm very faithful. I believe in momomogny. As George Michael says. That's a long word, innit? *Monogamy – can* say it proper, see! Cor, George Michael – I don't know what the world's coming to now banning his records 'cos it's stupid. I might do a record what gets banned like not I Want Your Sex but I Want *More* Sex but I'm only joking, ain't I? No, but it's nice to go home and know someone loves you and have a nice cuddle with somebody and it's great 'cos you're in love and that and that's the only moral code which I have, if you like.'

Father is waiting upstairs. With a wink and a cheery wave, Samantha Fox departs.

Chuck Berry

They called him The Inventor Of Rock'n'Roll. And this, apparently, gave him the right to ride roughshod over all of them for 30 years, extracting hefty wedges from luckless promoters, slighting his fellow musicians, short-changing his fans and subjecting fair maidens to his oily and unappetising advances . . .

CHUCK BERRY is a difficult man.

Towards the end of the recently-released Berry documentary film Hail! Hail! Rock 'n' Roll, Keith Richards is seen slumped on a chair, exhausted and exasperated. For the previous two weeks he has been rehearsing with Berry for Berry's 60th birthday concert at the Fox Theater, St Louis; he has endured the petulant outbursts of the legend when anyone so much as dares touch the great man's amplifier; he has engaged in heated debate about how the introductory guitar figure in Carol really goes; he has bashed all those old songs – Rock And Roll Music, Roll Over Beethoven, Johnny B. Goode, Nadine, No Particular Place To Go – into something approaching tight arrangements with scant operation from the grand old man himself.

And then on the big night what happens? Berry wilfully screws up Richards' labours by changing keys and altering arrangements as he sees fit, by throwing in bursts of unscheduled and singularly rotten guitar playing, and by acting the mischievous and awkward 'showman' the world had come to expect. It's almost as if Keith Richards cares more about Chuck Berry's music than Chuck Berry does and Keith is drained, all patience gone. Chuck, says Keith, has given him more headaches in a fortnight than Mick Jagger did during the entire Rolling Stones lifetime. Nonetheless, he adds with a fatigued smile of resignation, he cannot help liking the man . . .

The girl from Fabers (publishers of Chuck Berry: The Autobiography), on the other hand, cannot but loathe him. At 10 in the morning she is sitting in the coffee lounge of the Royal Garden Hotel, Kensington, wearing the haunted look that seems to descend on all those who come into contact with the Berry legend. She may be considerably younger than Keith Richards, and she may possess a full complement of teeth, but still she does a fair impression of Richards's filmed study of sorely tested tolerance. 'I hate Chuck Berry more than anyone else in the world,' she wearily declares. No, I don't think she likes him.

When Chuck Berry arrived in London two days ago to promote his film and his book and to play one concert at the Hammersmith Odeon, his first action, once settled into his Royal Garden suite, was to make a large and clumsy pass at the girl from the publishing house. The hotel chambermaids were merely complaining of pinched bottoms: this was a full-blown *pass*. And when the girl from the publishing house rejected the oily advance of this giant of rock 'n' roll, Chuck retreated into a mighty sulk, locking his doors to all comers. Forty press photographers turned up by invitation to snap the great man and were sent home shot-less when he declined to appear for their cameras.

The chairman of Fabers visited Mr Berry's suite with copies of the autobiography for the author to sign – and was sent packing by the great man who said he did not care to have his sleep disturbed by strangers. The man from The Times arrived to conduct a scheduled interview, was kept hanging around for seven hours (whilst Chuck lingered over a tardy three-egg breakfast, took a post-breakfast, took a post-breakfast nap and did whatever it is that sulking rock 'n' roll legends do) before, finally, he was granted an audience with the great man. The audience lasted all of three minutes – three minutes and Chuck decided he had chattered quite long enough. Everyone, it seems, is paying for the indiscretion of the girl from the publishing house who had the brazen cheek to say NO to Mr Chuck Berry, to turn her nose up at the distinct honour of a roll in his love nest.

I arrive at the hotel for the Q interview at the appointed time to be told these outrageous tales by the girl from the publishing house. The girl who does not like Mr Berry (because he is 'really disgusting') and who has engaged intermediaries to shuttle betwixt the Berry suite and the press gang camped out in the coffee lounge. The girl who never wants to clap eyes on Mr Berry again. 'I'm afraid you may have to wait around a long time,' I am informed. Chuck hasn't woken up yet (no-one would *dare* to wake him) and when he does, in his own good time, he'll be wanting his breakfast and goodness knows how long *that* will take . . . Chuck Berry is a difficult man, but the *good* news is that he seemed to be in a better frame of mind last night when he went off to be charming on Michael Aspel's chat show. (Though the story goes that he only agreed to appear on Aspel after a sum not unadjacent to two thousand dollars in used notes had been delivered to his suite. And when he was asked to perform Johnny B. Goode on the show, he refused saying, 'For second rate money, you get a second rate song.' He did a ragged and rather awful Memphis instead.)

Chuck Berry is a difficult man, but perhaps he *is* in a benevolent mood today, for morning has only just turned afternoon and I've been waiting a mere two hours when I am called to the lift to ascend to the legendary presence. Within the inner sanctum of his spacious suite, he sprawls in an easy chair, his legs straight out before him, his head resting on the chair back as he stares in boredom at the ceiling. With his slender moustache, his greased hair and his open beige shirt, he's somehow like a cross between a wizened spiv and an ageing lounge gigolo. Chuck Berry's eyes turn slowly from the ceiling toward me. Was that a nod of greeting I detected? Did a smile of friendship begin to play across his lips? Perhaps not. I sit before Chuck Berry, he leans leisurely forward to pick a Kool cigarette from the packet on the coffee table, and asks, in his sibilant, clearly enunciated voice, 'Did they tell you about the time?'

Did *who* tell me about *what* time?'

'Before we begin, you can have maybe three minutes of questions with your tape recorder and then, after, maybe some more questions.'

Three minutes. Is this going to be some revelatory, heart-to-heart confessional with the ultimate living legend of rock 'n' roll? Perhaps not. Chuck Berry is a difficult man . . .

Chuck Berry's book was largely written in 1979 when he was serving his third prison sentence – a short stretch in Lomproc Prison Camp, California, for tax evasion – and one had to hand it to Chuck: this autobiography is most definitely not ghost written (well, you'd have to *pay* a ghost, wouldn't you?) as is clear from his quaint and extravagant turn of phrase, particularly when he touches, as he often does, on the subject of his many sexual dalliances ('I embraced her in disbelief that I was about to enter the garden that she had spread before me,' he writes; 'I was ready as a sturdy log twixt two rolling stones,' he writes; 'My determination to get ahead with a bank account helped me manage to withdraw when we did wade nude in the nest,' he writes). It's a strange book: fascinating glimpses of rock 'n' roll, the infant years, and pre-Civil Rights prejudice in southern states being crowded out by Chuck's sexy memoirs and personal prejudices. He cares not for those who might try to part him from his money. He cares yet less for journalists. He doesn't like tape-recorded interviews because there's always the chance that he'll be misquoted. He doesn't like *un*-tape recorded interviews because there's always the chance that he'll be misquoted. Until recently he'd only permit *filmed* interviews ('visual-sound consultations') and he'd make sure these weren't tampered with after the fact 'by waving my hand before my face while answering questions to make it too obvious if they cut the scene to insert or omit anything.'

So here I am with my tape recorder and Chuck Berry and three minutes which is whittled down by his latest journalist-foiling ruse of pausing lengthily after each question, then cupping his hand over his ear and saying 'Once again?' You repeat the question and your precious time ticks away . . . Chuck Berry is an intractable customer . . .

'Once again?'

Would you say, Mr Berry, that you, single-handedly, invented rock 'n' roll?

'Single-handedly? Nope. I wouldn't say that I single-handedly invented rock 'n' roll. You see, there's all type of rock 'n' roll. There is *rock*. And there is roooooooll. See what I'm saying? And then there's rock 'n' roll which is rock 'n' roll, hahahaha. It's just a matter of whatever I've accomplished which is for others to say, I guess.'

How do you feel about those who look up to you in awe and say, *That* is the man who invented rock 'n' roll?

Pause. Eyes on the ceiling. The cupping of the hand. 'Once again?'

Repeat question.

'Actually, no feeling. I do not feel about such things.'

You have no feelings about the adulation you inspire?

'Once again?'

You have no feelings about the adulation you inspire?

'Nope.'

So you don't really care about your fans?

'My fans? What was that?'

Do you care about your fans?

'Oh, my *fans*. *Sure* I care about my fans. Because fans is money, hahaha. Muh-neeee! And who does *not* care about money? Me, *like* muh-neeee, haha.'

Throughout the above exchange, if you can call it that, Mr Chuck Berry, alleged instigator of this thing we call rock'n'roll, keeps one beady eye on his Rolex wristwatch. The precious time is ticking away and time, as we all know, is muh-neeee.

Chuck Berry is a man of few orthodox vices. He smokes his Kool cigarettes at a canter but he swore off the demon drink nearly half a century ago and he has always frowned upon drugs. His regular infidelity to the wife, Themetta (or 'Toddy'), he married in 1948, doesn't count as a sin in the great man's book: 'I keep my home fires burning. To say there must be no other women is a hypocrisy because that's something that is not written upon the heart. Pleasure is plea-suuuure! See what I'm saying?' he tells me with same strange logic. Which leaves only avarice. Chuck Berry likes muh-neeee, this much is clear, and stories of his pursuit of the folding stuff abound. We need not mention his first jail term, for bungled teenage armed robbery, or his third, tax evasion. (The second was for contravening the Mann Act, ie girl trouble).

We need only mention the tales of the man's stage career of the last two and more decades. He wrote some marvellous and imperishable songs in the '50s and early '60s, for sure; nobody had a gift for the wry lyric, the feeling for spry metre like Berry. But he seems to have spent the last 25 years desecrating his great songs for paying audiences around the globe. He just would take the money and run. A typical Chuck Berry appearance would go like this: minutes before showtime, the man would arrive, alone, guitar case in hand, and take delivery of concert fee in promoter's office; he'd walk on stage before pick-up backing band he'd never met (band's fee to be paid out of Berry's wodge only if they're up to scratch; no introductions – no 'How d'you do, Mr Berry, and what songs will we be playing tonight?' – no rehearsal), tune up perfunctorily and launch into whatever number popped into his head, hapless pick-up band struggling behind. A bit of crowd-pleasing duck walking, a few old faves with sloppy, idle guitar solos bunged on top, and after 45 minutes – on the dot – OFF.

Even if he were half way through a song . . . OFF. No encores. Bye bye. Forty-five minutes is what I'm paid for so 45 minutes you get, good-night.

In the film Hail! Hail! Rock 'n' Roll, Mr Berry is seen in his garage, a line of his swanky automobiles under polythene wraps. He doesn't want these cars but when he took them for trade-in, they didn't offer him enough muh-neeee. He cannot believe it. He leaves them to rot. And he tells us of how he once painted the interior of St Louis's Cosmopolitan Club (where he started out playing in the '50s) and how they paid him 450 dollars, which was such a lot of muh-neeee – and he kisses his fingers at the word – that he decided to give up music and be an interior decorator instead (until someone offered him even more muh-neeee – 800 dollars a week – to sing and play his guitar). And he tells of how he sees his guitars not as musical instruments but as 'Tools . . . Tax deductible, you know . . .' And others tell of how when Keith Richards and the band assembled for the concert featured in Hail! Hail! Rock 'n' Roll turned up for rehearsals at Berry's home, Berry Park, they found themselves stuck by the great man with a bill for equipment hire. A bill to appear in Berry's own film. Look after the cents and the dollars'll look after themselves (until the IRS catches up with you . . .)

'Once again?'

You have often been accused of being an avaricious man.

'I don't know what that means.'

Are you a greedy person?

'Greedy? A greedy person? You mean money? I just take what's my due. You see, sometimes before, I was taken advantage of. I was taken advantage of once. But not twice. That's the smart bit.'

He is referring here, one presumes, to his dealings with Chess Records to whom he signed in 1955, only to find that his first single, Maybellene, was credited not only to Berry but also (those were payola days) to the DJ Alan Freed and some guy named Russ Fratto. So Chuck had to split the royalties three ways for a song *he* had written, and it made him hopping mad. In the book, he fumes at the injustice of it all. But when I mention it today . . .

'I am not bitter because I realise the mistake was mine. The mistake was mine because I knew nothing about business and the accomplishment was theirs. Most commerce is an opportunity to achieve a product that is available and I was available and their accomplishment and my mistake put together is a perfect unity. I'd have done the same thing in their position. It's an incident, not an accident.'

So you didn't object to being ripped off by Chess?

'Once again?'

Repeat.

'Ripped off? Oh, by the way, it wasn't really ripped *off*. There's no such thing as being ripped *off*, of course, but that's under such things as stealing or burglary or something like that. So if I knew the culprit, of course, I'd have a grudge and I'd want him to pay the price. But if it's my own fault, if I leave my wallet on the kerb, I have no grudge against the person who picked it up. See what I'm saying?'

It's hard to imagine, somehow, Mr Chuck Berry leaving his wallet on the kerb.

'And that's about all the recording,' he says, consulting the Rolex and pointing a Kool in the rough direction of my tape recorder.

'That machine will have to come off now. That's about all the recording. But you can ask me more questions, I guess.'

And so, feeling impossibly fortunate to get a bonus on my three minutes, I ask him more questions (and find, to my surprise, that once the tape machine is off, and the notebook out, he drops the 'Once again?' tactic – I had begun to wonder if he were, perhaps, a trifle deaf). I ask him how he got on with Keith Richards during the filming of Hail! Hail! Rock 'n' Roll.

'Oh, well, you see, me and Keith, Keith Richards, we had our little problems, so to speak. No, let me say that another way. Keith Richards didn't have a problem with me but I certainly had my problems with *him*. Keith has a lot of problems, hahaha. Actually, I don't think that film is so good. They should have done it differently, but what do *they* know? I was in a film, Go Johnny Go, and I had a speaking part and that was 1958 – 30 years ago! So what do *they* know?'

I ask him about My Ding-A-Ling – that pitiful example of school-yard 'humour' which, in 1972, gave Mr Berry his biggest international hit ever – and suggest that it's a shame that he should be remembered for a song so infantile.

'A lot of people liked that song. A lot of people *like* that song. and I *LOVED* that song because that little, weeny song made my wallet so fat and happy, hahaha.'

I ask him what he feels about Mary Whitehouse who, in possibly the one supportable crusade of her career, tried to get My Ding-A-Ling banned.

'Well, Mary Whitehouse . . . I don't really know who the lady is but I heard about her. I think I was shown a picture of her, Mary Whitehouse. Mary Whitehouse – I guess the lady needs a little loving.'

And I ask how long – he's 61 now – he intends to keep performing.

'How long? How long, how long, how long, how loooooong, hahaha. Who knows? This is not my duty, I feel, you see? Not long, I guess. Not long. I like the money, yes, I like the muh-neee, but more than this, I like myself. I like my-self! *Greatly.*'

And with that the living legend stubs out his latest Kool, rises slowly to his feet and dawdles from the room without a by your leave. This, I take it, is a signal to indicate the end of 'consultation' – and as if in confirmation, the nervous intermediary pokes her head around the door and whispers 'Um, I think you'd better go now. You've had *twelve* minutes.'

Twelve minutes! And he didn't ask me for a stack of used dollar bills *once*, the cantankerous old bugger.

Bananarama

You nip into the studio, warble a bit, nip out and embark on a fresh round of televised formation jigging, giggling press encounters, hazy photo opportunities and all-purpose blotto behaviour passed off as 'promotion' – and then whinge about lack of artistic credibility.

THE THREE WOMEN who are Bananarama are sitting around the dining table in their press officer's West London abode and displaying their rare gift for petulance. Nothing is quite right. The chocolate cake is unpalatable, the pork sandwiches a disgrace, and the German TV crew who have set up equipment all over the house to film the group for a pop show segment are, it's plain, a pain in the triumvirate neck. With politesse, the TV director asks the girls to play Frustration – a juvenile dice game based on Ludo with which they have, in the past, tinkered away many an idle hour in the recording studio – for his camera. Sulkily, reluctantly, the girls comply. And now the director wishes the girls to step outside for one last shot in the afternoon sunlight. Sulkily, grumpily, the girls decline. 'Why can't they do it in *here*?' asks a Bananarama, *whiney voice*, pushing the side-plate of quarter-eaten cake away from her with a disdainful air. They do it in here . . .

'Thank you, ladies. Everything is good, thank you!' booms the elderly and enthusiastic German chief as he and his troops take their leave. His heartiness is hardly reciprocated: 'Bye,' say Bananarama mournfully as they fail to meet the director's gaze and continue with the game. The foreign crew are gone and there's a mutual sigh of relief. One more gruelling promotional duty performed – but another (a Q interview) to follow. It's a hard life . . .

Bananarama – Keren Woodward, Sarah Dallin and Jacqui O'Sullivan (who replaced Siobhan Fahey earlier this year when Siobhan settled for marital and maternal comfort in Los Angeles with husband Dave Stewart) are the most successful female group in British pop music history. Not that there's too much competition: The Vernons Girls, The Orchids, The Caravelles, The Modettes, The Raincoats, Amazulu, Girlschool and the rest – hardly a distinguished list. Still, Bananarama's ten Top 10 hits – light and frothy and harmless and enjoyable – in six years is an achievement of sorts. Back in the beginning, when they were bouncing up and down, looking like failed sirens as they smirked and pouted hesitantly in their grey track suits on Top Of The Pops, one expected them soon to go the way of all frivolous pop flesh: Haysi Fantayzee, Kajagoogoo, Belle Stars and JoBoxers – where are you now?

But Bananarama stayed with us, damned if they would shuffle off that mortal coil and are seeking to justify their existence, to explain what they were *trying to do* with their every public utterance, as if simply making jolly little pop tunes was somehow not enough. They are explaining – some might call it moaning – still. 'Look,' Keren Woodward will snap during the course of our interview, 'we don't want to be written off as three little bimbos who do nothing – as three puppets – because we did it all ourselves.' Her friend and colleague, Sarah Dallin, will echo the defensive sentiment: 'It's not that we want to be seen as serious, tortured artistes particularly, but, you know, credit where it's due. They always say that anybody could do what we do but no-one does, do they? Because there's no-one like us . . .'

The beginning was in 1981 when the three girls were all on the dole and habituees of any London club with a dancefloor and a drinks licence. For a giggle and a skylark, the trio began to sing, performing backing vocals on a B-side for third division one-hit-'wonders' Department S and whooping around to backing tapes in those same clubs. 'We used to take our backing along and just get drunk and go one stage and jump up and down,' says Keren. 'It was *brilliant!*'

They got to make a demo single, Aie A Mwana, which was taken up by London Records, and they got their photo in The Face magazine, which was spotted by Terry Hall of Fun Boy Three who rang up and asked them to sing on an album.

Keren: 'They just liked us because we were so unpompous and unglamorous and we wore moccasins and they wore moccasins so they thought we were alright. But we were shitting ourselves because we thought that they thought we were proper singers. But they let us play percussion and everything and Siobhan got into trouble with the cowbells. Their style was really shambolic and we were pretty shambolic so it sorted of fitted. It was brilliant.'

From the collaboration with Fun Boy Three came the hit single It Ain't What You Do It's The Way That You Do It. Bananarama, inexperienced, incompetent, were on the brink of success. What excitement!

Keren: 'It was so exciting because me and Sarah had never even been on a plane and suddenly to be flying all over Europe and experiencing free drinks was brilliant. I remember the first time I threw up in a sick bag on an aeroplane – it was heaven . . .'

Sarah: 'The free drinks, I must say, were a big turn on.'

Keren: 'We used to share rooms as well, didn't we? And she (Sarah) used to make me get up in the night and empty the waste bin because I'd been sick in it. It smelled . . .'

Over the years, Bananarama, through steady practice, have turned throwing up into something of an art form. The stories of blotto behaviour and activities of a tired and emotional nature are legion. There was the time when Sarah, somewhat the worse for drink (or 'out of my mind'), decided to set off a fire alarm in a Boston hotel; only the intervention of producer Pete Waterman, who claimed that Sarah was his daughter, saved her from a night behind bars. There was the time when the group sat in a New York restaurant studiously ignoring the boss of their American record company as they flung their glasses of tequila against the wall with optimum violence. There was the time when they were thrown out of a Newcastle club (where they were guests of honour) for tearing one another's clothes off ('a big beano where vests got ripped,' says Sarah) and the time when they were forcibly ejected from a German TV studio when Sarah collapsed against the set bringing it crashing down during a live broadcast ('We were a little bit tipsy to say the least,' says Keren). When relating such stories, Keren and Sarah collapse into heaps of coy giggles and they are pleased to tell one that when Siobhan left the group they hired Jacqui O'Sullivan 'because we'd never met her sober'. Antics on the sauce and paparazzi snaps of these girls looking hog-whimpering and worse in various night spots . . . is bad behaviour something that makes Bananarama proud? I ask. They suppress those nostalgia-fuelled giggles and go on the defensive.

Keren: 'It sounds really corny when you say "bad behaviour"

because it sounds like, Hey, rock 'n' roll, like you're trying to be outrageous.'

Sarah: 'We're just ourselves. It's just our dancefloor mentality, you know.'

Keren: 'The thing is people accept it from boys because that's the way boys in bands are supposed to behave but when it's these cute girls who are reasonably pretty and jump up and down on the telly, they can't take it. People can't cope with that mental drunken side of us. And it's worse when it's a controlled occasion. I really hate those sort of things where everyone is really pleasant like those BPI Awards meals where everyone's really poncey. It just makes me want to react and hit the bottle. I suppose it's reaction against authority which stems from childhood or the fact that we were all old punks with a rebellious attitude . . .'

Sarah: 'We hate those things with stars – the occasions where stars have to talk to stars.'

You can't have enjoyed joining in on the Band Aid single recording much then?

Keren: 'No, we didn't. It was excruciating. We just ended up giggling in the corner with George Michael. He's a killer . . .'

In 1982 Bananarama went into the studios with their first proper producers, Tony Swain and Steve Jolley (who made an international recording phenomenon of Alison Moyet). The girls' attitude in the studio seems to have been less than professional.

Keren: 'They used to send us home for giggling. Every time we went to sing a line we'd laugh and they'd send us home like naughty schoolgirls. Or we'd have our knitting down on the floor or we'd be playing Frustration and they'd say, Come and sing this line, and we'd be reluctant to leave our games. It was brilliant getting sent home for laughing . . .'

Sarah: 'But it was Steve Jolley's fault that we were giggling all the time – trying to play kiss-chase around the studio . . .'

It seems scarcely surprising, then, that the vocal performances on Bananarama's early hits – Shy Boy, Na Na Hey Hey Kiss Him Goodbye, Cruel Summer, Robert De Niro's Waiting – were, to use their own three words, 'not so hot'. And yet they are disinclined to shoulder the blame.

Keren: 'Swain and Jolley were much too meticulous about everything. Everything had to be so perfect and it's really hard with three people to get everything completely phrased the same. I think they really stifled us. They were such perfectionists that it took all the enjoyment out of recording . . .'

It is seldom, it would appear, that Bananarama are prepared to claim responsibility for their own shortcomings. The early videos – tra-la-la nonsense featuring shaggy 'acting', reluctant choreography and rather pathetic 'wild' camera angles usually showed the girls looking like Lonsdale sportsgirl harpies – these were somebody else's fault. 'The trouble with those videos was we were working with people who didn't have the first idea what we were about,' says Keren. 'We looked stupid, but that was down to working with people who aren't in tune with you.'

When I offer the complaint that I can never detect a vocal harmony on a Bananarama record, that too ' is somebody else's fault. 'There are stacks of harmonies on our records if you listen because it's one of our favourite things,' says Keren, 'but the trouble is most people who mix records mix harmonies low down so you can catch the melody. We spend hours doing harmonies but sometimes they don't get used in the final mix because they think it won't sell or whatever . . .'

Even Bananarama's current producers, Stock, Aitken and Water-man – creators of production-belt bubblegum (Rick Astley, Sinitta, Mel & Kim, Samantha Fox, Kylie Minogue *et al*) for the masses – come in for a share of flak from the grousing gals . . .

Keren: 'We go in to record and they say, OK, we've got some backing tracks. And we say, We're sorry but we don't like them. And they say, But they're smash hits. And we say, We don't care. And they say, We'll give them to Rick or Sinitta and then you'll be sorry. And we say, No we won't because we don't like them. And then we have to sit over them while they write other ones to our instructions. They get quite distressed . . .'

Sarah: 'I hate that interchangeable attitude they have – Well, if you don't do it Sinitta or Kylie will do it and it'll be a Number 1. It probably *will* be a Number 1 but we don't care because it's so vile . . .'

Keren: 'Pete Waterman says we're the most awkward act they've ever worked with. That's good . . .'

Awkward? Bananarama seem downright stroppy, at times. Stroppy, sulky, unmanageable. Ask the journalist who had set up an interview with the three girls on Hampstead Heath only to be told that Siobhan was unwell and would be unable to attend. Imagine his surprise when, up on the Heath, who should stroll by, tennis racket in hand and frisky as can be, but Ms Fahey? Ask the record company who ... well: 'The record company are always making stupid suggestions,' says Sarah, 'but that's their bad luck because we never do what they say because all they want is a few cleavage shots but it would lose the whole essence of our group if we went for all that tits and bums stuff and dressed like tarts ...'

Are Bananarama stroppy?

'I don't call it stroppy trying to get what you want,' says Keren. 'It's like if someone says, Can you do a photo session in a swimming costume sitting on the edge of the bath and get your tits out? and we won't do it, we're being stroppy. People only say we're stroppy because we're girls. Bros don't get asked to get their tits out, do they? It's pathetic. I'm not saying we don't make a fuss about things because we do, but it's really hard work promoting records, it's boring and it's physically tiring and it's crap and even when you're not doing anything you're going through the mental stress of it all. It ruins your life ...'

It's really hard work promoting records and it ruins your life – but to the casual observer it might seem that that's *all* that Bananarama do. They whisk into the studio and warble a bit; they whisk out again to PROMOTE. It is, is it not, widely suspected that Bananarama are nothing much more than hopeless and talentless bimbos. True?

Keren ponders the question and replies: 'That's too general. I think you should pinpoint our lack of talents, really.'

Alright. Bananarama cannot sing for toffee.

Keren: 'We *can* sing. We've always been good singers in the traditional white English female category, as opposed to ... well, none of us are like Aretha Franklin or great singers in that sense of the word. But we're more talented than people think because a lot of singers who are supposedly good singers have real trouble pitching and we never have that problem, actually.'

Sarah: 'We have perfect pop voices. The first person who said we can't sing was Mike Smith and look at Mike Smith.'

You can't dance.

Sarah: 'Well, it was very hard to dance to our early records because they weren't really dance records but when I see most people dancing in discos I think it's real cheek to say we can't dance.'

One last accusation (and popular belief). Bananarama – though their records may carry credits like Jolley/Swain/Fahey/Woodward and Stock/Aitken/Waterman/Dallin/Fahey/Woodward – could never write a song to save their lives.

Sarah: 'If people say we don't write songs, that's just people being stupid and it's something we don't have to justify.'

Keren: 'Of *course* we write songs. The first song I remember we wrote completely was Boy Trouble which was a B-side of Shy Boy and we did it on a keyboard – Johnny Fingers' keyboard, actually. Oh, no, the one we did on Johnny Fingers' keyboard was Give Us Back Our Cheap Fares which was an instrumental and quite political. We're not proficient enough musicians to sit and construct songs with chords and everything but it's rubbish to say we can't write songs. If we weren't girls, the suggestion would never even arise . . .'

I ask the girls to talk me through the creation of one of their songs. Let's take Robert De Niro's Waiting, for example.

Sarah: 'We just thought that was a brilliant title. Nobody had ever heard of Robert De Niro so we popularised him in England. From cult figure to top megastar . . .'

Keren: 'You want to talk about the music though?' Yes please. 'Well, we wrote the music with Swain and Jolley in Steve's house and we sang to them what we wanted and they programmed it. What happens is you get a drum beat going, like Grace Jones's Pull Up To The Bumper, and you get the bass in and you only really need the basics and you sing what you want and that's it. All you need is the basic chords to sing over. You don't need all the stupid little things . . .'

And with those technical details out of the way, we can discuss Robert De Niro – not the song, the man phenomenon. For, apparently, when Bob heard about the Bananarama song, he rang them up and asked them out for a drink. And . . . Keren: 'We were so nervous about meeting him that we got drunk before we even went out and he was wearing a Benny from Crossroads bobble hat and National Health glasses. He looked so unlike a movie star. We didn't talk much. It was hideous and we all got horribly drunk . . . and that's about it, really.'

Except . . .

'I threw up,' says Sarah.

Steve Davis

Welcome to the velveteen world of put-ball-in-hole-with-stick.
Its most seamless and well-heeled practitioner, ever among us
in lucrative ad campaigns, chummy TV game shows and star-
spangled pop ensembles, has a new hobby – rock publishing
and promotion. Interesting?

I N A SIDE ROAD off Romford High Street and its inelegant ranks
of building societies and electricity showrooms lies the Romford
Snooker Centre, headquarters of Barry Hearn's 'Matchroom'
empire. The window carries gigantic monochrome portraits of
Hearn's players – Terry Griffiths, Dennis Taylor, Jimmy White,
Willie Thorne, Neal Foulds, Tony Meo and Steve Davis.

Inside a selection of middle-aged, polyester clad secretaries bustle
about and, as I enter and announce that I am here for an interview
appointment with Steve Davis, they eye me with much suspicion.
A figure in a blaring Hawaiian-type shirt comes striding through
a door towards me: Barry Hearn, snooker impresario, Davis's
manager. 'Steve didn't tell me nothing about this,' he says. 'What
paper are you from?' Q Magazine, I reply. 'What's that then? Is
Steve booking his own interviews now or what?' I get the
impression that Hearn suspects me of being some kind of snooker
groupie, here on the off-chance of an encounter with Davis, the
famous Nugget, the Ginger Magician, but on hearing that 'Q' is,
in fact, a music magazine, his tone instantly changes to warmth.
'Oh, a *music* magazine. Like rock, man. I thought you meant 'Cue'
magazine – as in snooker. You were nearly out on your ear my
son, haha. Steve's into music now so I suppose *I'll* have to take
care of the snooker. I'll show you how to *screw* back off the blue,'
he leers. 'Hahaha . . .'

Upstairs in the snooker room, Steve Davis MBE, has his 'head
down over the table', practising in the single-minded fashion that

has made him the greatest player in the world. This room is no seedy, smoke-filled hall but a place of tasteless splendour, velveteen armchairs and the like. The lighting is subdued and the room is hushed – just the occasional 'click-click' of the balls on the baize and a murmured 'Shot, my son'. Steve Davis breaks off from practice to talk to me about his latest 'music-orientated' project which excites him so and we sit together in a corner, our voices barely above a whisper so as not to disturb his father and his father's friend who are playing at a nearby table. 'If this was the usual snooker sort of interview, I wouldn't have done it. You know, "I started playing when I was 14 and I won the World Championship when I was 23", because I'm fed up with that. But it's good to get some publicity for Voices From The Shadows . . .'

Some months ago, Davis caused some little surprise by promoting the avant-garde jazz-rock group Magma. The enterprise was not a wild success but at least it showed that there was something more to Steve Davis – the 'interesting' one – than just this perpetual snooker obsession. Now Davis has turned his attentions from un-listenable European rock to soul music by investing in a small-circulation soul magazine, Voices From The Shadows. It's based in Hull, it covers music of obscure black artists like the Reverend Cleophus Robinson, Sharon Song Byrd, Tyrone Burwell, Rodney Saulsberry and Tony Troutman, and there at the top of the mast-head it says: 'Managing Director: Steve Davis'.

What's it all about, O snooker supremo?

'Yeah, well, right,' says Davis, pausing to raise his eyebrows as his attention is diverted momentarily to the green baize upon which his father has just done an interesting safety shot or some-thing. 'Cor . . . Yeah. Um. Voices From The Shadows is . . . see my hobby has always been record buying. I think. Collecting – I don't know what you call it. Most geezers like to collect and it's a lot better than collecting stamps because I've always had a fascination for walking into a record shop and I think the first record I ever bought was either Argent's Hold Your Head Up or Neil Young's Heart of Gold . . .' The voice of Romford is now charged up and it speaks in a rapid, rambling vein. '. . . And as I got older I decided more what I liked and I went from at school liking the Canterbury jazz-rock kind of scene of Caravan and Soft Machine and Hatfield And The North and a load of strange groups like that and I then started getting more into American jazz funk and as I got more knowledgeable I started buying a lot more vocal-type music which I think as you get older you do tend to do because you tend to go more for feeling of voices as you get older and in my search for more black American vocal-type music I discovered Voices From The Shadows which was in a fanzine situation and it opened up singers I'd never heard of and so for that reason I thought it was important to keep the magazine going.'

A strange progression, is it not, from hippy music to obscure soul?

'Well, the hippy type of music that I started off on to me wasn't really hippy, it was just something I enjoyed. I think the first concert I ever went to was either a Soft Machine concert or a Caravan concert or it might have been a Magma concert – one of those. I refused to go along to Genesis concerts and preferred the Soft Machine which was 45-minute drum solos and inspirational sometimes and the other group I used to go and see was Gentle Giant which were . . . I don't know what they were, really. I've got all the albums. I used to have an Afghan and I used to go and see them – it stunk, the Afghan – but I never considered myself in that hippy vein and I never went along and smoked pot. I never did that and I never even noticed it in other people because I didn't even know what it was then when I was at school.'

It has been suggested in the past that, as a schoolboy in southeast London, Davis was less than popular – which is why he turned to the lonely pursuit of snooker in the first place. True?

'Yeah, I've read that, too. The papers distort things and they said that everybody hated me at school but I wouldn't say I was unpopular. I had a mate. Neil Rogers, his name was. But I was a loner at school and I was shy and everything I said came out all stupid so I wasn't a leader of a gang or whatever and probably what I do now has borne that out because to become a good snooker player, you have to spend a lot of time on your own practising, yeah, you do.'

It was Steve Davis's father, Bill, a snooker enthusiast, who turned Steve on to the 'sport' in the first place, taking the teenage son around the clubs and coaching him. By 1978, when Steve was 21, he'd become good enough to turn professional and in 1981 he won the World Championship for the first time. He is now, of course, immensely wealthy.

'Yeah, I've become very rich out of putting balls in holes. What's wrong with that? One year I was the most seen person on television apart from some newsreader who beat me to it. I like playing games and I think snooker is one of the ultimate games – it's like the working man's chess, if you like – and I'm very, very, very good at it. The only thing I've ever been good at is putting ball in holes with a stick but I don't need to be good at anything else because after snooker nothing else seems to matter, really. But it's not a money-orientated thing. It never was to start with and it never will be. The fact that I've made a fortune out of it is just a sort of bonus.'

If it's not a 'money-orientated thing', if money is secondary to the love for the game, why, then, has Davis felt the need to resort to such self-promotional tactics as becoming a TV host on the mildly embarrassing A Frame With Davis, a trifling Channel 4 entertainment in which Davis would stroll around a snooker table accompanied by sundry third-rate celebrities engaging in light banter?

'Well, it was all part of the PR, wasn't it? Even if you're the top snooker player, that's something you need. Plus it got quite good viewing figures. I did a very mediocre job to be honest but it was alright because all they did was they got comedians on and they just messed around on a snooker table which I thought was quite funny. All I did was say, Ladies and gentlemen, welcome to A Frame With Davis. On my left is Bernie Winters, on my right is Bobby Davro, and they just performed because they're pro-fessionals and it was the easiest thing in the world and I just had to ask a few questions. It's just something I done.'

Another PR exercise Davis 'done' was an appearance at the 1983 Conservative general election rally along with Bob Monkhouse and Tarby and Kenny 'Let's bomb Russia' Everett. Now that is some-thing he regrets:

'That was probably my biggest mistake getting involved in that because it gives opportunities for the knockers. Mind you, it was an experience sitting up close to Margaret Thatcher and watching her perform but it was a mistake for me to be there because it was bad for my image because it's a very important thing for a sports person to be divorced from politics. But that's just one mistake in a PR career that's been pretty well-organised.'

And it wasn't *Davis's* mistake, *was* it? It was Barry Hearn's mistake. For isn't Hearn the one who's groomed the boy and orchestrated the PR manoeuvres. Didn't Hearn *create* Steve Davis?

'It's very understandable that you should say that because Barry's a very larger than life character and he's the complete opposite to me. When I was 20 and turning professional, I had played snooker since the age of 14 and I had done very little else in my life and I was very unworldly wise and so in the early years very much Barry was my mentor, my leader of the sort of right way to be and I used to listen and do whatever he said. Barry's a very good psychologist as well as sharp at business. He used to coach me along the lines of interviews and what to say and that. But there's various things I've matured in now and I've done plenty of things in the entertainment world, you see. When I'm not a snooker player I tend to look at myself as a commodity and it's just part of the game. You can become addicted to being a commodity, sort of thing. They talk about other players being addicted to cocaine or whatever and I suppose my only vice is I am a little bit addicted to being used as a commodity and having an image. It's a little bit stupid, I suppose, because my only objective year in, year out is to make sure I can hit the centre cue through straight. But I do like being a commodity and being a character and having an image.'

Ah, the image. Steve Davis, the dedicated professional, nice boy, lives with his parents, a little bit dull, a little bit staid. Not for him the lifestyle of a cocaine-sniffing Kirk Stevens or a frenziedly 'bonking' Tony Knowles or a temperamental fisticuffing Alex Higgins. Steve Davis has bottom. He is Steve 'Interesting' Davis. It was Spitting Image who really manufactured this image for him, portraying him as this latex goon with a droning voice whose idea of a wild time is a glass of milk. If this hurt Davis, he's forgotten it now as he cashes in on the 'interesting' angle.

'I *am* interesting,' he says with a mirthless chuckle. 'So interesting that I've actually got a book coming out this Christmas that Penguin are doing which is How To Be Really Interesting by Steve Davis. It's good. It's got hints on how to be interesting with a lady – open up a Halifax Building Society account.' He snorts softly at the jape. 'My image on Spitting Image, I've made it work for me, you see.'

Perhaps by being Steve 'Interesting' Davis, the man manages to conceal the fact that he really *is* deadly dreary.

'Well, I suppose I *am* really boring but I quite enjoy it, really, because it gives you no hassle. What I've done is I've refused to act like a superstar. I see it as a crusade for the normal person who's absolutely brilliant at one thing but doesn't have any pretension in any other ways. I still retain so much normality that it gives people very little to write about so they think you're boring. If I have a choice I don't talk. If I go along to a party I'll just sit in the corner and watch other people enjoy themselves because that's my natural way. What's wrong with that? I'm in a sport that's flavour of the decade and is played by millions more kids than ever used to play it and I am the best player there is, without being big-headed, so what does it matter if I'm the most boring geezer that ever walked the earth? I've achieved something what not a lot of people could do so I think I've won the right to be boring and go to bed with a Marmite sandwich if that's what I want to do.'

Up the wooden stairs to Bedfordshire with an interesting Marmite sandwich. Steve Davis was once quoted as saying he preferred snooker to sex.

'Yeah, that's an example of learning not to open your mouth in interviews. What happened was this guy asked me, What's more important to you, sex or snooker? And I said Well, what's more important to *you*, your job or sex? To which he said, Well, my job's more important, to which I said, Same for me, and he just changed it all around and when I read it it was very embarrassing. Right after that appeared, I was playing in an exhibition and somebody shouted out the audience, Oh, you prefer snooker to sex, but we had a line prepared for it, because we thought it might happen, and I said, Well, no one's ever paid me for the other, which is totally accurate. Anyway, I've got a girlfriend but she's private, sort of thing.'

What of the Matchroom tours of the Far East? There are tales of snooker bimbos and kinky sex, of three-in-a-bed drug binges and all sorts. All *very* rock'n'roll, it sounds. But if Steve Davis has been witness to any untoward shenanigans, he's not saying.

'The Matchroom players when we're abroad are a very professional bunch. There's nothing rife in the snooker world other than individuals doing what individuals do,' he says with a tedious diplomacy. 'We've never had any problems out in the Far East together. I take a jar of Marmite and a couple of cans of baked beans so everything's alright.'

Once again Steve Davis's attention wanders to the snooker table where father Bill has just done something interesting with a ball. Ever thought of making a record, Steve?

'Um, I'm not Bobby Womack. I thought of taking up the piano

once but it would have got in the way of snooker practice. When you've set your life up to be the best snooker player in the world, there's not much room for much else. I only know the snooker world. Oh, but anyway, we *made* a record, didn't we? Snooker Loopy.'

Oh, yes, Snooker Loopy. A jamboree of Chas and Dave knees-up jollity which went, if memory serves, '*Snooker loopy, nuts are we/We and them and him and me,/We will see what we can do/With a load of balls and a snooker cue ...*' Performed by the Matchroom Mob.

'That was a momentous occasion. It actually got to Number 7 and there's lots of groups around that haven't had chart success that high which I think is quite funny, really, rather than frightening. Chas and Dave know a good tune when they see one. We had a follow-up, The Romford Rap, but it only got to Number 99 and we were going to go for an LP but we cracked up in the end. We disbanded quicker than ... what's the name of that group with the spider's webs all over them, geezer with the cobwebs all over him? Sigue Sigue Sputnik. Ha ha ha.'

Steve Davis affords a rare, if unconvincing, laugh. Are you snooker loopy, Steve? I enquire. This is intended as a light question to prompt, perhaps, some witty retort but Davis purses his lips, raises the eyebrows and addresses it with gravity.

'Yeah, I suppose I *am*, really. Take the World Championship – you put a hell of a lot of pressure into those two weeks and the mental pressure alone is the hardest thing in the world. I know we're getting paid a few quid for it but even so to cope with all that mental pressure washing over you makes me a very proud person. And I'm in a difficult situation being the top player because I don't tend to push myself in social situations with other players just in case they think I'm being smart. There could be jealousy or an envy situation because I'm the top I tend to let them make the first move, really. But I haven't heard any snidey talk, I don't think ...'

As we leave the Matchroom for a photo-opportunity in Romford's premier soul record shop – there is a little boy hovering in the street staring up at the portraits of Meo, Griffiths, Taylor, Davis MBE ('For services to snooker') *et al.* 'Do you like snooker, then?' Davis asks the boy. 'No!' snaps the scamp and dashes off down the road.

Davis follows him with his eyes. He is not smiling. He seems rendered speechless by the boy's response. He just can't understand it . . .

Ronnie Biggs

It's been a long stretch – from petty pilferer to over-romanticised lovable rascal to face-changing fugitive. But in exile he's 'gone straight' and turned bankable wag, philosopher, full-time lush and dubious tourist attraction.

'TAKE A TAXI from your hotel,' says the voice down the telephone, 'and when you get to my place, keep the driver and ring the bell and I'll sort him out to make sure he's not ripping you off. The taxi drivers in Rio, they're all thieves. All bloody thieves, ha ha ha.'

The voice belongs to one of the most notorious thieves of them all: Ronnie Biggs, Great Train Robber, renowned 'prisoner of Rio'.

As my taxi driver – who may or may not be a thief – somewhat recklessly negotiates the steep and winding cobbled streets that lead to Biggs's place in the bohemian Santa Teresa section of the city, he issues a large Brazilian cackle and declares in his fractured English 'I now where you goeeng. You go see the fuckeeng Beegs! Fuckeeng Beegs! Ha ha ha. Oh, fuckeeng Beegs is brilliant man. Brilliant man like your Margaret Thatcher and the General De Gaulle. In Brazil we love your fuckeeng Beegs.' Fuckeeng Beegs, it is clear, has become, along with the statue of Christ on the mountain, one of Rio's most treasured monuments. Fugitive, rascal and major tourist attraction.

And here is the man himself, padding barefoot across the wooden floor of his comfortable apartment, past the pool table, past a ramshackle stereo system and a record 'collection' that consists solely of The Sex Pistols' The Great Rock'n'Roll Swindle, to greet me. A tiny dog of indeterminate breed whimpers at his naked ankles as Biggs sits by an open window looking down across the city to the sea and assures me how 'super' it is to hear an English voice. At 59, the robber's hair is grey, the teeth are slightly soiled, but the face seems well-preserved and the skin is taut – a result, he says, of the plastic surgery he underwent in Paris in 1965 after his escape from Wandsworth. 'I guess I'd look pretty ghastly today if I hadn't had it done but it was very painful. Cripes! It hurt! But the guy who was organising it for me said, Christ, stop making a fuss, Biggsy, Elizabeth Taylor has it done every couple of years, ha ha ha.'

Cripes? Is this the expletive of a villain from the underworld? And where is the Cockney rhyming slang with which, if tabloid 'interviews' with Biggs are to be believed, his conversation is littered? In fact, the Biggs voice is gentle, almost refined, and an occasional 'bloody' is the strongest his language gets. Until, as I shall discover later, he's had a couple of drinks . . .

Under Brazilian law, Ronald Biggs is forbidden to work, but he gets by quite nicely by charging for press and TV interviews (this one's for free as Biggs is, ostensibly, plugging the film Prisoner of Rio for which he co-wrote the script and will receive 1.5 per cent of the profits) and for meeting groups of tourists. Off to sunkissed Rio? A mere 500 dollars – a snip! – will get you an audience with the great rogue. Then there's Ronnie's son Michael by girlfriend Raimunda de Castra. As the singer in Brazilian pre-teen pop troupe The Magic Balloon Gang, Mike made a small fortune before age crept up on him (he's 14 now) and he was forced to retire from the music business. It was Mike's money that bought the Biggs apartment. Then there are the T-shirts bearing the legend 'I know someone who went to Brazil and met Ronnie Biggs . . . honest!' which Biggs had made up and then flogged to tourists along Copacabana beach and then there's the night club Biggs has a stake in (Michael's money again) . . . 'Got to keep my act together,' says Ronnie. 'Got to keep cash in the coffers . . .' Before he came to Rio, before he reinvented himself as celebrity and tourist-point-of-interest, Ronnie Biggs had, of course, other ways of keeping the coffers filled.

The son of an honest and hard-working chef and toiling housewife, Biggs traces his descent into criminality to his evacuation as an 11-year-old from London to Cornwall. 'Bloody sadist the bloke was. If I came in five or 10 minutes late for tea, bed sentence was what this guy used to pronounce. I'd be lying there really hungry and I'd wait till everybody was asleep and sneak downstairs and raid the food cupboard leaving everything as I found it. So I was developing my skills as a burglar right there and then.'

Back in London as the war approached its end, Biggs attended a school of building where 'I started my old light-handed tricks'. He went 'stealing to order' for his fellow pupils. 'I used to make out a little list and go up the West End and steal all the stuff. I was good at it. Do you know a shop called Reeves in the Charing Cross Road? Well, that was my regular hunting ground. There's a real buzz in thieving. It's exciting, pitting your wits against the law. You can't beat that feeling. It just makes you feel good.'

Biggs was asked to leave the building school. He became a telephone engineer's mate 'and the bloke I was mate to was even more light-fingered than I was'. One weekend they 'turned over' a Yardley's perfume factory. He joined the Air Force and was given a dishonourable discharge when he was caught breaking into a shop. Slammed up on a six months stretch, Ronnie 'just went from bad to worse' . . . 'I can remember the first time I was detained I went to a place called Stamford House in London, and I remember sitting round with a gang of boys and we were all listening to this bloke Jackson and he was telling us how to break windows without making a noise. You put syrup on a piece of paper and stick it on the window and give it a tap and then take the paper off with a piece of glass stuck to it. You can pick up a pretty good education in prison, ha ha. I was always the prison bookmaker. When Never Say Die won the Derby in 1953, it was the biggest loss I ever took. From underneath my work-bench I paid out 66 ounces of tobacco in winning bets!' Ronnie Biggs laughs roundly at his memories of nefarious days.

In 1960 Biggs married a girl Charmian and, aged 31, decided to go 'straight' for the first time, working as a builder and carpenter. Good intentions did not last long for, in 1963, strapped for cash, he phoned up his 'old pal' Bruce Reynolds to ask him for a £500 loan and Bruce suggested something rather more tempting. 'He came up with this 40,000 quid minimum offer, and that was the sort of bait that was hard to refuse. I asked him for 24 hours to consider but I guess I only needed 24 seconds.' Reynolds had offered Biggs a place in a gang that were hoping to hold up a mail train in Buckinghamshire and strip it of its assets. August 1963 and the Great Train Robbers became 'criminals of the century'.

'I was nothing. I was just like the tea boy of the gang. But now I'm the most famous one of all, though I suppose old Buster

Edwards will be on my heels now that that pop singer chap, what's his name, Phil Collins, is in that film.'

Of the £2,631,784 train swag, Bigg's cut was £140,000. Not bad for a night's work – except, of course, he got caught. Nonetheless, he has no regrets. He'd do it all again. 'Oh, of course I'd do it again because it's given me the lifestyle I'd always dreamt of. There's a certain drudgery in working hard for a living. You get no mental peace. So, yes, I'd do it again. The only thing I regret is that it wasn't a clean crime. Had Jack Mills (the train driver who was coshed in the raid and died seven years later) not been struck down it would have made an enormous difference and I think there's every chance that the train gang would have been revered and worshipped by the public for putting one over on the establishment. I've never been involved in violence. I've never had a gun in my hand and the robbery there was three people who weren't even carrying coshes and I happened to be one of them. I'm not evil. I hate the idea of anybody considering me a criminal. I'm not a criminal.'

However, British law processes considered Biggs a criminal and he was banged up for 30 years. Yet, in 1965 Ronnie Biggs slipped over the wall of Wandsworth and out of the country. 'When I escaped, that's when I discovered vodka. Cripes! I was drinking a bottle in the afternoon and I found that it gave me these very erotic dreams. Have you ever found that? I thought I'd found the elixir of life.'

By 1970 Ronnie Biggs was living and working (his ill-gotten gains had all but gone on the escape and the surgery) in Australia with a new name and face. But the police were closing in. From the pages of a holiday brochure, he selected a fresh hiding place – Rio – and slipped off once more with a friend's passport. Then in 1974 (just as, he claims, he was preparing to give himself up and return to England to serve his time) he was apprehended by Slipper Of The Yard. 'Well, I wasn't going to be hauled back in cuffs like a screaming felon, was I?' Fortunately for Biggs, his girlfriend Raimunda was 'with child'. Under Brazilian law no father of Brazilian offspring can be extradited. Ronnie was safe and sound. And with his face across the pages of the Western press he could build a new career: cue the Biggsie Industry – books (his autobiography was published in 1981), TV interviews, documentaries, coffee commercials, hypes, pranks and wheezes. Ronnie Biggs the lovable reprobate, ageing petty scamp who'd raised two fingers to the stuffy Brits. Celebrity is something he clearly enjoys.

'Oh, yes, I love it, to be quite frank, yes. I get a kick out of being Good Old Ron ... Biggsy. I don't dislike it at all. I'm an entertainer now and I'm bloody good at it.'

One of Biggsy's 'best-loved' forays into the world of entertainment came in 1978 when, backed by Paul Cook and Steve Jones and a bloke passing himself off as Martin Borrman, he became the lead singer of the Sex Pistols on a single, No One Is Innocent (Punk Prayer by Ronnie Biggs), and in a segment of the Great Rock 'n' Roll Swindle film. What a lark that was.

'Yeah, what a lark, eh? I'm happy to say that I've got a good sense of humour and I like to preserve it. I met Malcolm McLaren and he said, Do you want to join in a bit of fun? so I said, Well, you know, if there's any loot in it! He said Can you sing? and I said No, and he said, So much the better. And then I sat down and wrote this No-one Is Innocent piece – well, McLaren wanted to call it Cosh The Driver but that was just the kind of ridiculous thing he liked to do. It was totally absurd to suggest something like that and all the workers in the printing presses refused to be involved in it.'

Biggsy's masterwork ran as follows: '*God save Martin Bormann/ And Nazis on the run/They wasn't being wicked, God/That was their idea of fun/God save Myra Hindley/God save Ian Brady/ Even though he's horrible/And she ain't what you call a lady ...*'

Biggs stands by his song: 'I did it with the intention of doing something of value. I didn't want to be accused of doing something that was just a heap of trash. And a far as I'm concerned I do have true sentiments in that song because what I'm saying is everybody merits salvation regardless of what they've done in the past. And I was willing to put my soul on the level with the villains in history as also meriting salvation.'

Martin Bormann, Nazi war criminal, merits salvation?

'Well, the way I see it is if God is going to save anybody then he's got to save everybody. It's no good asking for salvation for the Queen of England but not for somebody like Martin Bormann because if you did the principles of Christianity would break down. If you're going to apply the Christian principles, then you have to apply them totally and that's why I included Martin Bormann and

Myra Hindley and Ian Brady all of whom are guilty of quite heinous things.'

Are you saying that you believe in God, Ronnie?

'Yes, I am.' The man has become earnest and sombre. 'I do believe in God, yes. Yes. And more than I believe in God, I believe in the ideal of Christianity itself. If we could be true Christians, the whole world might be a far better place. Perhaps there will come a time when we understand this and go and just chew the cud in the field like cows do instead of wanting to slit each other's throats. Human life is very, very precious – it's like a million miracles all in one.'

It is hard to see this Christian soul, this philosopher gentleman, as the same person who appeared snarling in the Sex Pistols film in bondage gear with a hankie on his head – 'I don't think I looked like a buffoon. I thought I was quite a sexy little punk' – or as the one who has been portrayed in sensational tabloid reports as a coked-to-the-gills, sex-crazed dissolute with a penchant for voodoo ceremonials. As I mention these latter charges. Biggs puts up no great defence but simply chuckles.

Cocaine?

'Well, put it like this: I'm not a fiend, I'm not a junkie, but I'm no stranger to the hokey-cokey. This is Brazil. It's like eight dollars a gram in Brazil and what's it in London? Eighty pounds? And it's all rubbish anyway.'

Sex maniac?

'Cripes! Well, Brazilian girls are very, very beautiful. You'd have to be a bit of a homosexual or something not to notice that. Yes, I've had my flings but I'm settled down now.'

Voodoo?

'Ha ha. I guess I am into voodoo. Oh, yeah, I don't mind a bit of voodoo. My maid, you know, she's deeply involved in black magic and if there's anybody that needs sorting out she says write down the name of the person and leave it to me. She takes care of it. Raimunda and I took 16 Australian tour agents up to see this ceremony once and it freaked most of them out because it's kind of spooky. My maid turns into a prostitute with a witch's cackle and she started giving me these coquettish looks and she said I want to go for a walk with you so I said OK, where shall we go? and she said To Hell and I said Oh, great, I've never been there before. Nothing much happened, to be frank, but it's more than native flim-flam, you know. It's fantastically mind-boggling.'

So here is Ronnie Biggs with voodoo maid and swimming pool, leading his exotic and peculiar lifestyle. But is it right, one might ask, that this fugitive from justice should still be reaping rewards from a criminal past?

'Well, you always get the Bible thumping brigade who are going to step forward and say This is outrageous, this is scandalous, is Jack Mills's widow getting anything? I can only say, Well, what about all the people who are jumping on the bandwagon ie Jack Slipper, my old adversary? He's always on TV talking about me and does he part with half his earnings and send it off to Jack Mills's widow? I doubt that very much. The man is a buffoon. I can't expect to hope that the whole world is going to love me. The fact that I'm earning money from the misdeeds of my past must really get up their noses something terrible but I'm perfectly convinced that the majority of clear-thinking people in England would be in my favour about being pardoned. I would like to be pardoned – not that I'd come back to England if I was. I've been away so long now that in my soul I don't find there's anything I really miss about England. But it's always nice to hear an English voice. That's why chatting here with you gives me such great pleasure.'

The sun is now over the yardarm. Ronnie Biggs suggests we saunter down the hill for a drink and a meal. But before we can make our escape, the smart, stern figure of Raimunda enters to engage in a blazing row, conducted in Portuguese, with her mate. This is followed by a conciliatory kiss-up. 'Fiery woman,' Biggs winks at me. And then there is an encounter with Mike who is demanding money for a new pair of trainers. 'Fucking give me some money, man, you old cunt. You only gonna spend it getting pissed up!' bawls the surly adolescent. 'See he's picked up some good English,' Biggs winks at me.

In a seedy bar, Ronnie Biggs gulps local beers and pours out some troubles. The man has been ripped off. 'Malcolm McLaren ripped me off,' he says. 'That record got to Number 7, I believe, and I should have made all kinds of bread out of it. Needless to say, I was ripped off. I've got a hundred rip off stories and there will be more.' From here the conversation turns to snooker and to Margaret Thatcher ('A tough old cow') and to all the passing famous who have dropped in to see the ancient Biggs monument. 'The groups, you know, Rick Wakeman, Big Audio Dynamite, The Police. There's plenty enough English people who want to meet me. The Mission came up here for a barbecue, they're all good lads. I reckon they could be as big as The Beatles. And Simply Red, I met. I love that singer's voice – but there's so much soul in it, I reckon he must be gone on drugs, don't you? And I met Priscilla Presley – man, she was gone. Spaced out. Dear, oh dear.'

From here we wander into a local restaurant where we are greeted by a familiar sound. 'Fuckeeng Beegs!!' No, it is not the taxi driver but a massive bearded Brazilian who throws his arms, in the flailing mode of a drunk, around the robber. 'Fuckeeng Beegs' is evidently the accepted form of address for Ronnie in Rio. Drinking palm wine and beer, the Brazilian and Ronnie trade dirty jokes and banter with great gusto. 'Look at the arm of fuckeeng Beegs!' The Brazilian grabs Ronnie's forearm and waves it before my face. 'Ha ha ha, fuckeeng Beegs, drugs, drugs, drugs.' 'Ha ha ha, you're a fucking stupid drunkard!' roars Ronnie. 'I want seeeex with 12-year-old girls,' hisses the Brazilian. 'Ha, ha, ha!' roars Ronnie. And so it goes – until the bill arrives. I dutifully pay.

In the open air, Ronnie Biggs is swaying slightly. He places the arm of an old and trusted friend around my shoulders and demands that I return to Rio next August for 'my birthday celebrations – 60 glorious years' ... This prisoner of Rio – 'yeah, but what a fucking super prison, eh?' – marches with unsteady strides back up the hill towards home. A bark of 'It beats working down t'pit, ha ha!' and he is gone.

Yoko Ono

As an *avant garde* artist she was faintly endearing; as a
peacenik, naive but praiseworthy. But the '80s finds her an
agent of unlistenable records, a dispenser of daft cosmic twaddle and the suspiciously self-promotional curator of her husband's legacy.

YOKO ONO, frail and all in black, leans across the conference
table of her London hotel and reaches for the large bottle of
mineral water that's in front of me. 'Let's just move this,' she
says in her tiny voice. 'I like to see you when I'm talking. I can't
see your eyes.' As Ono's eyes are masked behind a pair of large
trademark sunglasses, it is a surprise that she can see much at all
in this darkened room. 'I can't see *your* eyes,' I say. Slowly she
removes the offending fashion accessories and gives me a stare
that's bordering on defiance. She follows this with a small and
nervous giggle. That's better.

Yoko Ono is in London to open an exhibition of her late husband's doodles and to promote the film Imagine which documents
Lennon's life and career in sympathetic, home-movie style. She is
not here, I have been warned by the PR persons, to discuss Albert
Goldman's already notorious book The Lives of John Lennon, in
which the husband is portrayed as an indolent, drug-soaked brute
of a man and his wife as a callous, manipulative opportunist. It
seems inevitable, however, that we *shall* discuss it. But first I ask
her if it is not a burden to carry on her shoulders the legacy of
Lennon, to be the sole curator of the Lennon museum, chair of the
Lennon industry. Why doesn't she let go?

'It is not a burden at *all*,' she replies sharply. 'First of all you
must realise that if John was alive now we would be living together
and I would be doing the same thing, which is to be with him and
to share various responsibilities and be promoting our work. So

47

what I'm doing is the same thing. Even the things that I did after John's death, like opening the Strawberry Fields in New York and 123 countries participated in it, those things are blessings. They are blessings that were given to us because of John's power.'

Well, that's some sort of answer, I suppose. Yoko Ono seems incapable of direct speech. Her sentences ramble waywardly and 'blessings' is a word she flings into conversation like so much confetti. One should not be too surprised. This is the woman who in a Christmas stocking-filler book called Rock'n'Roll Cuisine (comprised of 'funny' r'n'r recipes like Tony Butler's Guinness Stew and Rod Stewart's liquor-fuelled preparations) contributes this recipe: 'Dream Soup: Put a lot of sunshine in a large bowl. Mix it with your dream of your future. Spice it with a pinch of hope and laughter . . .' (And pass the sick bag.) This is the woman who planted acorns for peace, who composed what she called An Earth Play For Sun And Air (and released it as the Starpeace LP), who filmed loving travelogues of the human bottom, who spread 'messages of hope' to the world (with other half) via the dubious medium of the witless 'bed-in'. You could almost say that Yoko Ono is a . . . *hippy.* Are those bed-ins something she looks back on with pride, one wonders?

'Oh, yes,' she smiles. 'Pride and great joy. Those things we did were blessings. At the time we were doing it people used to sort of laugh at us – we were hoping that they would laugh *with* us but it didn't work out that way. But in the end, you see, it did have an effect. Last year when Reagan and Gorbachev had their summit and shook hands, I sort of felt, well, John and I did have an effect. I was saying to John in my mind, John, we did it!'

So by climbing into bed at the Amsterdam Hilton 20 years ago and summoning members of the press to witness the gesture, John and Yoko eventually made the world a safer place?

'Well, in the beginning John and I were quite alone in what we were saying, the only ones – but now 98 per cent of the *world,* I think, is really for peace. So I don't have to feel that I'm the only one doing anything anymore. It has been a long wait for me and John. We all have responsibilities and emotions to make it a better world for ourselves and for our children and people are now sharing those responsibilities with me and with John. It is a blessing. You see, there's a lot of things about John – the genius that you *don't* know about. When I say the genius that you don't know, you think, Oh, we know it all, but you'd be surprised. John was a person who was playing down what he was. Because certain messages you have to put in simple terms so that it would circulate very quickly and largely in the world. For instance, it is much better just to say "Peace and love" than make a very heady, intellectual kind of statement and John was trying to make his statements as simple as he could. But actually he was a very heady intellectual – an intellectual who was not smugly sitting on his intellectualism so he was even beyond the usual intellectuals.'

John Lennon met Yoko Ono on Monday, November 7, 1966 at the Indica art gallery in London. The hold that the diminutive Oriental 'artist' would soon have over the musician was viewed with suspicion and resentment by the other Beatles (and by the vast majority of Beatles fanatics). She was charged with being the Woman That Broke Up The Beatles – oh, mortal sin! Did Yoko Ono feel the loathing of the world?

'Well,' she says, and pauses for contemplation. She puts her sunglasses back on, takes them off again and pauses some more. 'Well . . . um, it took quite a while for us to realise that was happening because we were so close to each other, John and I, and we were busy trying to understand each other – exchange between us was more important so we just forgot the world. Little small things used to make us very happy, John and me, and everywhere we went we were so overjoyed that we felt like buying a house.' (And they often *did* buy a house.) 'And then when we started to notice the resentment of the world it hit us so suddenly so, um, I don't know. I just feel I was a scapegoat for other things.'

What things?

'Well, um, I don't know. It is too foggy. But, well, if they want to portray me as somebody who broke up The Beatles, somebody who controlled John, the people who write these trashy books have to make me into some incredibly powerful monster, you know. It's amazing. But I think that your common sense could probably tell you that there's no reason that anybody could be that powerful.

'Trashy books'. She said it. The forbidden topic has been introduced and I say the words 'Albert Goldman'. Yoko winces visibly. 'May I smoke?' she asks timidly, reaching into a black handbag for a mentholated snout. 'I stopped smoking six months ago and I felt like a very good girl – all clean – and then this book came out and I went right back to it. It's a blow on our confidence, shall we say?'

One can safely take it, then, that Yoko didn't find The Lives Of John Lennon a jolly good read?

She sighs and pulls in forlorn fashion upon her cigarette.

'Oh, oh, all those things in that book are so negative and cruel. It is terrible. It's amazing. John having dyslexia and diseases – that is wrong and negative and cruel and you can't prove it. We weren't totally normal, like normal people, because we were artists, but we weren't so bizarre. Yet John was supposed to pull my hair and I was supposed to put cat droppings under John's feet. This book makes us sound like totally bizarre people. And we were supposed to treat Sean badly. We *love* Sean. Ask Sean. It is terrible.'

And worse, in the book Goldman accuses Lennon of murder.

'That makes me *terribly upset*. It is terrible. How do I disprove these things? It is impossible.'

One of the most 'bizarre' accusations of all concerns not John but Yoko herself: Ms Ono, it seems, was (is?) a barking mad dabbler in the occult, taking off on whims on weird excursions to Latin America to consult with voodoo priestesses on topics ranging from the medical to how best too deal with her many enemies. Is this true, Yoko? Are you a devotee of the witchy arts?

Yoko Ono jerks upright in her chair and prods the table with an agitated index finger.

'Well, that's *another* thing,' she snaps. Her voice has become almost a fierce hiss of annoyance. 'That is the typical *WITCH-HUNT*!! See, when I was making this album, a feminist album called Feeling The Space – this is not a plug because it's not out anymore – I went to Salem in America and then I went to the hill where they burnt the witch and all that and it turns out this lady was not a witch but just a doctor, an intelligent doctor. And her house looked like that too, you know, a house like a nice intellectual would be living in. So what does that mean to *you*?'

Erm, I'm not entirely *sure*.

'Well, you *must* see what I am saying, don't you? What I am saying is that nobody is going to believe that I'm that powerful a person to control John and do these things they say. So they have to invent these fictions where I have taken a power from the above or from the below or something like that. You see they even say that Sean being born on October 9 (thus sharing his birthday with his father) was some calculated thing that we did, but *I* just took it as an incredible blessing.'

So if *that* book is such 'fictions', why doesn't the widow sue?

'People say that to me. People say, Why don't you just hide or escape from New York City because it's getting really bad? And they say, Why don't you sue? And I thought of all three possibilities. The first possibility, I wouldn't even hear of it. I didn't do anything bad so why should I hide or run? The second possibility – my own book. Well, if this doesn't give me a kick in my pants to write it, nothing would. But the thing is there is that side of me thinking, Who's going to believe my book after all this? But that's not very positive thinking so I shouldn't think about it. And the third possibility is suing, but suing is bringing focus to the negative. I must think in terms of energy and if I focus my attention on the negative, I am lending my energy to that which is negative. So I withdraw my energy from the negative and do something positive so that the positive energy will be focused and it is another blessing. It is incredible that the Imagine film is going to come out in October. (Another reference to John's birthday). It is incredible timing – the kind of timing that no human beings can really plan. So everything it is a blessing.'

There is one thing, surely, that could never be described as a 'blessing'. The unspeakable. The murder of a husband. The events of December 8, 1980 must have left their scars. Does Yoko not feel *angry*?

'Yes, angry,' she says, 'but angry towards what? I wasn't even given the pleasure of being angry towards something that was important. It wasn't worth focusing my energy and my attention on the guy who did it. This person was a deranged person, or whatever. It was a strange role I had to accept after John's death because I had to listen to tapes of his voice and watch many footages of us as if he were alive. It wasn't very easy. But I think some terrible things are usually hidden to us human beings to protect us from it all. You see, John and me were so intense in wanting to be together and every moment meant so much, it was as if we had a premonition that he would die but the premonition was hidden from us. This was a protective measure.'

But did John and Yoko always want to be together? What about the 'Lost Weekend' when the couple separated, John boorishly boozing in Los Angeles whilst the little woman stayed at home in New York? And what of Goldman's report that the couple were on the verge of divorce just before the murder? Yoko dismisses this second suggestion as unworthy of comment; as for the 'Lost Weekend', the words actually make her laugh. And Yoko Ono rarely laughs.

'Ah, the Lost Weekend! These phrases are so very funny because you start to use them yourself. The Lost Weekend, The Dakota Days, ha ha. Oh, you see I sent John away because it was a very logical thing to do and I have a very logical side to me, thank God. It was a very healthy thing to do. It was . . .' – let us guess – a 'blessing'? – '. . . a blessing. And then I let him come home. He could easily have just gone on writing silly songs but he just wanted to have a time to contemplate and go through some soul searching.'

The role Yoko accepted after John Lennon's death – the role of celebrity widow carrying with her for the world the memories of a deceased legend – attracted much criticism. She was accused of cashing in on her husband's death – particularly when she released her solo album Season Of Glass which carried on its cover a photograph of Lennon's shattered, bloodstained glasses.

'Well, this is very interesting,' says Yoko as I raise the charge. 'There is always the flak – Yoko cashing in on John's name, something like that. But gradually, I think, people are starting to understand what it is I am trying to do. There is always the flak and there always was the flak. Like with Sometime In New York City (John and Yoko Lennon's 1972 'radical' LP which included such offerings as Woman Is Nigger Of The World, John Sinclair and Ono's Born In A Prison) we got such flak for it, you know. At the time I was saying to John, Oh, we've got so much flak for this album that it might be that some time later we find that it has some incredible blessing! And when I went to Budapest recently, I realise that everybody is talking about Sometime In New York City and I was saying to John in my mind, John, we did it! Remember? And he was hearing me and smiling. And then I went to Moscow and there were lots of students gathering and they all know our music and one of them said, Do you think that the people in the West understand him? And I thought that was so sweet. John would smile to hear that blessing.'

It is hard sometimes not to feel a pang of pity for Yoko Ono, never blessed with an ounce of her husband's humour and trapped in a role of her own creation – the fragile, saddened celebrity widow. She seems somehow to *invite* hostility . . . and she seems to have somehow dodged my question about the Season Of Glass cover. This showed, did it not, some lack of taste?'

'No, I would stick by it. That made that album not commercial and the record company called me and said, Look, you have to change the cover otherwise we can't put it out because all the shops say they're not going to carry it, and I said, Well, we'll just have to take a chance. To have those glasses on the cover was important because it was a statement and you have to understand that it was like John *wanted* you guys to see those glasses. Because that was what was done to him. I *saw* what was done to him. It was worse than that cover shows. I've seen the worst of it and that cover was just like a very mild statement, a little message to you from John.'

Yoko also stands by the cover of Two Virgins, John and Yoko unlovely and unclothed. She claims that for the Imagine film she surrendered total control to its directors, David Wolper and Andrew Solt, only once interfering – when the camera panned up the Two Virgins sleeve. Yoko insisted that the shot should *not* be panned, because 'that was an art piece, that cover. It was a work of art and we decided to be shown that way exactly as a statement of art and when you pan it, it becomes a different thing and I didn't want it that way. I am still, you see, an artist. It might be an artist's arrogance but I really think that I have enough creative juice in me that I could make art anytime. I will be making music again but as you know the last record, Starpeace, was very controversial and the music world didn't take it too well so I think it's right to give a long vacation – space so they might get prepared for the next one.'

Not wishing to become too engaged in a discourse on Yoko Ono – The Music, I ask one final question. Are you happy, Yoko? She seems taken aback by such an enquiry, deliberating long before offering a response.

'Well . . . well . . . oh, I don't see how I *could* be happy now. But small things make me happy. Like this morning I woke up and the sky was blue and I thought, Thank you, thank you. I think that true happiness is just getting the normal blessing that we have the rights to – being human, being able to think clearly, to see the sun, to feel the rain, to breathe . . .'

This is all getting *very* 'hello clouds, hello sky'. It is time, I think, to take my leave. Her parting handshake is weedy and she is unsmiling as she says, 'So nice to meet you. It has been . . .'

She's not *really* going to say that word again, is she? She is.
'It has been a blessing.'

Edwina Currie

A pair of sharp stilettoes are clacking through the corridors of power. They support a fiercely garrulous Junior Minister who supports self-help for half-wits, seasonal tips for the senior citizen, and banal and insensitive pronouncements for the country's hapless crisp-munching electorate.

B
IG BEN has struck six over this Mother of Parliaments as the young and fiercely keen press officer leads me through the Commons' hushed and hallowed (and very seedy) halls towards his boss's lair. Approaching our destination – the office of the Rt. Hon. Member for Derbyshire South – the corridor's quiet is cruelly interrupted by the sound of stilettoes tapping a frantic tattoo upon the linoleum; we turn a corner to find the trim figure of the Parliamentary Under-Secretary for Health bearing down upon us as, summoned by the Division Bell, she scurries to cast a vote in the Scotland Housing Bill debate that's raging in the chamber below. 'Where's my journalist?' she demands of her press boy – and she scampers on by, carried upon clacking high heels, without pausing for an answer.

I am here, Mrs Currie, 'your' journalist is here. She seems *awfully fit* . . .

The offices of MPs within the House of Commons do not border on the palatial. The Currie den is minute: some sticks of tatty furniture and a veteran fridge – containing, unhappily, a bottle of bitter lemon and assorted other fun-free beverages – crammed into a space scarcely larger than a coffin. But although the room is short on grandeur, there's a noticeboard on the wall that's not so lacking in modesty. Here are pinned the fan letters ('Dear Mrs Currie, I just wanted to let you know that I think you are absolutely wonderful. I think you are fresh and energetic and speaking a lot of sense. Best wishes, Victoria'), press cutting highlights, assorted Currie 'satire' – cartoons, a New Statesman cover where her head's been grafted on to the body of a bikini-clad lovely. These politicians do so like to show they're able to 'laugh at themselves'. And, in pride of place, there's a piece of paper that bears this quotation: 'THE MOST SUCCESSFUL POLITICIAN IS HE WHO SAYS WHAT EVERYBODY IS THINKING MOST OFTEN AND IN THE LOUDEST VOICE.' Theodore Roosevelt said that. And Edwina Currie – she of self-help pronouncements designed for half-wits, she of the garrulous and grating delivery – evidently believes she is acting upon Teddy's words. She has adopted them as a *modus operandi* . . .

Edwina Currie, harridan of health, returns from voting in the chamber ('Housing in Scotland is *not* of enormous interest to my constituents,' she complains of this political chore). She greets me with a sturdy handshake and a savage grin, and settles down in the room's only chair. She is but a Junior Minister, a mere trifle in the corridors of power, yet Edwina Currie (Margaret apart) must be *the* most famous politician in Britain. 'Yes, you're right,' she tells me. 'It's very puzzling.' She feigns puzzlement with a hike of her alarming eyebrows. 'But in opinion polls I got a 78 per cent recognition. Not bad for a *Scouser, is* it?' She laughs.

Mrs Currie is, she will tell you, 'a Scouser'. She's *hugely* drawn to telling you: it's a device to engage the empathy of the common herd. It doesn't work. She's 'a Scouser' and she was born, Edwina Cohen, in Liverpool in 1946. Her father (now dead) was a tailor. He was also a socialist. He used to speak from soapboxes on Liverpool street corners. The daughter seems disparaging about the old man's politics. 'He didn't even vote. All he'd do was argue with the television set. I think that's what encouraged me to get involved with politics because it is simply not enough to *care* and then do nothing.'

Mrs Currie – Miss Cohen as was – is 'a Scouser' and so, while a pupil at the Liverpool Institute for Girls, she would often pop down, in a mildly modified school uniform, to what was described in Mersey Beat as 'Britain's Foremost Beat Music Centre', The Cavern.

'Oooh, it was so *evil*! There was noise and there were hot dogs and Coca-Cola, ha ha. We saw Gerry And The Pacemakers sing You'll Never Walk Alone and we all sang with them long before it became the main song for the Liverpool football clubs – and we had something called The Big Three. My friend June saw The Beatles and was in a totally ecstatic state. Then we'd take our sweaters off and go back to school.'

At this point Mrs Currie unfortunately remembers that she is a member of our Conservative government and so steers her concentration into a political siding to issue a giddy collection of statistical data on Liverpudlian population flux, and job creation enterprise. All of this is leading, no doubt, to some conclusion of Tory magnificence, but I foil the ruse by mentioning . . . America.

In 1965, with a year off between school and university, she took a ('disgustingly smelly') job in an industrial laboratory and made enough money to buy a return ticket to the States, where she had relatives.

'Just *unbelievable*. I was 18 and I found that much of American politics was very puzzling. While I was there President Johnson doubled the draft, the conscription for people to go in as ground troops to Vietnam. I had a particular friend, a boy of 18, who got his draft papers and his reaction was to go out and get drunk and I got so angry. I said, You haven't even been thinking about this, you don't know what your government wants you to do or why, you could get *killed*, don't you know what it's all about? And he said I don't know and I don't care. I was *horrified*.'

It's hard, somehow, to picture Mrs Currie as a peacenik. She's not. 'Well, you see, in Britain we have young men now – and women – who *volunteer* to join our forces and they know they'll be going to hot spots around the world – even in our own country, to Ulster – and they know they risk their lives and they *understand* what they are doing and why. I am quite sure of that. That's one of the great strengths of our country.'

So in America, Edwina was not smoking 'reefers', linking arms with the counter-culture and trying to levitate The Pentagon? *Gracious*, no.

'Oh, no, no, no, *no*. I am *not* a protester. I have never, *ever* been a joiner of demonstrations. There are better ways of achieving things.'

She went to Oxford and the LSE. She married an accountant, Raymond Currie. And in 1975 she became a 'representative of society' – a Birmingham City councillor. Eight years later and she was the Member of Parliament for Derbyshire South. In 1986 she was appointed Parliamentary Under-Secretary at the Department of Health. Almost immediately she became a political celebrity, derided for hasty, banal and insensitive pronouncements on the nation's health. Guidance for simpletons. There was, for starters, the infamous speech, delivered in Newcastle in 1986, in which she took Northerners to task on their dietary 'ignorance'. Everyone oop 'ere, she seemed to be saying, is a beer-swilling, fag-toting moron, going to fat and an early grave via a constant craving for crisps. 'Ah, crisps in Newcastle, hahaha.' A trill of laughter fills the room at the mention of this rib-tickling old chestnut. 'Some of these things amuse me. All I said about crisps in Newcastle was in response to a question about how expensive it is to eat a healthy diet. Now, in fact, that is a load of nonsense. It is possible to eat a healthy diet on any income. Even the Chinese manage it in China. And my response to this question was simply to say, Well, I dunno, we spend 800 million pounds a year on crisps in this country. And that got translated in all sorts of ways by the papers.

'But the interesting thing is when those headlines get written, it's quite clear that almost by *instinct* I have put my finger on something that's very important. There are the Guardian leader writers, the chattering classes, the people who decide what the rest of us should do around a dinner table in Hampstead – *bless* them, I think they're *wonderful*. But in the chip shop in Harrogate it's a different matter. I come from the North. I'm a Scouser. I grew up with people like that whose horizons were more limited, whose control of their own future was much less than for the chatterers of Hampstead, and so I do have a bit of an instinct for what ordinary people are thinking about.'

Really? Don't 'ordinary people' actually find her a bit of a bossy prod-nose, patronising them with advice on wrapping up warm for winter. 'Buy the long johns, find your woolly socks, check your hot water bottles and knit some gloves and scarves. Get your grandchildren to give you a woolly nightcap,' the High Priestess of Tact told our 'old folk' this September.

'Wrap up warm for winter, ha ha! I'm going to say that *again* on Friday. I've got another speech lined up saying the same thing. It's sound advice. Only this time I shall actually quote the Age Concern leaflet that I lifted it all from. Nothing I ever say is original. Nothing at all. You see, what happened with food and diet was that for many people in some parts of the country, they understood very clearly the link between diet and health. But in many parts of the country, particularly in the North where heart disease is at astronomically high levels, they thought that what I was saying was *bizarre*. They couldn't understand it. Do you really mean to tell me, Mrs Currie, that my breakfast is going to give me heart disease? And I'd say, Yes. And when they said, Rubbish, I'd say, It *isn't* rubbish. You don't expect them to jump up and down and agree with you and say how much they love you – you do it because it is necessary. And my message got across because it's finally dawned on people in Harrogate and Dewsbury that fat and bread may kill them.'

Edwina Currie, saviour of our nation's downtrodden. Edwina Currie, heroine of the businessman who once ran the risk of returning from trips abroad riddled with AIDS – until the minister's advice: 'Take the wife.'

'That was good, sensible advice,' she says. 'It had its impact and it's gone all round the world and I've had letters from people in all sorts of strange places thanking me for the advice.'

Edwina Currie, MP, appears to adore the attention her public utterances bring. One might fairly accuse her of being a raving and shameless self-publicist (some interviews in glossy 'lifestyle' magazines even featured Edwina's fashion faves – 'I'd love a real Chanel suit and some Janet Reger underwear'). There are those who have suggested that the woman could do with being deprived of the oxygen of publicity altogether.

'Some people can be very ignorant. They don't understand the job I'm trying to do. I mean, people nag me for interviews, pursue me round the world for interviews, and then they call me a shameless self-publicist. I think they've got a *nerve*, quite frankly. If part of the job is to get across a message to 56 million people then I can't do it by talking to them personally, we have to do it by using the media. I'm just trying to do the job I was appointed to do and that includes trying to persuade people to do less damage to themselves and to spend their money more wisely. We're looking at young people and smoking now, because we know that if people don't start smoking before they're 20, then the odds are very strong that they won't start smoking at all . . .'

By this point in the proceedings, I am *aching* for a snout. And *I* didn't start smoking until I was 25, I inform her. At this, Mrs Currie leans across toward me, batting her eyelids in a disconcertingly flirty fashion: 'Oh,' she says softly, but you don't look 25 *now*, if I may say so.'

Cripes. How lovely. And now the minister, showing admirable commitment to duty, attempts to cure me of my filthy ways:

'Cigarettes affect your hormones. You *do* know that, don't you? Men who are heavy smokers have fewer sperm floating around. Your sperm count will be lowered and if your wife smokes she will probably go into the menopause quicker and she's more likely to have a miscarriage and she's more likely to have certain key handicaps in her baby. Do you fancy that as an end result of what you're up to?' Mrs Currie gives me a pitying smile and adds: 'Does that help you?'

No, I could *murder* a snout.

Edwina Currie certainly likes to talk. The voice – nouveau posh with an abrasive edge, liable to fly off into unplaceable regional accents when she talks about her 'constituents' or of being 'a Scouser' – can prove wearying, making one almost rather wish that she had picked up instead on that *other* famous quote of Teddy Roosevelt's: 'Speak softly and carry a big stick.' The brashness of her approach to public life has hardly endeared her to her fellow parliamentarians (or so it's loudly whispered). They call her Vindaloo – 'That's not very original. *Honestly*, people think that they're producing the most original comments when they come out with this.' They call her Iron Tits – 'Nobody ever uses things like that to my face. If they *did*, well, I'm a Scouser – I can give as good as I get. Anyway, I think I'm a bit of a sex symbol; there's few enough of us in The House, hahaha.' They call her the Princess Michael of South Derbyshire – 'I think that's rather nice.'

'You don't go into politics to make friends,' she assures me, 'you go into politics to do what you feel is best for the country as a whole and that sometimes means taking on vested interests and challenging people. I always bear in mind the saying: 'People only throw stones at trees that bear fruit.' I think that's so true. But I tried something once or twice, to see if comments that were being made were an accurate reflection of what people thought about me. I would go into the Commons dining room and sit by myself at a table and within minutes it would fill up with people who wanted to sit with me and have a natter.'

Her Spitting Image puppet – Vampirella-styled harpy greedily feeding on the lifeblood of the National Health – she finds 'smashing'. It's a giggle and a skylark – and her 'constituents' think so too. Edwina Currie does not approve the idea that she might be the most hated woman in politics.

'Hated? Am I? How do you *know*? I'd be very disappointed if I was hated. My constituents are a big chunk of middle England. I have one of the largest constituencies in the country, South Derbyshire. My vote went up from 26,000 to 32,000 between 1983 and 1987. I've got one of the biggest Tory votes in the country. All I have to satisfy is my constituents, my family and myself. My constituents are optimistic; they work hard for themselves and their families and I do everything I can to help them. My constituents . . .'

Once again Mrs Currie has remembered that she is a member of our Conservative government and is showering me with stuff abut the 'socio-economic indicators' of her South Derbyshire faithful. I manage to despoil her concentration by invoking a name . . . her idol, Margaret Thatcher. One sometimes gets the impression that Edwina, with her orations so hopelessly thoughtless, might be something of a source of embarrassment to the Leaderene. Has she ever been summoned to the Beak's office for a stern wigging?

'Not at *all*. Oh no, no no. On my wall in my Department of Health office I have a letter from her saying 'Controversy is the stuff of politics. What we must not let it do is stop us doing what we know to be right. Yours, ever, Margaret.' I've framed it. And there it is. It's by the door and I look at it every time I go out. She is tremendous. I'm with her every inch of the way. She is an extraordinary person . . .'

And now the junior minister launches into a lengthy eulogy to the genius of her guru and chief, the Blessed Hilda. Over by the door, the press officer, who is taking down this conversation in shorthand in a notebook, is scribbling away furiously. How can he keep pace with this impassioned flow? How to halt the encomium? And appeal to the 'Scouser' in her – a further mention of The Beatles – does the trick. Do you still 'dig' The Fabs, Mrs C?

'Oh *dear*, yes. It was a long time ago. There are people alive now who don't remember John Lennon and I think that's so sad.'

Mrs Currie's eyes are misting over, watering profusely. Are these tears of sincerity – or is that an onion in her handbag?

'When he got shot I remember feeling a sense of grief that was so personal because although I didn't agree with a lot of what he said – some of it was just plain stupid – there was a good heart there. He only really wanted peace – not for himself and his family but peace for the world.' The Junior Minister seems quite choked. 'And . . . he was so gentle. And good. And it is so sad that some deranged mind took it into his head to deprive the rest of us of John. I still feel it. I still feel the grief. And I think *all* our generation feels it.'

Edwina Currie sighs forlornly and blinks back those tears. It takes but a moment for her to compose herself, though, for here she is – harshly, abruptly, (effortlessly) – reverting to her political, 'representative-of-society' mode.

'And there is a message here,' she declares sharply, 'because just that awful fact, John's death, is a good reason to be in politics because you do your best to ensure that the terrorists and the killers do *not* win! Wherever you can, you protect the public from people like that. And I feel better knowing that I'm doing my bit within this free society to preserve what is good about our standards and our quality of life.'

My time in the ministerial presence is up – but before I leave there's one last-ditch effort to save me from myself. She tells me of hospital wards full of smokers who have lost a leg, of hardened arteries and gangrene, of the 400 evil chemicals in cigarette smoke . . . 'Bite your nails instead!' she commands. 'It doesn't do you nearly as much harm as sticking a vegetable in your mouth and setting fire to it!'

Outside the gates of the Palace of Westminster, in the chill night air, I reach in my pocket for a friendly Marlboro. It tastes divine.

Eddie 'The Eagle' Edwards

He's such a perfect all-purpose commodity it's a wonder someone didn't invent him sooner. The perma-grinning pillock of the
piste, transformed by a news-starved media into a uniquely
British 'folk hero', is now ever available for inept publicity
stunts, bubbly personality slots, indeed anything at all (if the
price is right). But we Brits, we *love* a loser.

LAST NIGHT Eddie Edwards was out playing at 'celebrities' once
more – he was up in Birmingham, one of the judges of the Miss
Great Britain contest. And now, from the hall of Edwards's
Cheltenham home, his voice rings out as he tells a mate down the
telephone about all the evening's titillations. 'And then they did
this swimsuit parade. Cor! Hahahaha. Yuuur!'
On the settee of an ageing three-piece suite in the front room,
an elderly woman in a mauve housecoat and one slipper puzzles
over some knitting and asks me yet again if I have 'come far' . . .
'Hahaha, yeah, wooor!' the voice in the hall is rudely cackling.
'And this one girl, this one girl, had this really sort of minuscule
sort of silver swimsuit and the biggest pair of tits I've ever seen,
haw haw.' The grandmother, all of a dither with her needles,
appears not to notice the grandson's vulgarity. The room's other
occupants, vast soft toy figures, Dumbo the flying elephant and
Donald Duck, continue to fix me with goofy gazes.
His phone call completed, a track-suited and frantically beaming
Eddie Edwards bounds in. 'Hello! How about some tea, eh, Gran?'
He pats Dumbo on the head. 'That's Dumbo. I've got about 300
cuddly toys and things. Disney characters and things I've collected
and got from fans, I love them. Aren't they great?'
Eddie Edwards laughs. He seems quite determined to make an
impression on me as some kind of all-fizzing Mr Joviality. He skips
to the mantelpiece and its clutter of knick-knacks. 'This,' he says,
holding up a small and unimpressive perspex trophy, 'is what I got

presented when I did the Goofy Games for Disney – that was like It's A Knockout on American television. We had to jump through hoops and silly things like that. It was a good laugh. And this,' he points to a picture frame containing a typed piece of paper, 'was given to me by the Calgary Fire Department when I was at the Olympics. They wrote this poem for me – "He sails through the air with no ease at all/Our great Eagle, Eddie, he's having a ball/His pop bottle glasses can cause him to fall/But our hearts he has taken away . . ." Hahaha, Great! I've got lots of things all over the place like that and they mean everything to me. That's why I bought this house." Until recently, the Edwards family lived in a small terraced house down the road. But then Eddie made some money, so he bought this larger residence with a flat for himself in the basement. 'With my mum and dad living upstairs, they'll be able to keep an eye on the place because it would break my heart if my toys and things got stolen.'

On first acquaintance, Eddie Edwards seems quite simple . . .

Eddie Edwards was such a gift to the news gatherers called upon to cover the Winter Olympics, it is a wonder that no-one had thought of inventing someone like him earlier. The winter games – all Europeans with unpronounceable names and features indistinguishable beneath the helmets and goggles – were shot on 'personality' and the 'human angle' – and there'd certainly been nothing to stir up much British interest since Torvill and Dean retired from the amateur icecapades. Then along came Britain's first ever competitive ski-jumper, the 'jobbing plasterer from Cheltenham', this 'effervescent' and 'irrepressible' character of the goony features who was guaranteed to finish last. How the press warmed to his pluckiness. How our Des (Lynam) and David (Vine) enjoyed providing us all with those homely, heartwarming winks as they reported on the so-called Eagle's latest Devil-may-care ineptitude on the 'hill'. Thanks to Eddie Edwards, the media were once more able to broadcast those facile and fallacious messages about how brave little Britain always loves the underdog and how aren't we Brits so wonderful because of our doughty ability to laugh at ourselves (whilst the Krauts and the iron men of east Europe have absolutely no sense of humour and care only for victory-at-any-cost, the blaggards, etc.).

'Eddie "The Eagle" is clearly a man born out of his time. With his "never say die" and "jolly good sport" attitude he is a relic from a bygone age', said the Mail On Sunday. The Sun lavished acres of space on the 'madcap ski-jumper'. Today spoke of his 'remarkable personality, sheer guts and lovable eccentricity – he's the stuff from which empires are built', the Mirror would have the man as a 'glorious failure' and an 'intrepid hero' in the space of one soaraway sentence beneath a gigantic headline 'Go Eddie go!' . . . etc . . .

The papers were unanimous: 'The Eagle' made for topping copy and when he arrived back in Heathrow from the Olympics, he was greeted by hordes of press photographers who jockeyed violently for prime photo-opportunity sites, by reporters, by a leggy lovely who'd been employed by a vodka company to dress in a pink leotard and wield a banner bearing the perky legend 'Fiona! Vladivar Loves Eddie!', by cheering members of the public who'd been hooked by all the attention into thinking themselves 'fans' . . . Meanwhile, another 56 arriving passengers, the other members of Britain's Olympic team, were met by family members or no-one at all and slipped quietly away . . .

Telly and the press were much given to hailing this Eddie Edwards as a 'folk hero,' but really they had turned him into just another cheery celebrity, a commodity to fill up the space on Wogan and Headliners and sundry items of TV froth, available by arrangement for supermarket openings, for 'cheeky' photo-calls (posing with Page 3 girls a speciality), for almost any public function you might care to name. From snow slopes catastrophe to Mr Entertainment in one short step.

Eddie Edwards has taken his place on the three-piece suite and is 'doing' a lunch of jumbo egg-mayonnaise and tomato roll – though his mis-aligned jaw ('Eagle Has Crash Landed!' screamed the tabloids when he broke his collarbone in Innsbruck last week) and expansive overbite cause most of the contents to fly out and on to the floor. I ask 'The Eagle' whether he has ever, in his year of fame, analysed just why he is well-known. He peers at me through those spectacles so thick they magnify his eyes to cartoon-caricature proportions, nods and grunts through a mouthful of egg and crust. Yes, he has analysed it. He has a theory of sorts. A theory that borders on conceit. It is this:

'There's a number of reasons why I became so popular,' he says, laying aside the roll for a moment to expound his theories. 'One is because the Olympics is all about the taking part – it's not about the winning. But the Olympics have become so professional now, all they're thinking about is money, money, money – how much is Steve Lewis going to make (I gather he is referring to Carl Lewis here) and blah blah blah and all the sponsorship. And then *I* come along who is a complete amateur, this great guy who hasn't got any money, no training facilities, no trainer, nothing, but he's still made it to the Olympics, see, and he's just there for the love of his sport and for love of his country and they all love it. And they fall in love with me. I am a symbol of the Olympic spirit. I am a breath of fresh air . . .'

And that's not all.

'And also they could see that it was my dream to get to the Olympics and there's a lot of people out there who have sort of dreams like that but they lack the courage and the guts to go out there and grab that dream. But I've made that dream come true and so a lot of people are living their dreams through me. I give them all hope . . .'

The self-eulogy is becoming impassioned. It's as if this laughing stock of the piste has mistaken himself for a Martin Luther King.

'I'm sort of unique. Other ski-jumpers seem to think they're above everybody and they ignore everybody and they're jealous of me because they know I'm the best character in the sport. That's why I get all the attention. I am always happy and bubbly and jolly and always laughing and waving to the crowds and I'm giving people autographs and I've always got time for everybody and I'm bubbly and go-free and people love that. I'm the sort of David against Goliath sort of thing. The true British way. I went out there and fought for my country and I gave people hope and I cheered them up.'

The way he tells it, Edwards seems to suggest that it was almost inevitable, somehow preordained, that he should become a star. No such thing, of course – he got famous simply by accident, because the TV and the papers decided it should be so (so long as it suited them and filled up the space) – but Edwards's personality is unburdened by complications; there's no room for lurking self-doubt, no bewilderment at the position he has found himself in so suddenly. For the time being he is always there in the papers in wacky thumbs-aloft mode, ever pleased to act the goat. So very 'British'. Celebrity was thrust upon him and he is exploiting it for all it's worth (a lot) – though this wasn't entirely his own idea.

When, a year ago, 'The Eagle' became the news item of Calgary, his earning potential was spotted by an astute agent/manager who was quick to scoop up the buffoonish product. Simon Platz, a well-spoken man in his early thirties, a music biz entrepreneur who recently refounded Fly records, T. Rex's '70s label, is cagey when I ask him why he selected Eddie Edwards as a client. 'The papers were all over him,' Platz says, 'and it seemed like he could use some advice. I was just trying to help out.'

Platz's first act of benevolence, as soon as the Olympics were over, was to stick his new charge in a recording studio to forge that obligatory instant-celebrity creation, a novelty single. Fly, Eddie, Fly, it was called – a hugely forgettable singalong nonsense. (Since then, Edwards has appeared on disc again, on a rap number called Mr Ed for an LP called Dance Diverse on Mr Platz's label.) Doesn't Edwards feel a bit of a fraud posing as a pop singer?

'No!' goes 'The Eagle' with an infantile giggle that causes him to choke on a last portion of roll. 'It's a good laugh. Doing those records, it's quite nice and it's another side of my bubbly personality that people appreciate. We could bring out a Stock, Aitken and Waterman sort of boppy disco record that would be a Number 1 if we wanted to but I think people would see through that – they'd say, That's not him. It's a bit the same as if Rick Astley tried to become a sportsman. I don't really think somehow people would think it quite fitted in with his image, sort of thing.'

Edwards offers this shrewd analysis of the pitfalls of showbiz cross-categorisation with profound eyebrow-knitted seriousness. He has clearly worked out (or been told) that it is *vital* to maintain his role and image, step not from type. Under the guidance of Platz, he has gone from poor ski-jumper to recording artiste, 'author' (a hastily concocted hardback, Eddie The Eagle: My Story, 150 pages of towering banality), after-dinner speaker, beauty pageant con-noisseur, television desirable, and the rest. No celebrity chore too trifling for this opportunist (or his management).

'We've done more or less everything that's asked for us. And some people ring up and they're a bit hesitant and they say, Do you think Eddie would mind doing this – it's a bit dangerous, and all it is is jumping off a stool in a shopping centre or something. We'd jump off the top of the Post Office Tower if they wanted us to – if the money was alright. The only times we turn things down is when they sound dodgy . . .'

Dodgy? Memories of opening a Tourist Information Centre in

Devon, the time they couldn't locate an eagle outfit and he had to dress up as a chicken, move him to such convulsions of laughter that he is forced to resume his seat and remove his spectacles to wipe away the tears. But dressing in feathers to do a birdy party piece is not what Edwards means by 'dodgy'. 'Dodgy' means 'financially dodgy – that's the only time we turn things down, when they're iffy about the price. People think I'm a berk and I go along with that until it comes to the deal and then I go, You either come up with a better deal than that or you can stick it up your arse! And then they're surprised because I'm not a berk, ha ha.'

Eddie 'The Eagle' recently made £35,000 in one day for six personal appearances and if you want the alluring dignitary to spice up *your* function, you'll have to cough up at least £1,000 (per hour, plus expenses). Book well ahead – he is a busy fellow.

'How much am I worth? Hahaha, what a question!'

The papers have said he's made a quarter of a million in the past six months.

'Well, that's not a bad estimate but they don't know the half of it. That's the figures we give the papers for tax reasons because we know how the papers work and we feed them information that sometimes isn't quite correct. I won't tell the press what I've bought. I won't say to you, either.'

The interview started out with Edwards boasting of being a 'symbol of the Olympic spirit', a brave little Briton, plucky David battling for no reward against the European Goliaths of over-commercialised sport. And this is the image he strives to convey to the journalists from Austria and Switzerland who continually interrupt our conversation with telephone calls that are eagerly accepted. But as he chatters keenly to Q of his discovered sly business nous, of smart deals and financial adventures in celebrity land, he reveals himself to be more an example of dynamic Thatcherism – humble man makes money for nothing – than an emblem of de Coubertin's Olympic ideal.

'I've got my manager and I've got about 15 or 20 agents around the world and I've got solicitors and financial advisers and consultants, so it's a big business and if half the projects we've got in 1989 come off, we stand to do very, very, very well. Probably, I wouldn't have to work again.'

And he reels off the projects. He is unstoppable. There is a planned extravaganza for the opening of a Las Vegas hotel, a US kiddies' ski club, possibly a movie of his life story, a production company to make commercials (look forward to Eddie Edwards, the people's friend, in advertising campaigns for Cadbury's Creme Eggs, Woman's Own, After Eight Mints and a 'major car company' . . .).

One might be racked with jealousy at this massive financial gain – but, of course, there is always a sour side to this gay celebrity carousel, is there not? When I ask him if he has no qualms about a prominence based, as it is, on such slender foundations, he misses the point. I was hoping he might crack and confess 'Yes, yes, isn't it stupid that a sporting nonentity such as I should be propelled into the media spotlight where there's always a warm cushion waiting upon the TVam sofa? I don't really understand it, to be honest'. Instead, he leans toward me and assumes an air of saddened sincerity.

'It's a very lonely world.'

It is terribly sad.

'I meet a lot of people that try to use me. People want to be my friend but only because I'm famous and they want to be seen with me. Especially girls. I've met some many different girls that have been real bitches. I went out with one girl and she got rung up by a journalist and all of a sudden there was this story where she said, "He dumped me because I wouldn't go to bed with him". It drove me potty. The whole thing drives me potty sometimes. I am very wary of girls . . .'

Oh, well. It will all be over soon, won't it? The public are fickle, celebrity is fleeting, the Edwards face will, surely, soon be forgotten. How much mileage is there in the 'jolly-good-loser' story anyway? I put this to Simon Platz. The manager, less than convincingly, rejects the proposition, saying, 'When Eddie had his accident in Innsbruck, he was on the front page of the Sun and the Guardian. That shows his appeal is across the board and growing . . .' The Eagle himself, of course, is quite incapable of entertaining any thought that he might one day be a 'nobody' again.

'Oh, no, I don't think that because I don't think the public will *ever* get sick of me because I'm still the same bubbly person I always was and I'm still a bit unique and always laughing and I live life to the full and I know so many people who work in a bank and they come up to me and they say, I absolutely *hate* working in the bank, and they wish they could be like me, you see. And . . .'

The Eagle pauses. I suspect he's got another of his insightful celebrity analyses on the brew . . .

'And I'm not a child molester or a rapist or something like that. I think people appreciate that . . .'

Bros

Travel, they say, broadens the mind. Consider the case of the twins Goss. There's travel aplenty as Bros embark upon their inaugural visit to the New World. But what lofty insights has their voyage vouchsafed them? 'We've got *messages*,' they promise.

'**V**ERNA!' cries Luke Goss, the drummer. 'Verna! Can I have another triple Hennessey's please, darl?'

Verna, beleagurered waitress of the St Paul Hotel. St Paul Minnesota – clearly unused to ministering to the needs of upstart pop combos from the United Kingdom and their unruly entourages – obliges and Luke Goss drains the glass. For his supper tonight, Luke Goss dressed in routine Bros fatigues (bestudded black T-shirt, jeans a-ripped at the knees and held up by a belt with a gargantuan, taste-free buckle featuring the Rolls-Royce motif), is having an ample platter of pasta for starters and as a main course he thinks he'll try the beef. 'Verna? This beef. Has it got bones in it?' 'Er, no, sir,' replies the patient Verna. 'It's . . . it's beef.' 'Oh, right, I'll have the beef. Twice!' 'Er, they're *very large* portions, sir,' explains the stoical Verna. 'Yeh, and I'm *very* hungry, hahaha!'

At the far end of the table Matt Goss, the singer, is filming the proceedings, this slap-up American feed, with a video camera. His lens alights on Dave who is munching buttered bread. Dave is Bros's hairdresser, the only man in the world, apparently, who can do the Bros cut just so. Dave was flown out from England this afternoon because the boys had run out of hair-gel and felt in need of his particular snip. As Dave eats, Matt makes crude scoffing noises into the vid-cam's built-in microphone. Should be a hoot when viewed.

'Bros is like a very anti-drugs band,' Luke is telling me as he tucks into his boneless beef. 'You know, man,' he is warning me, 'drugs are very, very dangerous. They scare the shit out of me. Cocaine. Evil. Don't do it. I've seen heroin once in my life. My dad (Mr Alan Goss was a policeman) showed us a bag of heroin after a bust. It makes you think . . . Verna! Give us another triple Hennessey's!'

Poor Verna arrives with a large measure of brandy and Luke's second order of beef. He rejects the latter – 'Full up now, Verna' – drinks the former. Already seemingly well-versed in the ways of proto-excessive rock star behaviour. Luke Goss and his twin brother Matt are just 20.

Bros, Britain's biggest current mass pop phenomenon, are on their first tour of these United States. The group – Matt 'n' Luke and the stalwart backing musos (bass player Craig Logan, the one no-one fancied, is already but a dim memory) – are supporting the blonde and perky teen pet Debbie Gibson (as sponsored by Natural Wonder Cosmetics) on a continental jaunt. But things are not going so well. Bros may be 'huge' in Blighty and points elsewhere (Europe, Australia, Japan) but in America they're unknown – and peeved about it. 'In a couple of years or so,' they tell me defiantly and in unison, 'we'll be selling out Shea Stadium.' Maybe or maybe not. But for the moment they're just a support act to Debbie, strutting their stuff in the confines of Debbie's twee, tot-orientated fairy-tale castle stage set; and Debbie's not selling very many tickets at all.

The St Paul Civic Center seats 8,000 people. For the Debbie Gibson Natural Wonder Cosmetic experience there are less than 2,000 in the place. Pre-teenage girls in Gibson-styled fedoras with younger sisters in Care Bear rompers clutching the hands of reluctant and apologetic-looking parents who've shelled out big bucks on this regrettable musical event, for the most part. As Bros bound on to the stage at 7.30 p.m. on the dot – Matt nervously shrilling, '*We're from* London so we need some help, OK?' and the backing musos striking up a failed call-and-response/product-recognition cry of 'B-R-O-S! B-R-O-S!' – the atmosphere could not be cut with a knife or with any other available kitchen utensil. There is no atmosphere to cut. The Bros 'set' is undeniably 'tight' . . . the first hit I Owe You Nothing, Don't Bite The Hand, and I Quit (featuring Matt's quaint philosophical rumination 'Most of my friends were strangers when I met them'), peppered with sturdy and strident electric guitar solos . . . respectable 'rock' music. Bros do the 'biz' but apart from one small girl who flings one small furry toy in the general direction of the pirouetting singer, there is no audience reaction to speak of whatsoever. On stage things begin to go horribly wrong. Matt is muttering sheepish apologies about 'technical problems'. 'This has never happened to us before,' he whimpers. Brother Luke looks distraught. After a fourth song (a version of Stevie Wonder's Higher Ground) and a 15-minute set, Bros depart the stage. Apparently, I later learn, the 'click track' has gone awry (this means that the drummer finds it impossible to keep in time) and something has gone wonky in the keyboard sample department (this means that its impossible for Bros to 'deliver' any more of their celebrated numbers).

Matt Goss and Luke Goss are in tears of frustration. 'Me and my bruv, we're *professionals*,' Luke is saying. 'Something like this, it's – this is the honest truth – it's an insult to our art, d'you know what I mean?' The American video director, here to shoot a Bros promo, replete with frugging foxtresses, for the new single, Chocolate In A Box in the twin city of Minneapolis in the morning, courageously feigns enthusiasm; he's never seen Bros before but 'Wow, these guys, they're so *channelled*!' he exclaims. One does not care to enquire just what he means. He seems quite mad . . . Out front the toddlers couldn't give a damn. Roll on Debbie Gibson and bed . . .

Matt: 'This tour . . . I've been down in the dumps. I've been depressed . . .'

Luke: 'Matt is *this* weak. He's so sensitive . . .'

Matt: 'Everything affects me. Luke looks after me. He protects me. He's physically trained his body now so that comments and problems don't even get into his brain. Not because he's thick. Because he's trained himself to disregard it. But I'm like a dartboard. Sharp things go in, you know . . .'

Luke: 'I cry probably three or four times a week. That's my release. But Matt the other night he was was so tense, I was absolutely terrified. He was on the bed and it took us two hours to try and relax his body. He just couldn't move his body at all and it took me six cups of tea to figure it out. I thought he was going to have a nervous breakdown. I thought this tour was over and that's the truth. He was a nervous wreck and I . . . I have to look after him . . . these people are fucking us up. These people in this industry are fucking us up. It's the whole . . .'

Matt: 'It fucking scares the shit out of me . . .'

Luke: 'It's the whole vibe . . .'

Matt: 'I don't want the press to know how weak I am. Because they'll *get* me.'

Luke: 'It's the whole vibe of his business. It's so lonely, sometimes . . . It's so lonely . . .'

Britain's biggest current mass pop phenomenon are, as we speak, a little the worse for wear, a trifle tired and emotional. We are in the wee wee hours. A post-mortem on the Civic Center fiasco has been conducted at length in the Goss twins' hotel bedrooms. Soundmen have been fired, Goss twins are hopping mad. 'We're so professional,' runs the thinking and the corporate speech. 'We *demand* professionalism from the people behind us. We *pay* them.'

Bros are downcast on this grey Minnesota night. They have let their 'fans' down. (No, I dare not tell them there were no Bros fans in that Civic Center audience). But the bristling confidence of young men with bristling haircuts is, nonetheless, very much in evidence. Luke leans forward in the hotel foyer sofa and says, 'But we don't want this to be a whinge about this one bad gig and that, know what I mean? It's important that you set the record straight about Bros.' 'Yeh,' says Matt. 'You've flown all this way and you're our release. We want you to set the record straight about Bros.'

This responsibility is somewhat daunting. No matter: let me try. Matt Goss would like you to know that, contrary to popular belief, he *can* actually sing.

Matt: I'll fucking . . . I'll go and take on anyone because I know my voice. I can take on anyone, any white singer who wants to give me a go. I'll give him one and . . .' Luke interrupts. 'Yeh, yeh, and they talk about your voice and my drums never even get *mentioned and* . . . 'Matt says. 'Yeh, Lukey, but *my* voice, I'm professional like you are and . . .' And Luke says, 'But listen, 'cos I listen to my drums sometimes and I think, yeh, I'm pretty good.' And Matt says, 'Yeh, *'course* you're good. Lukey, you're the *best* and what I'm trying to say about the singing . . .' And . . . 'Yeh, but hold on, hold on, listen, Matt . . .' Interviewing these South London heart-throbs, evidently brimming with twin sibling rivalry, is possibly one of life's less simple tasks. 'I've never said this before but my drums is so professional, man, know what I mean? Mike Rutherford asked me to play on his album. Mike And The Mechanics asked me to do the album, right? And on the Bros album (The Time) I played it all live – bang bang – took me up to 27 hours a track but I did it all live because I'm such a professional!'

So, do not suggest that the golden boys cannot sing or play. It gets their goat and I am here to set the record straight. Worse even than this to the Peckham twins is the insulting intimation that Bros are just one more disposable commodity fabricated by the business-wise – in this case manager Tom Watkins – for teen consumption. Watkins, it is supposed, is solely responsible for the Bros look, the 'style', even the music. I am here to set the record straight . . .

'*Listen*,' says Matt, approaching fury. 'I will tell you *now* that Tom Watkins has fuck *all* to do with my career and . . .' Hold on, Matt, bruvs, hold on.' Luke is similarly apoplectic. 'Tom Watkins is not involved with my career. Listen, I'll tell you what happens. We're suggested something and we say yes or no and . . .' The interruption interlude will now go into overdrive . . .

Matt: 'See, people think Tom Watkins saw us when we had long hair and decided to cut it off . . .'

Luke: 'Yeh, he *did* see us when we had long hair but we did know what was going down and we actually went into a barber's shop on our own and had our hair cut off for ourselves and . . .'

Luke: 'And we had our hair cut off and we walked into Tom Watkins's office and everybody laughed at us. That's the honest truth.'

Matt: 'Yeh, that's the honest truth because all Bros was was something that needed sticky bits put on it . . .'

Luke: 'It was made a bit more solid . . .'

Matt: 'But we don't need it anymore because we're now a snow-ball that needs a bit of a shove along now and then and Tom is a brilliant manager but . . .'

Luke: 'Tom is very extrovert and blase and a brilliant manager but he's done TV and we don't want our manager going on and saying he's a genius and he's a hitmaker. Bollocks! Sometimes he's a bit too big for his boots.'

Matt: 'Hold on, Tom is brilliant, I wouldn't want any other manager . . .'

Luke: 'I tell you, Matt, 50 per cent of his ideas are rubbish. Absolute rubbish . . .'

Matt: 'Yeh, but I wouldn't have any other manager on the planet because . . .'

Luke: 'Because a great band needs a great manager. *We're* a great band. We need a great manager because you don't put a diamond on a silver setting, right? You put it on an 18-carat gold setting or platinum. Right? Like, you can't make chicken soup of out chicken *shit*. That's very apt.'

Matt: 'But it's like Tom's the greatest manager on the planet but on The Time he didn't have one lyrical input because he's not a musician . . .'

Luke: 'He can write some good songs, thought.'

Matt: 'No, I'm talking about *our* stuff, right?'

And so it continues. The twins in disjointed argument. I am supposed to be their 'release' but I am failing singularly to get a word in edgewise. 'Lukey, let's not talk about this,' says Matt, finally. 'We're on tour; it's the tour.'

Immediately before embarking on this tour, Bros performed at Wembley Stadium to 65,000 of their highly enthusiastic fans. That was the proudest moment on their lives, they will tell you. Everything since has been anti-climax.

Matt: 'Idealistic feelings can be very soothing. You know when I played Wembley Stadium, do you know what it looked like to me? 70,000 people in slow motion. There wasn't one bit of hate there.'

Luke: 'No hate there.'

Matt: 'It was 70,000 people all tuned into the same thing. It was almost like playing to a city of love.'

Luke: 'It *was* a city of love. You could feel it. A mini-city of love full of natural energy. It was all love and people were hugging and that's what Bros is about. We've got messages.'

Matt: 'If we do nothing else apart from trying to spread love and trying to spread awareness and honesty, then I'll be a very happy person.'

Luke: 'That sounds, like, really corny but deep down I am a hippy. I love the idea of love and happiness for everyone. I love that. And we can spread that to our fans. It may sound corny but we're like God. Take drugs, for example. We're aware of our responsibility so we put a big no entry sign next to our throats. No drugs, drink but drink in moderation, beware of AIDS, beware of diseases. Whatever, we make people aware.'

Matt: 'It's like when I write a song I know that three and a half million fans are definitely going to listen to this song and you just go . . . phew!'

Luke: 'And our fans, for a start, our fans are the best.'

Matt: 'They're our lifeblood, I love them.'

Luke: 'They love us and they're individual. Is your kid on cocaine? Is your kid smoking pot? Is your kid getting pissed out of her brain every night? Or has she got a Bros poster in her room and is she driving you mad listening to the Bros album every night? Which would you rather have?'

Bros fans – Brosettes – have been perceived, however, as little monsters. There's the Peckham Posse, a gang of particularly obsessive admirers who have been known to turn on rival fans with sharp instruments in piques of jealousy. The Goss boys won't have a word spoken against their public. They take it as criticism of *themselves* and leap to the defensive. 'For God's sake,' says Matt, 'we're Britain's lads. We're Britain's boys and we're not doing a bad job around the world to represent Britain's music.' 'It makes me sick,' agrees the brother. 'We're Britain's lads and people in England should be proud of us but they're all so pessimistic. Why do some people want to hate us so much? Some of the slagging in the press is so incredibly nasty. We've never told a journalist before that it bothers us because we don't want to lower our defences.' 'But it *does* piss us off,' says Matt, softly, almost threateningly. 'It really . . . pisses us off.'

They have been on tour in northern America for just three weeks and already Bros feel that they've got 'the road' in their blood systems. Ah, the road. 'The road,' says Luke. 'Thinking about it, the road is my life.' 'I love the road,' says Matt. 'I love the coach from the bottom of my heart. Because I get to drink, I get to get drunk – not drunk as in pissed but a bit tipsy – and I get to play Nintendo baseball (*exciting video game*). The coach . . . The road is my world. That's the honest truth.'

Later on the boys will show me some of their road movies – home flicks they've shot on the amateur video camera. Skylarks and Spinal Tapism. Here's the saxophone player in a state of some disrepair, he's talking of 'knobbing' and displaying his private parts. Here's the bass player in hog-whimpering state; he is bending over a hotel toilet bowl and, egged on by his young bosses, throwing up his supper. The vulgar clips reel on. Ah, the innocence of youth. 'This is how we unwind,' explains Matt. 'This is our release from the whole vibe of this business.' Luke: ''Cos it's a lonely business.' Matt nods dolefully. 'Lonely.'

Lonely but worth it. They take a great deal of their pride in their work and their luck. 'We're in such a lucky position to be able to influence people's lives and to give people so much love and pleasure.'

Matt: 'They compare us to Wham!, the Bay City Rollers and

The Beatles. And if they want to compare us with three bands that have actually made history, that's fine – but my level of history making will go into a further level. I'm not going to stop writing music and I'm not going to stop performing. People *believe* in us. Our only obstacle is the people who *don't*...'

Keith Floyd

First find your galloping gourmet, a rakish 'hands-on' purveyor of recipes and rib-tickling anecdote. Add just a *soupçon* of anarchy, the faintest flavour of rock'n'roll, garnish with a bow-tie, place on television and serve, lukewarm, as often as possible.

T IS shortly after midday and Keith Floyd sits slumped in the bar of his London hotel, the smart Warldorf, nursing his favour-ite tipple. Bell's and ice. Dressed in crumpled suit, white shirt, that ever-present bow-tie (crimson), dark glasses slung around his neck on a chain, he looks somewhat the worse for wear, a battered roue from some slightly seedy gentleman's club. Last night the televisual cook was up late, hitting the 'Vodkatinis', celebrating the publication of his latest book, A Feast of Floyd (recipes and rib-tickling anecdote).

The hair o' the dog Guinness he had earlier in the pub round the corner failed to restore him to normalcy; the Bell's isn't working much better. The man feels grim. He lights another Marlboro – 'a merry Marlboro,' he has it – and I suggest that such copious cigarette consumption may be less than beneficial to a gourmet's palate. 'Horseshit!' he rasps, his eyes clamped resolutely shut.

Later in the restaurant (the smart Langan's Brasserie) – after a crawling taxi ride that has convinced him that London is the pits of the earth – Floyd is still in morose mood.

'Oh, Gawd,' he groans, 'looks at them all!' His arm gestures at the tables lined with business folk troughing into stout lunch. 'They're all pinstripes. They're all making deals. They're all trying to sell things. Miserable. Miserable. It's all fucking shit!' Oo-er. 'Ha ha ha!' The venomous laugh rings out across the room. 'As Dylan said, *Money doesn't talk, it swears*. I'll go with that . . .'

Maybe his chosen meal – simple fare: chicken 'with lots of bread sauce and lots of spuds' – will coax Britain's most celebrated TV 'chef' into a more amiable frame . . .

Keith Floyd was born in 1943 at Folly Farm outside Reading. He remembers having 'terrible spots' and an early interest in and appetite for food. 'Lots of things came out of the garden: real food.' Despite 'humble' origins (his father was a meter tester for the electricity board), he went to the public school (Wellington, in Somerset, where England's keenest man, Jeffrey Archer, was Captain of everything) and got into the rugger team. 'When we went away for matches, we'd have great teas.'

He left at 16 and joined the Bristol Evening News (where he had his own column, 'prosaically called Youth Notes', and where Tom Stoppard also worked: 'Stoppard and his gang would sit at the back of the newsroom looking like Jean Genet with black glasses and leather jackets, smoking Gitanes'). He found the life of a journalist 'too pressured', however, and soon joined the army instead. What on earth possessed a young man with a taste for wine, for a feed and the good life to take this course, one wonders?

'It was an absolute whim,' Floyd confesses. 'I went to see a Michael Caine film called Zulu and it was absolutely goddamned fucking brilliant. Don't shoot till you see the whites of their eyes, hahaha, soldiers getting pissed and the preacher going mad and incestuously assaulting his daughter. It sparked off a dash of romanticism, so the next morning I walked into a recruiting office and joined the army. And, of course, it was as boring as hell. In Germany playing with tanks. Boring as shit. But it did enable me to drink lots of German wine . . .'

After the army, Floyd did menial tasks – 'peeling potatoes, catering for the BBC, any old shit' – until, eventually, he could afford to open his own restaurant. He's been cooking stuff ever since. And a BBC producer, David Pritchard, who dropped in at a Floyd restaurant five or so years ago was so impressed with Floyd's 'hands-on' style of catering management – swaying before his customers, nibbling their spuds and supping their wine and treating them to impromptu renditions of First World War poetry (Owen, Sassoon, Graves) or the Bob Dylan songbook for no evident reason – that he (Pritchard) decided to put Floyd on the telly. And the rest, as they say, is history. Floyd On Fish, Floyd On Food, Floyd On France, Floyd On Britain And Ireland, Keith Floyd a galloping gourmet sticking his fingers in the bouillabaise and tossing back the wine with gusto, acting the eccentric, plummy goat for the delight of the viewing millions.

Keith Floyd, TV personality, was soon infinitely more famous than Keith Floyd, cook. Ask him if he feels comfortable with a celebrity status that's been gained or thrust upon him in his middle-age and Floyd lurches forward for his Bell's as if he's received a sharp poke from a cattle-prod.

'Celebrity?' he snarls. '*Ce-leb*-rity?' he sneers. 'It's a heap of shit! You get frightened to go out. People you'd like to speak to don't speak to you because they're too polite to interfere with your privacy. People you don't want to speak to hound you to death. Everybody thinks you're incredibly rich when you're not. Every-body thinks you're a dickhead – and one thing I am not is a dickhead. And there is no-one . . .' he sighs and pauses and fumbles for a merry Marlboro, 'there is no-one to talk to. *That* is the trouble with being a fucking celebrity. No-one *believes* you if you say you're lonely or you're worried or you're depressed. They just don't believe you because . . . because you're the goddamned Man On The Telly.'

The Man On The Telly, the man in the wilting bow-tie, looks close to tears. It's lonely at the top (or thereabouts). He seems, in many ways, a highly unstable solution.

'They're all out to get you,' he says. 'I never asked for any of this and I don't give a shit if all this stops. The French have an expression for being ripped off which is to be 'plumed' – you know, all your feathers pulled out one by one. But my expression is better. What they – the public, the shits in television, the shits on the newspapers – *really* do is they pull your entrails out through your arsehole and then they throw you away when you've got no guts left.'

Shits on the newspapers. The hounded Man On The Telly has had a bellyful of them. They've said he drinks 472 bottles of Scotch before he rises of a morning. 'That's horseshit!' he cries, calling for a fresh beaker of the hard stuff. 'A drunk couldn't write eight books and make 25 television programmes in three-and-a-half-years. It couldn't be done. I never drink at home . . . because I never go home, haha . . .'

There's been an obligatory sex 'scandal' – TV CHEF TRIFLED WITH ME IN HOTEL FLING – Bride's Fury (News Of The World) – in which Floyd's lovemaking 'prowess' was described as 'exciting as eating a mouldy cheese sandwich'. They've called him a 'potbel-

lied Lothario' and a 'Bentley-driving bounder'. They've lovingly
dwelled on his two failed marriages ('It takes *two* to make a
marriage fail and that's all I've got to say about *that*,' he tells me)
and they've painted him as a toff buffoon. Sadly, he does not see
the funny side.

'All that . . .' He shakes his head disconsolately. 'All that . . . it
hurts like hell. Really does. And it's better to be thought a fool
and keep your mouth shut than it is to open it and prove beyond
all doubt that you are a fool. You can't get involved. But it hurts
your sister or your uncle or your mother or your daughter and I
think it's *shit*. But Hemingway said, *Never complain and never
explain*. I'll go with that . . .'

A fierce hangover can wreak a terrible vengeance upon a man's
sense of well-being. Keith Floyd is tinkering with his 'shades' and
acting the paranoid, misunderstood, woebegone wretch. 'People,'
he says, 'people . . . I know I piss people off. Quite a lot of them.
Take my producer (David Pritchard). David will tell you that I'm
the most difficult, awkward, obnoxious, single-minded, arrogant
fuckpig that ever slid across this earth.'

'And *are* you?'

'What? *No!* One thing I am not is an arsehole. But David is a
bastard and he'll tell you I'm a bastard because we have absolutely
nothing in common except a desire to make brilliant programmes.
I wear hand-made shoes. I like suede waistcoats. David doesn't.
He thinks I'm slightly right of Vlad The Impaler and I'm not. And
he doesn't like Elvis Presley which is inexcusable. And he doesn't
like Dylan. And he likes drinking 20 pints of Bass and I like
drinking 20 bottles of wine. And I'm not a dickhead but everybody
thinks I am a dickhead. Christ!'

Come, come, bleak fellow. There must be some joy in the life of
a somewhat anarchistic celeb in a dicky bow, surely? Up to a point,
The Man On The Telly agrees.

'Well, I make a lot of people happy. I know that. Sometimes
being The Man On The Telly – particularly when I went to LWT
to present their rotten Clive James On Television thing which any
glove puppet could do – feels like being raped – though I don't
know what it's like to be raped – but sometimes . . . I'm innovative.
I can see a good idea coming. The shows I do aren't cooking
programmes, they're a gastronomic Sesame Street. It's to do with
giving people a chance to enjoy themselves, to give them a chance

to see where the box is that they can open. I give people something, you see. And at the risk of talking myself into Pseuds' Corner, there has to be an antidote to the performing Keith Floyd. It sounds utterly crass but you can't laugh until you cry. You've got to be aware of some pain, you have to be hungry before you can *give*. I don't care who you are – Jesus Christ or the postman – the reason you're *giving* is you hope that something might drift back your way at the end of the day, something that's meaningful and warm.'

Somewhere in the midst of this monologue, I find myself failing to catch Keith Floyd's drift. I ask whether he's referring to a belief in, ahem, 'karma'. The Man On The Telly gives me a withering look. 'No.' Oh. 'I'm quite happy to commercially exploit what I do. After all, that's what we're all here for and anybody who tells you we're here for any other reason is a barefaced hypocrite. You've got to get as much money as you can and then bugger off.' But, Mr Floyd, money doesn't talk, it swears.

'You get as much money as you can *without* selling your soul . . .'

Finally. Lashings of bread sauce, bottles of wine are appearing on the table. An appetising sight and Floyd seems no longer so out of sorts. He raises a glass to his lips.

'You know, I went to the Sun Studios in Memphis and somebody tried to put a Rocky Stallone record on!'

I beg your pardon?

'No, what's he called? That jerk. That bloke who wears the McEnroe tennis band?'

Um . . .

'Springsteen! They tried to put a Bruce Springsteen record on in Sun Studios where it all began. You can't have that sort of thing.'

Keith Floyd feels quite passionate about rock music. He is happy to decribe himself as a rock'n'roll cook. He perks up considerably when I ask him about the first record he ever bought – he can't remember but it was something by Elvis – and he is afforded an opportunity to recall selling all his fishing tackle, when a boy, to go out and squander money on pop discs.

'Most people, when I'm interviewed ask me what my favourite meal is. What a boring question. This is *great* to talk about something other than food. Someone like me who knows all the words to Purple People Eater has no time for Bruce Springsteen, hahaha. On a good day I know all the words to the classic songs – because I *had* all the classic songs, the lot. I sold *everything* to buy rock 'n' roll. Little Richard and Jerry Lee Lewis and, of course, Elvis. I felt Dion And The Belmonts and Fabian were in the crap division of the whole lot but *Elvis* . . . Do you know Elvis never had any blue suede shoes? Forty-five years old and I discover that. Talk about being *plumed* . . .'

Did Keith Floyd every fancy himself as a sort of rock singer? one enquires. The Man On The Telly bangs a bottle of wine down upon the table and cries: 'I *am* a rock singer! It's just that, like Kris Kristofferson said, I guess I'm just the river that never made it to the sea . . . That line rips me *right* down the middle . . .'

Floyd talks of The Beatles. 'I love the nasty Lennon songs. He's got a *powerful* bitterness . . . I inadvertently caught, on the World Service, Part 28 of Paul McCartney by Paul McCartney. Episode 57 and he's going around the place talking as if there never was a John Lennon. That is wrong. McCartney can't hack it. Sorry, I don't like that. All McCartney ever did was Yesterday and he's an arsehole. Why can't these people tell the *truth*?'

Floyd talks of Bob Dylan. 'The first time I properly listened to Dylan I was cooking in a restaurant. As I always am when big events happen. Like the daught of my birther . . . er, the birth of my daughter.' Floyd is nicely into his cups now and sparkling as he does when he *is* The Man On The Telly. 'Hahaha, you'll *always* find me in the kitchen at parties. I am a fucking stove. Merry Marlboro! Er, what were we talking about?' Dylan. 'Yes, yes, and there I was in the kitchen and Kennedy was shot and they dragged Dylan out on to the stage of a television studio and he sang *How many roads must a man walk down before they he knows he's a man* (sic) and it fucking gobsmacked me. Fuck! Previously I'd seen Dylan as a bit of an art student and a bit too into Woody Guthrie and a bit of a pseud because he never was Woody Guthrie and he never was Jack Kerouac and he never was James Dean and he never was anybody. But then I found out that what Dylan was really good for was when your relationships break up, and mine always do, and you're sliding into this abyss of gloom and you haven't really got the vindictive energy that you should have, Dylan's there saying what you should be saying which is . . .' Which is? 'Which is . . . *I wish that for just one time you could stand inside my shoes, you'd know what a drag it is to see you* . . . Ha! . . . Fuck. Dylan is probably one of the greatest poets of the twentieth century. How he exposed the bleeding nerve of people's consciences I don't know. Because I don't think he's that clever. But . . . *And even the Presi-*

dent of the United States must sometimes stand naked ... that is *remarkable.'*

Keith Floyd, food buff, eccentric, heart-throb by appointment to the gentry, and rock enthusiast, made a pop record once. It wasn't very good, it seems. Keith Floyd is launching into the dessert wine now and enjoying it very much indeed.

'Hugh Cornwell. Hugh Cornwell of The Stranglers. He is a very nice man. Very lonely. We recorded a song together that was never released. It was called The Goose Goes In, or something like that, a terrible sort of funk record about geese. The best bit of the whole thing was we ripped off a line from Led Zeppelin – it was a rock'n'roll recipe, you see – and I went, *Squeeze my le-mon 'til the juuuuuice runs dooown ma leg*! Ha ha ha ha. It was brilliant! And on the B-side was Old Shep – me doing a Richard Burton Old Shep with one of the girls from Fuzzbox singing high above it (Floyd attempts a weedy falsetto), *When I was a boy* ... Ha ha. It was shit.'

Keith Floyd has opened a pub in Devon called The Malsters Arms. When he's made a lot of money that's where he'll bugger off to. He loves the pub. Much more than he does 'this temporary thing of being popular on The Telly.'

'My pub's quite good,' he says. 'It's got pickled eggs that I've made and a jukebox. I've got Lean On Me, Bill Withers, When A Man Loves A Woman, Percy Sledge, Blueberry Hill, Fats Domino, Be Bop A Lula, Gene Vincent, Elvis's Old Shep and Take My Hand, Precious Lord. There's 186 songs on the fucking thing. I can't remember them all. Positively 4th Street, Just Like A Woman, Like A Rolling Stone. I'm Not In Love, 10cc. Argent. Fucking good band, Argent. But you can't have Bruce Springsteen on the fucking thing. And no U2. Absolutely *not* Nights In White Satin, I Am The Walrus. Brilliant ...'

Who the hell does Keith Floyd think he is? It's so very hard to tell, isn't it? Ask him and he'll pick up a bottle of wine and say, 'Well, it's all written on the label on the back of this bottle, really. It's in French. French is such a beautiful language.' And he'll afford a somewhat faltering translation: 'Lovingly brought up by masters of the shade ... the issue, the child of many different well-known grapes ... inundated with sun, this, um, this privileged position enables us to obtain an alcoholic richness and wonderful aromas.

Isn't that lovely? It's like, *I started out on Burgundy and soon hit the harder stuff* but it is all there. You've got to get sunshine into your television programmes and into your life and into your food. Give joy. I can give joy, great joy. I can also end up in Pseuds' Corner – Shit. I mean, who gives a bucket of horseshit? Let's have some more wine . . .'

Albert Goldman

What shadowy figure is this, that flits from tomb to tomb in rock'n'roll's graveyard? What dark purpose directs him to disinter the stars' venerated remains, and cast his cold, unpitying eye over their reputations? These perplexing questions raise another, even more compelling query.

T HE ODOUR OF the hotel room, that bears an unwelcoming faded gold Number 9 upon its outer door, is that of stale tobacco, the stink of dirty old journalists summoned here to pay homage to an elderly professor from the Americas. The most grotesque object in this Cave of Knightsbridge Comforts is the elderly professor, the infamous biographer, himself. Padding like an intemperate cleaning woman around the king-sized bed – what a bed! – with its coverlet of blood-purple, he tuts and fusses as he empties the ashtrays of their suffocating burdens. Steel-framed spectacles cling to his head like some life-sucking parasite. He turns his moon face as he hears the intruders from Q magazine trespassing within the inner sanctum, his eyebrows twitch and quiver like mating cockroaches on a flophouse floor, and his mouth creaks ajar, a slender, crimson gash in decaying flesh. 'Hello . . .'

Well, that's how Albert Goldman – for it is he – might have written this introduction, given his penchant for overblown, sub-Gothic, 'mock-heroic' spectacular. the written style with which he opened his infamous accounts of the lives of Elvis Presley and John Lennon. In reality, the man I meet emptying ashtrays in a Knightsbridge hotel room, where he is staying whilst he does PR duties on the paperback publication of The Lives Of John Lennon, looks, at first sight, to be quite an amiable old codger. Shoulders hunched within a sensible beige jersey, grey threads, beaming smile of greeting (though the teeth could do with some attention). It is only when he laughs that you think, perhaps, the man could be quite mad. It's a high-pitched squittering cackle, rather unnerving. The publicity gel from Bantam Books asks him if he would like some coffee or some sandwiches or anything and he bellows. 'No! Bring me a big bag of COCAINE!! And some of those disposable SYRINGES!!' And then comes the laugh. 'Hehheh-hehHEH!!'

What a card.

Albert Goldman is famous, notorious, for just two things. 1: He told the world, in his 1981 book Elvis, that Presley was a drug-sozzled, cheeseburger-guzzling, nappy-wearing goon who had few redeeming human features and whose records weren't really much good. 2: He told the world, in last year's The Lives of John Lennon, that Lennon was a drug-sozzled, pseudo-political, hypocritical quasi-sociopath who had few redeeming human features and whose records weren't really much good. That is how Goldman got rich. That is why he is reviled by so many devotees of the deceased rock gods in question. A character assassin, a pitiless grave robber, they've called him. The ageing biographer (very late fifties going on sixties) grins enormously and issues forth his maniacal cackle. 'Grave robber! Hehhehhehhehheh. Uh, I feel that is unjust.'

And then the ancient professor of English Literature, who taught at Columbia University for 20 years, springs to his own defence in a florid and overconsidered manner that shall be, as I find, characteristic of many of his answers. 'We live in a time that is sentimental,' he says. 'Through the hard-boiled racket of the modern world, there's a lot of oozing sentimentality and it's hard for people to take an adult view of anything because they're barely adult. And when you take an unsentimental view, as I did with Elvis and John, you're always accused of being cruel. Blake wrote very eloquently on the whole subject.' A short lecture on the eloquence of William Blake here followed – but let us pass over that and examine events that led up to Albert Goldman's current status as most 'controversial' pop biographer of the age.

Albert Goldman was born in Pittsburgh many, many years ago. He went to drama school, Carnegie Tech ('at the same time as Andy Warhol, in fact') and he joined the navy where he 'met people who were well-educated, who said, Shame on you, you haven't read James Joyce.' So he enrolled at the University of Chicago to acquire a 'proper education', got a master's degree in Eng Lit and ended up teaching in New York. On the side he wrote music criticism for the New Leader, Life and Esquire. 'I didn't have a formal training in music but I think I have a better perception of music than I have of literature. I spent most of my life listening to music. Literature I would do in my spare time, hehheh-hehhehHEH!'

He wrote about classical music, he wrote about jazz, in the late '60s he was writing about rock. 'I got into rock pretty late. The Doors was the first band I ever saw live and it disposed me very much to write about it.' Albert Goldman snaps his fingers – click, click, click. Perhaps this is his rendition of LA Woman; perhaps he is trying to indicate that he is 'hip to the beat', or something. 'Rock was fascinating to me because it evolved very rapidly into an entire culture, you could step inside the rock world and feel it all around you, 360 degrees. It was alive and spontaneous and growing and developing all kinds of kinks and expanding and reaching like a vast mushrooming growth of instant culture. But unfortunately it can instantly collapse, too. It went up like a rocket and down like a stick and in the early '70s when I saw the likes of Elton John and Bowie and that lot, I thought, Uh-oh, it's no longer for me.'

Intrigued by the so-called 'counter-culture', Goldman quit his day job in the '70s and took off on the drug trail. He spent two and a half years in Colombia. 'I lived in that world with two different smuggling gangs and I wrote an unpublished book that deals with all our merry pranks, hehheh. I couldn't publish the book because you had the police on one side and smugglers on the other and it's not a good place for the rockers to be in, hehHEH! I was rocking too HARD! Dope I didn't see as any great sin. This was Robin Hood. Drug smuggling was romantic.'

Evidently, Goldman saw himself as a latter-day Jack Kerouac, or somesuch, but arriving back in New York in 1977 – 'my worldly working capital was 50 dollars and a bottle of Black Label scotch' – he wrote a book about the disco scene (a 'scene' he thinks was 'exciting'; a book, persuasively titled Disco, he considers 'brilliant').

And then came Elvis.

Albert Goldman had, he claims, no 'significant' attitude about Elvis when he was asked to write and began to research his book. 'I had no idea what I was getting into. I mean, I just had never paid any attention to Elvis. I thought he was preposterous after his early records. A male impersonator, hehheh. A male sex object for the over-thirties ladies. Las Vegas. Pretty preposterous. That was the only attitude I had to Elvis. I only agreed to write the book to make some money. But when I began to see how Elvis lived, I got a pretty strong take off it. It was all so *revolting*!'

Goldman's Elvis is, indeed, 'revolting' – the queasy saga of a jiggling-jowled entertainer bloated on excess, stuffed with stupidity, surrounded by apes and morons. Didn't Albert Goldman feel at all, er, guilty about painting such a grotesque portrait of a man who was in no position to defend himself (i.e. dead)? No.

'No, I don't think so. Because I didn't *destroy* him. Even if I'd wished to, I didn't succeed because the myth is now stronger than ever, more irrational than ever, more *profitable* than ever. One doesn't have the power to destroy a myth. History is no match for myth. Myth is what we instinctively are disposed to believe, history is what we laboriously learn and readily forget. Writing a history of Elvis was an unequal combat. I wanted to combat a myth. For me it became a moral cause. To fight these manias. But I have no illusions about my success. The Elvis myth lives on, stronger than ever.'

Unsurprisingly, Goldman's book was not received with glee by the hard-core Presley fans. As Goldman discovered, it is hardly a bright idea to cross swords with the hard-core Presley fans. They can turn distinctly nasty.

'Elvis fans are like religious fanatics!' cries the man, with another of his ear-splitting sniggerings. 'And the Elvis fans were *highly* organised. The moment my book came out, the fans in the clubs down south all received my address, my telephone number and orders to go after me. And at the height of the hullabaloo a bullet came whistling through my window into my office and missed me. By about eight inches, I'd calculate, hehhehHEH!' The professor seems to find the furore that might have ended his life a hugely amusing skylark. Did he take some perverse delight in being a marked man?

'Well, of *course* I didn't,' he says with a wry smile that almost belies the answer. 'No one wants to be Mr Nasty. I'm a nice *guy*! It's *frightening* when the loonies are out to get you! But, I mean, I've had a *lot* of frightening experiences in my career.' He talks again of the 'drug game' in Colombia; he talks – with much satisfaction as he adds further 'colour' to this long life that he'd like you to know has been lived on the 'edge' – of the time he was doing some investigative journalism into the death of Bruce Lee and got drugged and kidnapped in Hong Kong. Well!

'After that what is *frightening*, you know?' he cried with a merry gleam. Elvis fans with guns, pshaw. 'Elvis fans aren't so exceptional. The hue and cry that came with the Lennon book was *far* worse than Elvis; U2 put out a song inciting all the loonies to come and kill me. There was an incredible chorus of denunciation. A persecution. Organised. People vowing to get me and all that stuff. It is frightening when you see the U2 thing, these self-righteous, smug jerks inciting people to murder me, because you have to realise how many crazies there are out there listening to this stuff and absorbing it. How many Mark David Chapmans are sitting there in their sweat saying, Kill, Kill? How many people jerking off on these outrageous lies and accusations about me and out to get me? That's why, when the book came out, I went to Italy where all is calm and serene. Observed the explosion from a distance, hehhehhehHEH!'

A bullet whistling by his head after Elvis, why, then, did he dive in again to demean if not demolish, over hundreds of pages, another greatly revered (and dead) icon of pop? Goldman claims that he had no intention of disparaging Lennon when he embarked upon his second pop biography.

'I think I was setting out to balance the stink over Elvis with an account of someone I genuinely admired. I had identified with John and I felt a great deal of empathy with John. But, I found out, obviously I was just like all the fans. I was deceived by the illusion, the myth. When you compare Elvis with Lennon, whom I genuinely admired, you would have to say that Elvis, for all his grotesquery, at least managed to have a bit of fun, whereas John was an innately melancholy, depressed being who denied himself things. He wouldn't eat, wouldn't drink, wouldn't screw for long periods of time. He was Jack Sprat who ate no fat. Unattractive and life denying. It was a very disillusioning experience to write about John Lennon. And well before I'd finished the damned book I felt, Oh my God, you've done it *again*. My best friend said Albert, you can do it once – desecrating the grave of a lauded pop singer – but you can't get away with it twice. But there I was, I couldn't back out. To do that would have been cowardly . . .'

Goldman's book of Lennon is stuffed with cod psychology – Lennon as mad multiple personality, violent victim of traumatic childhood. Goldman is, you see, a fan of Freud. 'Freud defines the hysteric as the one who must play all the parts, assume all the roles. That is John. Borderline psychosis by anybody's standards. He was *nuts.* John on record is many, many people. I always used to say that John was the Peter Seller (*sic*) of song. Yes, I suppose I was a fan of John, *loved* John before I started this book but, well, Freud defines love as the overestimation of the beloved object.' At this, the Goldman eyebrows twitch and there's a smile, bordering on smug, that says... well, who knows? A tommy-gun-fashioned HehhehehhehHEH! swiftly follows to disturb any reverie...

Goldman's book of Lennon is stuffed with supposition – *perhaps* Lennon killed a sailor in Hamburg, *perhaps* Lennon believed he was responsible for Stuart Sutcliffe's death, *perhaps* etc., etc. – based upon the hearsay of faded/dead junkies like guitarist Jesse Ed Davis and sundry persons who delivered smack to the Lennon portals. 'Well,' says the author, 'if you're going to rule out people who are fond of drugs, I don't know who you would interview in the rock world. And I think if I'd had more witnesses and they were more candid, John Lennon would have turned out *worse.* Contrary to what the press made of my book, which was that was continually making John worse than life, I would say I was continually, but unconsciously, making him *better.* And that, I would say, is one of the defects of the book.'

Does Albert Goldman give one fig for the still living persons he may have offended with his written works? Absolutely no.

Paul McCartney, whom Goldman depicts as a self-serving weed, has dismissed the Lennon book as 'trash'. (Well, he would, wouldn't he?). 'Paul McCARtney.' Goldman chews disgustedly on the name as if it's some gigantic lump of gristle. 'Paul McCARtney. Hah! Paul McCartney is certainly not anyone whose judgement of this book you ought to take seriously. I was never fond of Paul.' Evidently. 'Paul is that familiar figure with the straw boater and the cane and the dancing shoes and the line of practised patter, hehehehehHEH! Mr Entertainment. The man is a marshmallow!'

Yoko Ono, who's painted as some batty and manipulative witch, has called Goldman an 'assassin' possessed by 'negative energy'. (Well, she would, wouldn't she?). 'Yoko Ono – hehhehehhehHEH!' This particular cackle shakes the very foundation of the hotel. 'Well, you certainly don't have to have the slightest doubt about my portrait of Yoko. If I make her look terrible, so what? That's what she is. She's silly. She's a silly billy. She put cat droppings under John's feet, hehhehheh. I spoke to people who saw her do that. She's a rich girl and she's just *awful.* She's a neighbour of mine, actually, so I can't avoid seeing her – but there's never any intercourse, hehhehHEH!'

And all the rest of the rock fraternity can go straight to hell, as far as Albert Goldman is concerned. He *despises* rock music. 'Rock, I think, should just be totally bulldozed to the sidelines. I just find it this hideous cultural totalitarianism. It's so establishment and so self-righteous and full of shit. All this wretched doggerel writing and, oh God, it's a classic example of how a sort of libertarian revolution can turn right round and become the worst sort of tyranny. And now, of course, they're all doing charity, they're giving milk away to babies, you know, they're back to all the showbusiness tricks to disguise who they *really* are. How *dare* they? The *arrogance*! There just is no popular culture for adults anymore. There is, of course, culture for 40-year-old adolescents. The Rolling Stones on their wheelchair tour, hehheheh, their drug survivor celebration, and The Who being resuscitated and taken out of their embalming wrappings. God, these people were telling you never to trust anyone over 30!

As John Lennon said (*Goldman assumes the least convincing 'scouse' accent in recorded history*), You don't think we're going to be doing this when we're 40, do you? And at 40 he was out there doing it, hehHEH! That's funny!'

Is there *anybody* that Albert Goldman admires? It would seem not. 'Who would I admire? I don't see a lot.' Bob Dylan, the poet, perhaps? Stupid question. '*Dylan*? HuhphrumphHEH!' He was just a sufferer of diarrhoea of the mouth, droning and sawing and grinding away in a spurious hill-billy style. I remember when Nashville Skyline came out, I wrote in Life a *mildly* sarcastic review and I was instantly fired. HehHEH! It's one of the rules about pop heroes, you cannot say *anything* against them. Put one little scratch in the veneer of one of these pop stars and . . . *apocalypse*! But I don't think any of these people mean anything, do they? They are all illusions. Not an attractive lot, the heroes of the modern world.'

So no more heroes anymore for A. Goldman.

'As you grow older, you sober up and you realise that your own heroes were just like John Lennon. They were people that you saw through a mist of distorting illusion. They were, in reality, insignificant or grotesque. Who *are* these pop stars? People cherish the idea of a pop star taking an interest in politics, like John Lennon pretended to, as if that were so wonderful – it's like if a monkey were to talk, that would be a miracle. If a pop star makes a joke, it seems to be infinitely more funny than if anybody else made the same joke. The whole thing is full of shit, fans and the press in a kind of synergy back and forth jerking each other off. I'm sick of it.'

Rest assured, readers, Albert Goldman will not be destroying *your* favourite popster in print in the forseeable future. He doesn't need the money, doesn't want the 'hassle' and would rather be writing about 'proper' historical figures. He reckons he might have a bash at Casanova. 'No psychosis with *that* baby!'

As I get up to depart, Goldman blocks the exit and, with arms folded, launches into a quite unsolicited account of the homosexual antics of Brian Epstein and Brian's supposed death in some sordid orgy. What do I think of the gay SM 'scene' in London? he asks. Golly, Mr Goldman, I haven't the foggiest. He wants to discuss homosexual death rituals. Oo-er. I want to leave. It would seem that this man really does relish the seedy side of human nature. No, no, hehheh, he protests. With Elvis and Lennon 'it was good for me to get down in the muck and dirt and dig around a bit,' he says. 'But you can't do it *all* your life. It's too *revolting*.'

Gary Glitter

It is the festive season. Peace on earth. Goodwill to all men. But when the portly panto-horse of pop lurches forth upon his annual outing, trussed up in foil like a Christmas turkey, parading ever more lacklustre editions of his moronic glam-rock concoction, there's precious few tidings of comfort and joy.

WEDGING HIMSELF WITH effort into a most negligible pair of silver spangled trouserlettes. Gary Glitter is struck by the possibilities of a mirth-making ruse. He thrusts his hand down trouser fronts, revealing a tufty expanse of pubic hair, and waggles obscenely therein. 'Aw haw!' he cackles, leering at the Q photographer. '*That* made yer blush!' He seems most impressed with this primitive laddishness.

The words 'leader' and 'rock'n'roll' are never far from Mr Glitter's lips. I'm the *leader*, aw *haw*!' he insists on crying at every available opportunity during our meeting. 'THE LEADER!' screams the motif on the back of one of his many grotesque jackets. And he wants all Q readers to know that he is *consumed* by rock'n'roll. 'There's nothing so uplifting, so *spiritual* as rock'n'roll,' he informs me, authoritatively. But just now, as he tucks himself into another exquisitely awful outfit, here at the Fulham home of his 'costumier', Gary, one-time Portly Pilot of Pop, the panto showhorse, glam buffoon, wants to talk to us about . . . body hair. He confesses that the hair on his head is going to grey and that he dyes it constantly, but look at *this*, he says, tugging open his outer shirt and showing off his abundant clump of chest plumes, he never dyes *this*; he tried it once and it went all matted and strange – 'It looked hideous, it just doesn't work' – and as for the pubic hair, well, 'me pubes haven't gone grey at *all*, isn't that *funny*?' Funny ha ha or funny peculiar?

'Why hasn't Kim Basinger rung me today?' guffaws the lad. And

95

then, as he so often does, he raises a painted eyebrow (he shaved the brows off when he was doing the Rocky Horror Show in Australia in 1978; they never grew back again; he has to pencil them in) and assumes the slightly dotty, gawpy look that is his trademark . . . Ladies and gentlemen, Gary Glitter, camp relic . . .

Paul Gadd, born 46 years ago, wanted to be a 'rock'n'roll' singer the minute he saw Elvis Presley in Loving You – 'at the Gaumont in Sutton, I think it was. I just thought Elvis was so *funny*,' he says. 'The whole idea of the audience screaming and shouting tickled me. Also I wanted to sing so that I could get my leg over. That's the thing about this fame lark, it's a great way to pull girls.'

Paul Gadd never *did* quite make is as a proper 'rock'n'roll' singer; he grew up, instead, to be an 'entertainer', a figure of fun, a bit of a laff. Which is the next best thing . . . perhaps.

It was as Paul Raven, he made his first record in 1959. 'It was awful because I was a rock'n'roll singer and they gave me this song called Alone In The Night which was in a minor key. I'd never even *heard* of a minor key. 'In the early '60s, he got a job as a warm up man on a celebrated television pop show. I know this because it says so in the exceedingly badly-drawn strip cartoon catalogue of a career in the Gary Glitter Album 1975 . . . *But fate moves in strange ways and soon Gary was offered a job as warm up man on Ready Steady Go!* . . . Gary's balloon: *Mum, I've got a job on television!* . . . Mum's balloon: *Oh I am pleased for you* . . .

Gary claims that at Ready Steady Go! he was 'fairly responsible for getting Donovan on the show and starting his career,' as if this is something to be immensely proud of; but he 'got bored with telling the audience to scream and shout for The Beatles and The Animals and The Rolling Stones', he wanted to 'pursue my own recording career' and, 'if you didn't speak with a Northern accent in the mid '60s you couldn't get a gig in London' (unless, perchance, you were The Kinks, The Stones, little Dave Clark and his 5, a thousand others). So he went, Paul Raven & Boston International, to Germany, to Hamburg, to the Star Club, to do some already outmoded 'rock'n'roll' (Elvis and Chuck Berry and Gene Vincent) for a living wage. Germany was 'great': Gary Glitter thinks back to days on the Reeperbahn with laddish nostalgia; Paul Raven was, he says, more debauched, even, than The Beatles in *their* Hamburg phase.

He raises a painted, prominent eyebrow. He leers. He cackles.

'Aw haw. I was *far* more debauched than those Northerners. *Far* more, I'd say. Imagine living on the Reeperbahn in the late '60s. Cor! Sex? I must have seen everything. *Everything*. I grew up very quickly. It was like being thrown into Sodom and Gormorrah. It was 24-hour sex and it was easy. Everything was there. I first was aware of transvestites as well, and things like that, and sex changes and all those sort of things that I never saw in England. Great stuff!'

He did the mandatory drugs, too.

'Oh yeah, we took all the horrible drugs going . . . I was talking to Paul McCartney about it once and we both remembered that there used to be a little old lady in the Star Club's ladies toilets who would sell these all-night keep-you-awake tablets, speed, lorry drivers specials and things. Cor! And that's where it all started because I later went on to cocaine and stuff like that.'

In 1970, the lad returned from the decadent land and teamed up with producer/arranger Mike Leander – chiefly noted for his work on Marianne Faithful's soppy hit As Tears Go By – to create the pop monstrosity that was Gary Glitter. Other names were considered, according to George Tremlett's seminal pop biog The Gary Glitter Story . . . Terry Tinsel, Vicky Vomit, Turk Thrust, Horace Hydrogen and Stanley Sparkle. But Gary Glitter it was. And they created this minimalist bish-bash-bosh 'sound', featuring ape-like shouts of 'Hey!', and Gary clambered into grotesque and glistering outfits, and thus 'glitter rock' was born. The first moronic concoction, Rock & Roll (Parts 1 & 2), was a hit all over the world in 1972. The rest, as they say is history.

Gary Glitter is proud of his pop prowess: 'Mike would get on the drums and I'd start shouting rubbish over it and then we'd put the drums down and then we'd build up the tracks just like they're doing now. We were quite avant-garde at the time . . .' But not *that* proud: 'Rock & Roll came about by accident actually because we wrote it and we ran out of money so we remixed it and I threw in a load of Hey Heys on it and hand claps – and I got voted as being the best songwriter of the year by the Ivor Novello Awards. George Michael won that recently. Quite right, too. But *my* song – if you read the sheet music, all it's got written on it is, *Hey Hey Hey Ugugug shshsh fartfart*, you know. It's rubbish. And my lyrics have never been any better since. You know, anything too complicated and we throw it straight in the bin . . .'

Gary Glitter got big and famous by being utterly ludicrous, looking thoroughly stupid on Top Of The Pops (backed by the equally ridiculous-looking Glitter Band – just *dig* the Ray Dorset-styled sideburns and the gargantuan shoulder pads of John Rossall, saxophone player supreme); going Hey! and Hey! again astride a motorcycle, raising the eyebrow and acting the goat in great, huge boots. But these were strange times the old boy was living in and the little girls, deluded, just *loved* it.

'Oh, yeah. Cor! It was *raunchy* on the road, aw haw,' pipes the lad who never quite grew up. 'It was *very* good. I used to take my pick of girls, you know. I remember Helsinki, looking out the hotel window and there was 4,000 girls waiting – at *least* 4,000 because I was counting, I was standing there on the balcony and I'd get the binoculars and I was saying. Send me up that one. I'll have that one. And *that* one. It was *that* easy . . .'

Gary Glitter was ludicrous. With this he agrees. 'Ludicrous? Absolutely! But I'm *much* more ludicrous nowadays.' He was a less than skilled singer who just got lucky with a glitter-bonded paunch and perky eyebrows. With this he does *not* agree.

'I always *claim* not to be a great singer but that's because I try and underplay everything I do because otherwise it can sound a little pompous. I think. But *actually*, I'm a *great* singer. Really. I can sing really well. I've got a very good voice for a rock'n'roll singer and if you bother to listen to my records you'll see that. The trouble is nobody's ever *wanted* me to be a great singer. They *certainly* don't want me to be a great singer *these* days.'

No, they want him to be the elderly swinger going to fat with cucumber slices on his eyes in ads for British Rail Studentcards. They want him to be a fat old hoot of a coot, trussed up in foil like the Christmas turkey, a barrage balloon disguised as Michael Jackson's nightmare with a wilting hosepipe down the trousers. A parody. The Portly Pilot of Pop . . .

'The Portly Pilot of Pop?' says Gary, eyeing me with no little suspicion. 'The Portly Pilot? Are these the words you're going to use in your article?' Probably. 'But I'm not particularly fat any more.' (It is true that he has shed some pounds of late, since he forswore the rock'n'roll mouthwash.) 'I'm *old*, of course!' Oh, here comes that quip he's been cracking for far too long. 'I just put two pounds of concrete in my face to get over here. Polyfilla! Aw haw!'

'And yes, I am a parody. Always was and always will be and proud of it. So what? I'm a parody only because to *me* rock 'n' roll is supposed to be *fun*. It's *got* to be *fun*. If I don't get a giggle out of it, what's the point? It goes back to Elvis, really. I always thought that Elvis was doing it for a laugh because every time he did a little wiggle or something there would be a big grin on his face like he was trying to say, Oh, that's a good one, try that on and see what happens. And that's exactly what *I* do. I put cucumbers on my eyes and sit on British Rail hoardings and if people have a good laugh out of it, I get pleasure.'

Sounds *just* like Elvis, does it not?

'So, I'm very happy to be the Portly Pilot of Pop, as you put it. I give people pleasure. I have a laugh and . . .' – here it comes again – '. . . I'll keep having a laugh until all the Polyfilla in London has run out. In 10 years there won't be enough Polyfilla left to put in the cracks, aw haw.'

These days Gary Glitter goes out of a Christmas with The Gary Glitter Gang Show, which consists of lots of barmy costumes and ancient GG hits and is the nearest thing you can get to panto without Terry Scott booming away as an ugly sister. It is a laugh. It keeps the wolf from the door . . .

In 1976, after four years at the tip top, and 11 – count 'em – successive Top Ten hits, Gary Glitter 'retired'. Mr Glitter sighs. He rattles on about the 'pressures of the road', about how within three years he went to Australia – he was big in Australia – some 20 times and how he had to be protected down there from frenzied fans, ferried from airport to concert hall in tanks and/or ambulances with 'people all screaming and jumping on the top.' He was a wreck. He was exhausted. He wanted to chuck it all in and try to settle down with a paramour called Mary Medalee. This last bit came as quite a surprise to many of his detractors who, dazzled and irked by the camp and the kitsch, presumed that the mincing superstar leaned towards the lavender, was 'not as other men' . . .

'I am *not* gay. I'm not gay and I suppose it's funny that people thought I was but I used to share an office with David Bowie, at least he was down the corridor, and Marc (Bolan) used to come in and we were all showbizzy rock'n'rollers into costumes and all the camp things and so people thought we were *all* gay. But it wasn't like that. I mean. I got my idea for the big shoulders and the platform shoes from Jean Genet, a play which was set in a *brothel*. Heterosexual stuff. Nothing gay about that. I mean, I *like* men, actually, I think they're really *funny*, you know. But I don't like their anatomy. That's it. It does not turn me on. But it wouldn't worry me if I was gay. It wouldn't worry me at *all*. I'd just take it in my stride like everything else . . .'

We digress. Gary Glitter's 'retirement' was not a raging success. The love match was a flop – 'She lasted about four months, Mary' – and the would-be recluse was declared massively bankrupt. 'Financially, Gary Glitter is secure – the managerial skills of Mike Leander have seen to that,' it tells us on page 135 of Tremlett's The Gary Glitter Story (published 1974). Unfortunately, this was not true. Gary was living it up like some barking and biffy Rock God. In a mansion. With Rolls-Royces and new-fangled Range Rovers, antique furnishings, coiffeured hedges and all sorts.

'I had everything. I had a fridge where the champagne would come out automatically on a robot arm the minute you pressed the button. It was gadget time. If somebody invented a gadget, it seemed like a good idea to have it. I don't know why. Probably because I was stoned out of my box all the time. I had a house with 10 bedrooms and I thought I had to fill the bedrooms every night so there was non-stop rock'n'roll partying all the time. And I had an outdoor swimming pool which I'd keep at 70 degrees all through the winter so you could see the steam coming off it like a sauna. And stuff like that. And in my own bedroom, which cost £50,000 to do up, I had these electric curtains which were hand-made silk with little electric motors which used to go mad so the curtains were swishing all over the place out of control like a poltergeist was swinging on them . . . It was very funny because at the bankruptcy hearing, the judge looked at me and said, £6,000 pounds for curtains? Can this *possibly* be right? . . . Yes, m'lud . . . Aw haw.'

So, declared bankrupt, Gary Glitter had to go back to work. Ten years ago the 'comeback' began. Again not initially, entirely successful. 'When I retired it was on News At Ten, man! Gary Glitter retires! It's funny how the British press are inclined to go with the gloom and the down side of things. When I said, Hey, I'm making a comeback, nobody wanted to know.'

For years, in the early '80s, all the British press – the tabloids – wanted to know about Gary Glitter was what a disgusting mess he was. He was still drinking heavily, they said. 'That is true. I was drinking loads of vodka and taking too much cocaine. Revolting, really.' He was perpetually attempting suicide. 'No, that's not true. I made some mistakes with pills and I was hospitalised twice but those were accidents.' He beat up his girlfriend Alison Brown and threatened to chop his hand off with a meat cleaver (this from the News of The World). 'No!'

'But those sort of stories did bring it home to me that I might be becoming some kind of monster. There's no smoke without fire, is there? So I cleaned up my act . . .'

Since early 1987, Gary Glitter has been off the sauce and off the hokey-cokey and he feels a better man for it. He feels great. 'I feel great!' His glam parody routine, even if the late-lamented Glitter Band are no longer by his side, has them falling about in the aisles.

'People believe in me now,' he says, fixing me with a look that says Mr Sincere, though it's hard to take him seriously – ever – what with all those layers of make-up and that perpetually elevating eyebrow. 'I *know* I was drinking too much. I *know* I was taking too many drugs and I was a monster and a bit badly behaved, but that's all over and people know that and they love me for it. I've cleaned up my act completely. And what I'd like to say is that I've found the glitter *inside* of me as opposed to just having the glitter on the *outside*. Nowadays, I feel *worthy* of being loved by an audience. I'm no longer dirt. I'm *loved* . . .'

Gary Glitter is loved. The lovable showhorse, the preposterous popinjay, the aged King/Queen of glam. The grand parody. A sort of establishment figure, national treasure, a bit like the Queen Mum (only his clothes are even worse). Loved.

Don't you ever feel inclined to be *serious*? Wouldn't you like to, say, try and save the planet through music, do a 'concept album', with no Heys, about rainforests and the human condition? Or something? Do you want to play the fool *all* your life?

'Play the fool? I'm not a fool. I'm a parody, sure, but not a fool. I make a decent living out of singing. That's not being a fool. And on Boys Will Be Boys (1984) I *did* get a little bit deeper. But that album never really did that well. You see, every time I get too involved in things like that, in Green issues, or any of those, nobody really wants to hear it from me. But there's more kind of I Want To Save The Planet stuff, in my music and on my latest album, which is live from Glasgow, than there is on U2 or any of those types. When you get 10,000 people singing Be Bop A Lula, like I did in Glasgow, there is more vibe, there is more good feeling on that, there's more *love* on that, than there is on most records you could mention.'

Gary Glitter as tool for betterment of the planet, political force. Sounds a bit hopeless and unlikely, does it not? He hikes up that eyebrow. He opens his mouth wide and does the madcap Glitter-face of yesteryear, today and forever.

'But I *am* political. I do it *subliminally*! Cor! There's a long word I never used before . . . I do it *subliminally* and I think I'm pretty powerful. I mean, some of my dinner parties, some of the gang go out and do all the talking and I'm the funny little Buddha sitting in the corner.'

What are you talking about?

'I have *power*. I'm the leader of the gang. I *am* power. Power with love, love rock'n'roll and power, power to . . . you know? Do you know what I'm saying? *That*'s what I'm talking about.'

And with that, Gary Glitter asks his costumier to help him into a pair of thigh-high boots. 'Cor! *These* are as tight as a you know what, aw haw!'

Do you *really* want to be in his gang?

Jerry Lee Lewis

The Killer is at large again, the firebrand ivory-thumper with the legendarily short fuse. And 30 years of bankruptcy, busts, mayhem-making and messy divorce have transparently failed to dislodge the notion that he is the God-sent creator of rock'n'roll.

THE *ODDEST* COUPLE are sitting side by side on the sofa. Bar the obvious – common conquered 'drinking problems' – the two would seem to have little or nothing in common. 'Cor!' says Jimmy Greaves, ex-footballer, man-of-the-people with the withered moustache. 'Cor! 'Ere I am sitting next to a legend. Makes yer think, don't it?' The wizened gentleman of some 54 summers, whose once rampant curls have gone tame and grey, turns to the jaunty footballing person-cum-celebrity at his side, fixes him with a beady look and says, in a gracious drawl from Louisiana, 'Sir? Uh, pardon sir, but I don't understand what you're saying.' Greavsie, for once, is nonplussed.

It's half past seven in the morning and Jerry Lee Lewis, aka 'The Killer', rock'n'roll maniac, is making an appearance on TV-am. In the 'hospitality' room, where we are watching the proceedings on a screen, Lewis's management person is still congratulating himself on getting Lewis, the much-married mayhem-maker, to the Camden Lock studios at all. An hour or so earlier when Lewis was awoken for this early bird promotional appearance, he flew into one of his regular tantrums, warned the management person that if he didn't leave the master to his slumbers, there would be fisticuffs, spilt blood or worse. A flaming, wailing, cussing row, but then suddenly and without warning, Jerry Lee was transformed into a compliant kitten asking, 'Hey, aren't we supposed to be in some Goddamned TV studios?'

And here he is, ill at ease and unsmiling on the televisual settee, sporting an ill-fitting, fringed black suede jacket, whilst the cheery presenters, Mike Morris and Richard Keys, ply him with polite enquiries.

Thanks to the dull Hollywood biopic, Great Balls Of Fire (based on Lewis's ex-wife Myra's book of the same name). Jerry Lee is, momentarily at least, a household name once more. He's in London for a one-off concert (he was supposed to play the show two weeks ago but, due to 'illness', he missed the plane) and, supposedly, to help promote the film (for which he performed the music). 'Let's take a look at the film,' suggest Mike and Richard, and we see a clip of Dennis Quaid (Jerry Lee) and Winona Ryder (Myra) in domestic high-jinks situation. The real-life Jerry Lee is asked to comment. He looks somewhat baffled.

'Can't understand a word that boy says,' murmurs Jerry Lee of Quaid, and, 'Who was that girl supposed to be? Which wife was that?' (With six wives thus far and counting, the man's confusion is perhaps understandable.)

'It must be difficult making a film based on the lives of people still living,' suggests Richard, helpfully.

'Sir?' replied Jerry Lee. 'Sir? I don't understand what you're saying.'

'Golly,' gushes Mike, 'golly, what an adventurous life you've led, eh?' At which Jerry goes rambling on, Southern-wise, about Religion. 'Sir, I base my life on God Almighty, the son Jesus Christ, the third part of The Trinity, the Holy Ghost . . .'

Er, yes, Mike and Richard seem enormously relieved to cut to a weather update.

Jerry Lee Lewis, firebrand ivory-thumper from Ferriday, Louisiana, has had a remarkably 'adventurous' life, of course. Expelled from the fundamentalist Southwestern Bible Institute in Waxahachie, Texas, when he was 15 (for playing sinful 'boogie-woogie' music on the pianoforte), he decided not to be a preacher after all, but to play music, the 'Devil's music'. And, it would seem, to live a Devil's life. Thirty years of bankruptcy and of busts: he's been indicted for one million dollars' worth of unpaid taxes, been sued for cancelled shows and defaulted payments on cars, homes and airplanes; of messy D.I.V.O.R.C.E. (three), family shenanigans (the 'controversial' third marriage to his 13-year-old cousin Myra that nearly ended his career) and tragedy . . . the deaths of two sons and of two wives; in 1982, Jaren (his fourth wife) drowned in a swimming pool, in 1983 Shawn (his fifth) succumbed (apparently) to an overdose of methadone (and Jerry Lee, the only person present at the death, wasn't even called upon to testify at the coroner's inquest); of drugs (Placidyl and amphetamines, Biphetamines, Dexedrine, cocaine, by his own admission) and drink (wine, Jack Daniel's) and reckless behaviour.

In 1976, he shot his bass player Norman 'Butch' Owens (an accident: Butch visited Jerry in his home and the boys started drinking and Jerry pulled out a .357 Magnum and said, 'I'm gonna shoot that Coca-Cola bottle over there or my name ain't Jerry Lee Lewis'; the bottle survived but Butch got two bullets in the chest). The same year he overturned and wrecked his Rolls-Royce in Tennessee after driving his daughter Phoebe to school, and he turned up at Elvis Presley's Graceland home and, when the guard wouldn't let him in, began waving a .38 Derringer pistol.

There's been a riot of self-abuse, ill-health in a million hospital beds: broken nose, ulcers, wonky gall bladder, respiratory problems, exhaustion, ruptured stomach have been amongst the man's ailments. Once, when he was lying in one of those beds, his wife Jaren pressed for Jerry Lee's commitment to a mental institution. The Killer simply tore the tubes from his nose and arm and stormed home threatening to kill anyone who signed commitment papers. He installed an iron door on his bedroom, loaded his home with more guns . . .

In 1982 he underwent a brief period of 'repentance', instigated by his cousin, the disgraced preacher Jimmy Swaggart. It made little difference. Jerry Lee, still an ornery critter, missing concerts, insulting audiences if he does deign to show, ever playing the original 'wild man' of rock (and country). Barking mad really, and surprising everybody here today by actually turning up at dawn for an appearance on British breakfast telly . . .

His inquisition-by-sofa at an end, Jerry Lee Lewis walks at my side, with shoulders bowed and civil nods to passers-by, to the TV-am canteen where he takes a breakfast of four huge sticky buns. The crusty crackpot lays down his Sherlock Holmes-styled pipe, a constant companion though he never seems to light the thing (a gun substitute, perhaps?) and, with no absence of violence, tears the buns apart, rejecting all the raisins. Ugh. Raisins, like so many things in life, tax Jerry Lee Lewis's patience to the limit. 'All these Goddamned raisins,' he curses under his breath. He gestures to the mutilated confections lying plate-less on the table and, in his politest Southern drawl, asks me if I would care for a piece, 'young man'. Politely I decline and frame my opening question.

Mr Lewis, you are, are you not . . .

A pointing index finger right between my eyes stops me in my tracks.

'What magazine are you from, boy?' he asks in a tone that's well, threatening, Southern courteousness snapping into menace just like that.

I'm from Q magazine, I squeak. The finger draws closer to my forehead.

'Is this gonna be written down in your magazine the way I'm talking here now, or are you just gonna take this and write it like you *WANT* to?'

I try to assure The Killer that I am an honourable man.

'OK, boy, OK now, but some of these people do that, you know. They take my words and write them like they WANT to. You're not gonna do that. I'd like to have that *UNDERSTOOD*.'

Understood, I croak. *Thoroughly* understood.

'OK now. So what's your question, young man?'

Erm, Mr Lewis, you are, are you not . . .

Mr Lewis interrupts me again. This time not with a stern finger but with a slice of his Good Time Religion.

'I don't base my life on the human being,' he says, 'I base my life on God Almighty, the son Jesus Christ, the third party of the Trinity, the Holy Ghost. That's where my loyalty lies and that's where my loyalty will always be. The rest of it . . . we're just passing through here. Here today, gone tomorrow. But the soul lives on. That's what I look forward to when I die. Standing before God on Judgement Day and going home. Yes, sir . . .'

The man goes quiet, smiles a strange smile. I pipe up. Mr Lewis you are, are you not, the King of Rock'n'Roll?

'Well, young man. I really wouldn't want to be branded with the name of King of Rock'n'Roll. That's a farfetched question. But I guess you could call me the King of Music.'

The King of *all* music?

'See, Jerry Lee Lewis has had 74 Number 1 records,' says The Killer (what reference work there is to justify this extravagant claim is hard to imagine), '74 Number 1 records, back-to-back both sides Number 1 at the same time in the charts, in a row, two of them in a row, four Number 1 records, two records been out at once. Ain't nobody else ever done that, not even Elvis Presley.'

Ah, Elvis Presley. Stories of Jerry Lee Lewis's consuming jealousy of Presley are legion. The gun at Gracelands incident; the filling station that Jerry Lee once, reportedly, pulled up at and, finding that they sold Presley discs but none of his, smashed to pieces; the concert at London's Rainbow in 1976, Jerry Lee stalking the stage and muttering 'Elvis? Elvis? Elvis is just a kid!'; and the remark he made when he heard of Elvis's death . . . 'I am glad,' he told a country magazine. 'Just another one out of the way. I mean, Elvis this, Elvis that. All we hear is Elvis. What the hell did Elvis do except take dope that I couldn't get hold of?'

I put this to the so-called Killer and he chuckles wildly.

'Huh huh huh! I don't believe I remember *that*! Huh huh huh. I don't . . . huh huh huh huh . . . no, I don't . . . huh *huh* . . .' The beady eyes fill with tears of mirth. 'Huh *HUH*! I don't recall *that* statement. How does that go again?'

Just another one out of the way . . .

'Well, young man, huh huh, something like that was said. See, sometimes it's better to smile than to cry, you know. I have a way about myself, about joking a lot, saying things. Elvis was the same. So I made a statement that was similar to something like that only it was joking, playing. I didn't mean that I was *glad* Elvis Presley was dead. That would be a very stupid statement for anybody to make. Besides, Elvis is not gone, anyway. He's never gone. He just took a vacation.'

Does Jerry Lee expect to meet up with his old rival when Jerry Lee 'goes home'?

'Huh huh! I can't say about *Elvis*! It'd just be good if I could account for *myself*. Everybody's got to give accounts of themselves.' Abruptly, Lewis's mood changes again. The index finger prods the air once more and the man is glowering at me with something approaching fury. 'Don't nit-pick me, boy!' he hisses. 'You mention Elvis Presley to me again, you keep digging me about something like that, you're gonna *upset* me. You mention Elvis Presley to me again and I'm gonna *kill* you, so help me God. Don't tell me what to do, OK?'

I am stumped for words. But as suddenly as it has arrived, the rage abates.

'But, ah, that's a good question you just asked me about Elvis Presley. I would *hope* someday to meet Elvis Presley up there. It'd be great. I hope you're right . . . Old Chuck Berry might even make it, huh huh huh!'

I begin to ask this temperamental legend about the wives, the chequered past of marital conflict, but he's not having *that*.

'You're nit-picking me, boy. History is history. You keep talking about history and I don't think anybody really cares too much about the history of Jerry Lee Lewis. They want to know about what Jerry Lee Lewis is going to be like tomorrow and the next day. I still have a lot of hit records in me yet. If God's willing, we're gonna have some more hit records. If the Lord's with us. If the creek don't rise. Jerry Lee Lewis is Jerry Lee Lewis and he's number one Jerry Lee Lewis. We're talking about Jerry Lee Lewis, right now, we're not talking about John D. Rockefeller or Jimmy Swaggart. We'er talking about Jerry Lee Lewis. Jerry Lee Lewis is an individual and he is Jerry Lee Lewis and there will never be another entertainer and there will never be another talent like Jerry Lee Lewis. It's not my fault. It's what God put on me. That's the way it is and a lot of people are upset about it and a lot of people are jealous about it and they can't handle it and they never could handle it and they never will handle it and I don't particularly give a damn if they do handle it. I can handle it! I have the God-given talent!'

At the following night's Hammersmith Odeon concert, Jerry Lee handled it well enough, swooping his right hand over the keys like always, tripping out those high register trills, singing You Win Again with fine voice, mocking Elvis with Jailhouse Rock, leaping up from the piano stool to bawl out his bass player – 'D'you know how the song goes, boy?' – looking sturdily unimpressed when a gaggle of 'superstars' (Van Morrison and a flock of guitarists – Brian May, Stuart Adamson, Dave Davies) appeared to 'pay tribute' and/or attempt to steal the old man's thunder. A God-given talent doing old Lucifer's tunes . . .

'A talent from the Lord. You can't handle it. *NOBODY* can handle it. Except for old Jerry Lee, huh! Anything else you need to know?

Are you a difficult man to live with. Mr Lewis?

'I don't think so. I don't think so. I think if you check back with anybody I was ever married to before, you'll find out that they'll tell you that I wasn't quite as hard to live with as they thought I was. And I have a beautiful little boy now, nearly three years old, and I love my little boy and I have a daughter, 26 years old, and she's a good little lady, and I have my wife with me on this trip . . . Looks like I'm working for another divorce, huh huh huh huh! But I'm telling you this, boy, I don't want you talking about my wives. I want *that* understood.'

At this point, Jerry Lee's attention is distracted by the sight of Lizzie Webb, TV-am's morning exercise personage, who has entered the room and is standing at the canteen counter.

'I'd like to have that understood, too!' he roars, gazing at the frizzy figure of Ms Webb, a lecher's glint in his eyes, and chucking me roughly on the arm as if I were one of his drinking buddies. 'Ah *hah*!' he growls. 'Fiery, fiery me! Huh huh!' He shakes his head and grins at me as if we were together in some laddish ogling conspiracy. 'Lawdy, lawdy! Lawdy, Miss Clawdy! Yeah!'

Dear me. Will I ever recapture the man's attention from Ms Webb? 'Lawdy, lawdeeeee!' Excuse me Mr Lewis, do you believe you are playing the 'Devil's music'?

'I don't really know what you're talking about, young man.' Well . . .

'Things change and the years go by and they call it the Devil's music. It could very well be Satan's music. He could have very well been the director one time, who knows? He probably had a lot to do with it.'

One doesn't want to 'nit-pick' further by delving into history, but would Jerry Lee Lewis have ever become quite such a 'legend' if he hadn't kicked over a piano stool one day?

'Golly that's going back a long time ago, young man. But let me see . . . I was doing a stage show and I was talking to Carl Perkins and he said, *Do* something, because I was just sitting at the piano. So I said, Well, I'm going to stand up and play, we'll try that. But when I did stand up, the piano stool got hung in my boot. So I had to kick it away and it fell over and it scared me to death, you know, but the audience just went crazy, wild. I thought, Hey, Jerry Lee Lewis, there's something here. It was all a mistake, huh huh huh . . .'

And one doesn't want to 'upset' The Killer by touching again on the ticklish topic of wives. But Myra, the 13-year-old, she's the subject of the film he's supposed to be here promoting. When he first arrived in Britain in 1958, the juvenile cousin on his arm, the press were displeased. 'So Jerry Lee Lewis and his malodorous little circus have been given the old heave-ho by Britain's theatre managers,' went the Daily Sketch. 'It will be no bad thing for British show business – or for our young rock'n'roll fans either – if the unsavoury saga of Jerry Lee Lewis ends up as a cautionary tale . . .'

'Huh huh!' goes Jerry Lee. 'Well, the English press only wrote the truth. They told it like it was. I told it like it was. When I first stepped off the airplane, I told them exactly who I was and who she was and what was going on. It wouldn't be right if I went hiding the truth. Jerry Lee Lewis is an honest man. But this Jerry Lee Lewis movie is not an honest movie. That boy (Quaid) is saying things in the movie like when I left England, he's saying England can kiss my ass. That's *bad*. I never said that. That makes me sad that they put these dirty words in my mouth. But I want to say to you, young man, that I have no regrets about my life, no sir, no sir. I am living and I am breathing and I got a beautiful little boy and I live my life by God's Holy Commandmants . . .'

You've broken quite a lot of those 'commandments', have you not?

The fire and the fury is back, of course.

'Don't nit-pick me boy.' He jabs a finger into my tape recorder and threatens to smash it and then kill me (again). 'Don't nit-pick *ME*! I still got a life to go, you hear? Don't tell me what to do. There is no shame on Jerry Lee Lewis. Jerry Lee Lewis is Jerry Lee Lewis and Jerry Lee Lewis knows the Holy Ghost and there is no regrets . . .'

And there, evidently, he wants to leave it, for he leaps to his feet, snatches his pipe from the table and slaps me sharply on the back with the other, practically knocking the stuffing from me. 'Well, I've *enjoyed* it, son!' he bellows, indicating that the interview is at an end. 'I can't tell you no more about Jerry Lee Lewis . . . I can tell you about *that*!' He winks and gestures towards another TV-am female person at the canteen counter. 'Huh huh, *lawdy*!' he goes. He chucks me on the arm, he grips my hand, and the man, who minutes before was threatening to kill me, reverts to his old deferential and Southern manner. 'I hope I haven't offended anyone with what I been saying, young man. It is not the purpose of Jerry Lee Lewis to offend. No, sir . . .'

Jeremy Beadle

Laugh as he humiliates another unsuspecting citizen. Hoot as he smirkingly informs them he's come to build a nuclear reactor on their grandmother. But . . . *not really!* For he is TV's unlovable practical joker, the condescending perpetrator of concealed-camera japes, the Prince of Pranks.

A SLIGHT FIGURE with strangely sculptured beard skips friskily on to the stage of the 'world famous' (Edwardian seedy) City Varieties Music Hall. 'Hello boys and girls!' he pipes with alarming gusto as he slaps his thigh with a certain zest. 'Do you know who *I* am?' One hundred tiny voices (the theatre is three quarters empty, this matinee) squeal the response: 'Jer-em-y Beadle!!' 'No, no no!' chortles 'Britain's most popular television prankster', the self-styled 'mischief maker'. 'I am . . . *Wishee Washee!*'

Here he is, Beadle, a star of panto in Leeds, top of the bill over such illustrious names as Paul Stead ('Radio Aire's youngest daytime presenter'). Samantha Jane ('has appeared in many "pop" videos for chart toppers Black Lace') and Mystina ('has thrice been voted Best Lady Magician in the UK'). As Aladdin's rather 'zany' brother, Beadle is called upon to tell some rather disappointing jokes – there's 'Do you have an outstanding bill?' 'What do you think I am – a pelican?', boom boom, and there's a jape featuring an unusual brassière, 'A Leeds United bra: plenty of support but no cups', boom boom – which fail singularly to tickle the audience's funny bone. And, true to form, for this is what has made him a national figure, he summons members of the audience on to the stage for public humiliation capers. He points with his malformed hand at one small boy and barks, 'Why are your flies undone?' (they aren't); one can see the poor boy's blushes from the Circle Gallery. In jest, he tells a tiny girl that, although all other victims have left the stage with a gift bag, there's no present for her (there is). The girl, unfortunately, fails to see the 'funny side' and is distressingly close to tears before the assembled company ...

Aladdin (Craig Deegan) marries Princess Balroubador (the alluring Heidi Manton), Mystina performs a magic trick with a firecracker and a handkerchief and does a lot of adept cartwheels, and Jeremy Beadle steps into the footlights to deliver his parting Beadle's About catchphrase: 'And remember ... *next* time, it could be *you!*' Not very scintillating as catchphrases go and, in the circumstances, utterly irrelevant, but there we have it. In the orchestra pit, the three-man band go into the breezy and annoying refrains of the Beadle's About signature tune yet again; several still alert children in the audience decide to sing along yet again, thus providing the 'tune' with its undemanding lyric: '*Watch out, Beadle's about/ Watch out, Beadle's about/ You'd better watch out 'COS Beadle's about* ...' The curtain falls. Fin.

In the minute, genteel, decaying 'star' dressing room of the City Varieties, Jeremy Beadle has already changed out of his unconvincing 'Old Peking' stagewear into a more leisurely track suit. 'Hello!' he cried. 'I'm Jeremy Beadle!' He says this with *much* fervour, as if being Jeremy Beadle is the most exciting human possibility on the planet. Perhaps it is. Cunningly, he pre-empts my 'What-are-you-doing-in-some-terrible-old-northern-panto-when-you-surely-don't-need-the-money?' inquiry by gesturing about the grimy dressing room walls and gushing 'Look! Do you know this was once Charlie Chaplin's dressing room? It's the only reason I took this job. Charlie *Chaplin*! I love it. I love it to pieces ... You know, I could make more money in three hours of my other work, TV and consultancy and stuff, than I can in three *weeks* of this. But I *love* working with the pros.'

The pros being, um, Paul Stead, Mystina and the alluring Heidi Manton?

'Yeah. They're *pros*! They're wonderful because they have a *need* to be seen. It's in their blood. Their motivation, like all celebrities and would-be celebrities, is one of vanity and conceit. Whereas I am *not* vain or conceited. Both of those things are very low on my list of priorities. I have a very low vanity point. I am not that good when it comes to being a celebrity, you see. I don't preen. I don't really give a *fuck* what people think about me ...'

Which is probably just as well. And so we retire to the bar, where photographs in black and white of celebrities of old – Sir

Harold Secombe, the bloke who used to present The Good Old Days, lots of forgotten music hall turns of the North – are hanging on the flock wallpaper-covered walls. Jeremy orders coffee. He never drinks alcohol when he's working (or 'on the job', as he wittily calls his pantomine exercises). Jeremy starts to talk. Jeremy likes to talk.

He talks of his childhood. He was born, out of wedlock, 42 years ago in Kent, brought up on a 'very rough' council estate. 'My great friend Leslie Grantham, Dirty Den, once said to me, "There's one thing I never understood about you, Beadle. How did you survive St Paul's Cray with a name like Jeremy?" I thought that was *great*!'

He went to secondary modern school in Orpington and was expelled, at 15, for the super prank of hanging a pair of trousers on a flag pole. 'I always used to get terribly bored at school and so I created mischief and mayhem for which I was regularly beaten, and eventually expelled. Nowadays I get paid huge sums of *money* for creating mischief and mayhem. And people *love* me for creating mischief and mayhem. It's great, isn't it?'

After school, Beadle took a variety of jobs – lavatory attendant, barman, dustman, baker, hospital porter; as a 'bit of a hippy' he went around Europe and 'got kicked out of Italy and Holland and Austria and Denmark, all for vagrancy'. He became a co-editor of Time Out from the magazine's third issue and attempted to start similar 'alternative' what's on guides in Manchester and the North-west. 'They died.'

Then Beadle moved into the world of rock'n'roll as a promoter. He helped to organise the Bickershaw Festival of 1971. 'I brought over The Grateful Dead, New Riders Of The Purple Sage, Cheech & Chong, Captain Beefheart, Dr John,' the man says with a glint of pride. 'On the Sunday when The Grateful Dead came out there was this blistering sunset and they played a set like *mad*! Bliss! . . . But, really, The Grateful Dead insisted on 18 first-class return air fares and all the creature comforts and it was a real struggle and I remember Jerry Garcia being interviewed by the press and he was sitting in the back of a trailer which we'd paid for and stocked out for him and he said, I'm really enjoying taking these capitalist shits to town. And I thought, Fucking hell, you know, excuse me while I die, Jerry. He made sure all the creature comforts were there and then he attacked us for arranging them . . . Dr John was weird and Captain Beefheart was *extraordinary*. He

113

looked at me and I felt like a freckle on a rabbit's bum. God knows what was in him at the time. I think he was out of it . . .'

Beadle also helped to organise the first ever rock'n'roll show at Wembley – Chuck Berry, Bo Diddley, Jerry Lee Lewis, Little Richard, Bill Haley. He's got a feast of yarns about *that*, he assures me. Pray tell.

'Bo Diddley got his trousers nicked, hahaha. We paid Chuck Berry in used teenagers, hahaha. Jerry Lee Lewis arrived really late and I was trying to get him into a dressing room and he said, Just tell me one thing, boy: you ain't put me next to any niggers, have you? And the joke was I'd actually put him next to Little Richard. And then Little Richard overstayed his welcome. He just played on and on. Meanwhile, Chuck Berry's waiting to get on and he's getting more and more agitated – the show has to end at 12 and it's twenty to. Little Richard finally comes off and Chuck Berry's so furious, he comes to me and says, "You take me down to Little Richard's dressing room now!" and we walk in and Little Richard's sitting there with this fur coat – it's got to be 30 grand's worth of mistreated animal – and he's obviously totally out of his head, shouting, "They *love* me! They *love* me!" And Chuck Berry says, "Fuck you, boy. Love *you*, boy? They're waiting for *me*! You ever eat in my town, boy, you're gonna eat my shit!" And I'm going, "Ah, yes, well, very good, Mr Berry. Can we get on stage now, please?" '

Tickled by the memory, Beadle assumes a monstrous grin. 'It's interesting, isn't it? People only know me for leaping out on little ladies, for being Beadle, the floating fantasy. They've no idea about my history. Chuck Berry, what a bloke, haha!'

Ah, heady days. But the giddy world of rock was not for him, it seems.

'I didn't like the music business because it was full of liggers. The music business was all image and no substance. And drugs. I just hated the drugs. I've always been vehemently anti-drugs, primarily because they're anti-social. Drugs make people very introverted and it's very selfish. I often found myself trying to have a conversation with somebody and they were mooning over an orange. I hated that. I'm a motivator and I need *feedback*.'

So Beadle began writing for the telly, doing research for Russell Harty, providing material for Kenny Everett and the quiz show Celebrity Squares. He helped to compile The Book Of Lists and wrote a book of his own, The Intimate Sex Lives Of The Famous

('With a face like mine, you can only *read* about it, heehee.') In the late '70s, he hosted a late night phone-in on London's LBC radio. Madge from Tottenham would ring up and Beadle would ask her what colour knickers she was wearing. That sort of thing.

'It was wild and naughty!' the man enthuses. 'It has been much imitated, I'm very greatly flattered to say. You know, I remember the Sun headlines used to claim that the Sun created the word bonking, but *I* used to use the word bonking *regularly* on my show. It was one of the great features of the show. I used to say to callers, Done any good bonking lately? It was a real laugh. It's a bit much of the Sun to take credit for putting that word in the dictionary.'

The proud creator of the noble word 'bonk' eventually got the sack from LBC for being too 'saucy' or too 'raunchy' or whatever. But this maker of monkey business soon popped up again, with some hidden camera tomfoolery on London Weekend Television's Game For A Laugh, the japes that would make him so very (in)famous.

'Game For A Laugh was a hole in one, a massive sensation. And I became TV's cheeky prankster! Ha *HA*! Game For A Laugh changed the face of the viewing habits of the British public. Do you know, it's extraordinary but when they celebrated 21 years of LWT, Game For A Laugh never got one mention. Beadle never gets a mention at LWT because, while they love the viewing figures, I think they're slightly embarrassed by me. They think I'm low-brow, or something. But what people don't understand is it takes greater skill and intelligence to produce light entertainment than it does to produce documentaries. I could go and write and produce a documentary tomorrow with no problem. But with my brain I am a mischief maker and in the end I genuinely enjoy making people laugh. It thrills me to pieces. I meet people in the street and they say to me, I fell off the chair laughing at your programme, and it gives me such a kick I can't tell you.'

For a decade now the British public has been invited to guffaw at the rib-tickling practical japes of Beadle. Beadle's About is watched by more than 13 million people. What usually happens is Beadle's crew turn up on some poor fool's front lawn and they pretend they're from the council and have come to erect a sub post office or something. Then the 'victim' swears a lot (rude words bleeped out and signalled with a comical BEEP bubble on the screen). Then

Beadle turns up dressed as a policeman. He takes off his false beard. 'Victim' realises he/she has been 'had', rocks with laughter and merriment, swears a lot. Either that or fun is poked at persons of the fat persuasion because, Beadle says, 'Fat is funny.' What a hoot it all is.

Jeremy Beadle does not take criticism of his trivial style of entertainment lightly. Call him a buffoon and he'll titter in agreement – 'Heehee, it's not a man's job, is it?' – but will go on to tell you that *actually* he's got a brain and a lot of books too, and that his producer is an 'academic' and a genius.

Call him an irritant and he'll cry fury, say, 'It's only certain snobby sections that find me irritating – and they claim not to watch my show anyway, so what do *they* know? If you walked through the streets with me now, everybody would be going, Hurrah! Beadle's about! Watch out! They love it. The affection I get from the public is incredible. I get *mobbed*. I know it sounds stupid but I do. There's an *enormous* affection for the programme and an enormous affection for me because the public know that it's an affectionate tease.'

Call his programme, well, appalling rubbish and he'll tell you, 'The show might be nonsense, but it's *fun* and it's certainly not rubbish. It's practical jokes and I love practical jokes to pieces. The show that we produce is the Rolls-Royce of hidden camera shows in the world. We've taken it way beyond Candid Camera. The show is all about showing how wonderful the great British public are. Despite enormous provocation, they always come out on top. And whatever you say, there is no element of humiliation involved in what I do whatsoever. Because I care very much, *deeply*, about people . . . And let me tell you, I take great pride in the fact we produce a show that kids like at the same level of comprehension as adults. The joke goes right across the board and is understood – and that's a *real* skill.'

If you're being set up for one of Beadle's hair-raising pranks, a team of researchers will be despatched to make sure that you're a jolly good sport and game for a laugh beforehand. They will also find out whether you are likely to have a heart attack and die on the spot if your pride and joy of a motor car gets tipped into a lake or they build a pretend nuclear reactor atop your bungalow or whatever.

'The show is run like a military operation,' says Beadle. 'I would have been very good in wartime. The first question we ask is, Is there any medical reason why we shouldn't play this joke on your husband or your wife? And they say No. And we say, Has he or she visited the doctor recently? And they say, No. That is being thorough. I mean, the press often accuse me of invading privacy but that's such a load of twaddle. I read this drivel and I think it tells you more about the sexual frustrations of the writer than anything else. If they didn't have the forum of the paper, they'd be doing something *bizarre* . . .'

Beadle's team of thorough researchers will also make sure a) that you will recognise your merry-making host, b) that you are not the kind of person who is likely to hit the silly supremo when the 'joke' is revealed. Strangely enough, Beadle has *never* been abused by a 'victim'. 'Never, ever have I been attacked by the public. The public love me. The only abuse I get is from the press.'

He seems to have a bit of a bee in his bonnet about the press. 'I take all the abuse. It's either me or Cilla. There's no criticism, it's just plain abuse. It's sad. The British press used, until recently, to be the cream. But then you realise that there are only two things that rise: cream and bastards. All I know is that the public love the show and I just get slagged off. it doesn't affect me because I've never worried what people think of me. But the press have actually been saying that somebody should punch Beadle in the face. They've been saying, Isn't it about time Beadle got a pasting? Now that is incitement to assault, which is illegal. They're inciting people to attack me and that is outrageous and indeed illegal. And it must *stop*.'

Our cheeky skylarker bangs his clenched fist upon the table. Somewhat embarrassed by his wrath, he instantly changes the subject. 'But you know,' he says with, believe it or not, a *wink*, 'it's enormous fun being Beadle. *Great* fun being Beadle. The great thing about being Beadle is I can pick up the phone and play with the world's biggest toys. I can ring up the Royal Navy and say, Will you lend me a destroyer? and because I'm Beadle, they'll say, Yeah, sure. I don't like being a celebrity, but I do like being Beadle.'

Wouldn't you like to be anything else? Something, perhaps, more serious, respectable, acceptable? The frolicsome one pauses. 'What? . . . Er, what do I want to do? *Tell* me, what do I want to do when I grow up. People are always saying to me, Why don't you grow up? And I'm thinking, Well, I'm doing alright, really. I'm just genuinely lucky. Napoleon, before he promoted any man to a general, asked them one question. Are you lucky? That is a *brilliant* question ... I discovered where Napoleon's penis was, you know ...'

Mercifully, there is no time to discover more about the whereabouts of Napoleon's penis, for the evening audience, the family crowd, is arriving and Beadle must once more transform himself into Wishee Washee for its delight.

He will not apologise for being Beadle, for doing what Beadle does. 'After all,' he says, with another wink and a grin as big as Kansas, 'in the end it's only rock'n'roll. Isn't it?'

Jerry Hall

WANTED: drawling Southern belle with modelling experience, fun-loving socialite/raunchsome rock star's moll with sidelines in amateur dramatics, swimwear design and promoting beefy hot drinks. Position suits professional person, practised at playing the dumb blonde.

WE TAP SOFTLY and politely upon the dressing room door – nameplate: 'Miss Jerry Hall' – in the Lyric Theatre, Shaftesbury Avenue, and it's tugged, fairly *wrenched*, open by this peroxide Amazon, beaming beneath acres of lipstick, drawling Southern-wise, like Scarlett O'Hara on the sauce, 'Wayull, and how ahre youwew!!?' You'd think she had never been quite so delighted to see anyone in her life. 'Cayum *eehyounn*!' she goes, battily fluttering the eyebrows set within the overlong face and baring a set of monstrously gleaming, somewhat equine nashers. In her left hand she brandishes a vase of flowers, and there are similar bloom-filled vessels lined all along the mirror counter.

'Just leeyook at all these flowers!' she says, gesturing dangerously with the vase at her florist shop-styled display. 'I just leeyuvre flowyers. They're from all my friends. Aren't they nahce? Aren't *people* nahce?'

Flowers, one must admit, are sometimes very nice, but these ones have been there in water since the play she's performing in, Bus Stop, opened a week ago. The dressing room now has a certain less-than-pleasant fragrance. Observing that we have noticed this fact, Ms Hall turns up her ample nose and all but bellows, 'Eeyuh, this duressing room smeeyewulls! Mah curleaning lady, she's so nahce and surweet, she just cayun't bayear to throw my flowyers away!' At this she laughs a laugh that's almost a whinny, a thing born in the throat that comes out the nose and is almost impossible to express on the printed page ... something like 'Shn-awwwslnifffhuhhihhyawl.'

I will refrain, from here on, from attempting to translate Ms Hall's utterances phonetically. You would get a dreadful headache. Suffice it to say, she is clearly very proud of her Southern accent. She exaggerates, uses it, in combination with fluttering eyelashes, as a flirting device – 'What, li'l meeyuh?' – just like Scarlett/Vivien Leigh did in Gone With The Wind. But if riled or angered, the accent slips; she loses it and she sounds, of a sudden, not some Southern belle but more like ... well, *Mick*.

'Hi, Chris! How are *you*?' We have been interrupted (again ... someone came scuttling in with Ms Hall's tea and then a make-up lady came to pop her head round the door and say 'Hi!' and then there was a bearded bloke relaying some message about Saturday's matinee and now there's assistant director Chris Pickles, dropping by for pre-performance salutations.) 'Hi, Chris! How are you? Wasn't Ben *sweet*? Did you meet him? He's so sweet. He *loves* the play!'

Chris looks rather blank.

'Ben Kingsley.' Jerry darts a look at me to see if *I* have registered the name of the famed British Thespian.

'Ben Kingsley. He just *loves* the play.'

Chris perks into action. 'Oh, yeah, *Ben*. Ben was saying in the interval how he *adored* it. It was really nice to have such an open, honest reaction.'

Jerry: 'Sure *was*! Byeeee!'

Chris: 'Byeeee!'

Jerry (to me): 'Isn't Chris *sweet*?' (How on earth should *I* know? I only saw the geezer for a few seconds, but Jerry Hall seems to imagine – or wants you to imagine she imagines – that *everybody* is sweet and *nahce*.) 'Oh he's so sweet. Everyone in the play is so sweet and nahce, all the people in the theatre are so nahce, it's just like having a family. They're so sweet and so supportive and so positive, full of energy, and so sweet that it's really ...'

Sweet?

'... nahce.'

Jerry Hall, dressed in simple sweater and jeans, though made up to the gills, stalks her dressing room, fussing with her hair and dabbing at her flowers, saying just how very delighted she is to be here, starring in the West End.

'I think the West End is wonderful. And you know, this is a really sweet play. It has lovely messages . . .'

Bus Stop, written in 1955 by William Inge, is pretty trifling, sub-Tennessee Williams stuff, concerning the fractured relationship between a would-be rodeo cowboy Bo Decker (played by David Cassidy's younger brother Shaun) and a would-be showgirl singer Cherie (Hall), who are stuck in a Kansas diner during a snowstorm. Maybe you have seen the 1956 film staring Marilyn Monroe. Jerry Hall is not Marilyn Monroe (her feet are too big), and reviews have been 'mixed', as they say, some unkind gentlemen suggesting that Ms Hall is to the art of Thespis what Yves St Laurent is to speedway. To be polite, Ms Hall is adequate in the part (called upon to lounge upon the diner's counter and sing That Old Black Magic out of tune, she proves that when it comes to singing off key, she's the tops). Ms Hall does not take kindly to criticism of her craft. She sits, slowly crosses her legs, slowly ignites a Marlboro Light and blows the smoke out with something approaching a snarl.

'Some of the reviews were nahce but, you know, they picked on me a lot about being too tall, which is so stupid because everybody *knows* I'm tall. But they just wanted to pick on me and be bitchy and stuff.'

Paranoid tendencies dissipate and Hall composes herself once more into a life-loving Southern belle.

'But I've gotten *wonderful* letters. All my friends liked it and I've been offered four other plays and two movies,' – she is positively beaming – 'so it's very good for my career.'

Ah, career. Thus far, the career has consisted of highly-paid modelling and, more important, being the much publicised paramour of Mick Jagger. She doesn't *need* the money that the West End offers but, well . . .

'I have a whole lot of creative energy and I have all these big ideas and I want to entertain people. It's something that's in you from childhood, this desperately wanting to please and entertain people. It's like a gift, or something. Maybe it's that. It's different with Mick.'

Ask Jerry Hall about herself and her response often, somehow, turns to things Mick.

'Mick dreams music. He hears music, you know. He's always hearing songs in his head. It's some sort of special talent. With me, I like to do different projects because if you have too much energy, it can go bad on you if you don't do something about it. I just *have* to work because if I don't work I tend to rearrange the furniture all the time.'

Jerry Hall was born in Mesquite, Texas about 35 years ago ('about' = age in some dispute). Her father was a truck driver, transporting explosive chemicals across America. Her mother was a medical records librarian. The girl had to share a bed with three sisters, which sounds frightfully Southern-impoverished-romantic and Dolly Partonesque but 'we weren't like dirt poor, you know, we weren't really white trash, we were just sort of on the verge of being regular suburban lower-middle-class American. I have *never* had to starve.'

It was mother who taught Jerry that a woman should be a cook in the kitchen, a maid in the living room, a whore in the bedroom.

'Oh, *that* old quote. I try not to say those things anymore. When I was modelling, I was hanging out with wild people and the reporters would want me to say some wild quote. I used to be quite good at that stuff.'

Yes, it was Ms Hall who offered this valuable snippet of advice on how to keep a man to gals everywhere: 'Even if you only have two seconds, drop everything and give him a blow job.' She laughs her whinnying laugh, a disconcerting sound.

'Oh, that's dumb. I don't say those things anymore . . . Actually my mother was a bit old-fashioned, really. She did believe that the man was the king of the castle and that you should try and please them and she thought if you were nahce and sexy you got a lot more out of life.'

Does Hall believe that 'man is the king of the castle'?

'I don't know because I feel very liberated. I've always made more money than the men in my job. I've always worked and I've had my own money and done what I like with it. And actually Mick is actually much better at organising, you know, things to do with the house than I am. I like to do the decorating and invite people and entertain them but he's much more practical.'

What? You mean Mick Jagger, latter-day rock Lothario, can change a fuse?

'A feeyews? What's that? I dunno. He's good with his *hands* haha.'

Oo-er, sounds a bit rude.

'I wouldn't say I was the sort of typical unliberated, you know, housewifey thing. But I suppose man is still king of the castle . . . if he's got some *muhney*, hahaha . . .'

Hall has always been drawn to men with *muhney*, it seems. Flings with David Ogilvy and former racing mogul Robert Sangster, relationships with Bryan Ferry and Mick. But she does not wish to dwell upon the men in her past.

'No, no nah, I don't want to talk about all that. I'm sick of talking about that. I'm sick of talking about Bryan. I'm sick of talking about Mick.' (Really?) 'I don't want to talk about all that. The English press can be pretty ghastly, can't they? They sure can.' All she will say about Bryan is, 'He was great fun around the house.' The rest is silence.

Jerry Hall, girl from Mesquite, worked at Dairy Queen, dishing up ice cream, before her mother encouraged her to take up modelling.

'Everybody said I was nahce and pretty and photogenic but I was tall and thin and I used to be very upset about it. I'd cry and *crah* and stuff but my mother said, Well, you know, look at this girl Twiggy, she's really well known and she's skinnier than you are and she's made it, so maybe you can do that. And my school picture came out *real* good. It gave me a happy feeling.'

So she left Texas when she was 16 (or thereabouts), came to Europe and was discovered by Helmut Newton, billed as the new Verushka, and the rest, as they say, is history. Catwalks and the covers of all the high-class magazines and piles and piles of dough. This top model person now has her own swimwear 'collection' . . .

'I *lerve* choosing fabrics. I *lerve* design. I do it all myself. Sometimes when I see somebody on the beach that I don't know and they're wearing all my swimsuits, I get the *biggest* thrill. It's called Jerry Hall Swimwear . . .' (a plug) '. . . for lack of imagination. It's about the third most successful swimwear line in the world.'

Golly! And she has a proper acting career – of sorts. She was in the thoroughly tiresome Urban Cowboy (starring John Travolta) for about two seconds; she was in Batman for about 10 seconds, scuttling in and out of rooms with shopping bags as Jack Nicholson's bimbo girlfriend ('Boy, was Batman a success!' she exclaims, almost taking the credit herself). But she is probably best known to the casual viewer for her appearances in telly commercials for Applause (a chocolate bar confection) and Bovril (a peculiar beverage). In one of the Bovril ads, for Chicken Bovril, the glamourpuss was called upon to dress up in a stupid chicken suit. Not very dignified, was it?

'Oh, that was *fuhn*! I've been so lucky in my career because most of my commercials are kind of tongue-in-cheek and have a lot of irony and I lerve that. Dressing up as a chicken is kinda funny, you know. It's not a hard, dumb sell. And all the products I do are quite good. I've never done commercials for things that I thought were awful.'

You mean you actually *like* Bovril?

'I *lerve* it!' she says, brand loyal to the last. 'I lerve it, I swear. I drink it all the time. Have you ever tried the Chicken Bovril?'

No.'

'I *swear*, if you don't like the beef, the Chicken Bovril is very good. I like the beef Bovril, too. My mother had this beef wine and iron tonic that we had to drink and we were brought up on cows, you know, beef, beef, beef for breakfast, lunch and dinner so I *lerve* the beef Bovril. I think it strengthens me.'

Jerry Hall takes a sip of tea and lights another cigarette. She's said she thinks the English tabloid press is 'ghastly' but, in fact, the newspapers have always been unusually soft on Jerry Hall. They rave on about her striking looks and her glamour and her impeccable nahceness; they've never done a scandalous number on her. When she got into her spot of trouble in Barbados, arrested on drugs charges, they rose in her defence crying this-is-not-a-fair-cop-hands-off-our-Jerry and that sort of thing. The entertainment correspondent of the Daily Mail fed her mints every day in court.

So how was Barbados? She draws heavily upon her cigarette, summoning up her righteous anger. The accent slips.

'That was so awful. So stupid. As if *I* would go through customs with a cardboard box full of 20 pounds of marijuana. It was the dumbest thing I'd ever heard of. I actually *didn't* go through customs. What happened was I asked my butler to send my sweaters from the States and my butler sent them and someone picked them up and put them in the wrong locker at the airport and then they put my name on this other box (*the marijuana-stuffed box, that is*) and I went to collect it and, God, it was like a nightmare. It was like something so *awful*, you can't possibly imagine. You can't imagine that that could ever happen in the civilised world. But they're so idiotic there in Barbados; they are all fools and they're horrible and they were getting bugged about their drug problem and they were trying to blame it on somebody well known.

It was just pathetic. But the judge was very sweet and nahce . . . and the customs man got fired for it.' Well, 'I mean, I don't even *like* drugs, you know. You can ask Mick. When I first met him, I didn't even drink and he used to laugh in my face, huhhuh. I drink now, because alcohol is very good for your blood . . .'

To the vulgar newspapers, and others, Jerry Hall represents some kind of Queen of London Society. Seen at all the best parties with the nobs and the toffs and the Billy Connollys of this world. She denies this all, of course, says she's really just a hard worker and a homebody with no time on her hands for playing the flitting socialite. It's just that, you see, photographers tend to snap her whenever she deigns to attend some frolicsome function or other. They like to have her pic in their publications because she's, well nahce and pretty . . .

'I don't think I'm a Queen of Society, I don't think that's true at all. It makes me laugh when I read that. I think, God, I spend so much time working and staying home with the kids. But I like the Summer season. In the Summer there's lots of parties. Don't you go to them?'

No. She throws me a look of pity.

'Oh, that's sad. In the Winter there's dinners and stuff and charity events, you know, but most of the parties happen in the Summer, with all the events, the horse-racing and the tennis and this and that. I love it.'

She plays a dumb blonde act, batting the lashes and tossing back the peroxide mane and pouting and flirting and purring (except when the accent slips) with gusto, does Ms Hall. Is the act genuine, one wonders, or is it something she learned at her mother's knee, to please and entertain and get her way? Is she a woman of artifice?

'I've heard them say that but, you know, Little House On The Prairie (*dreadful American TV series with Michael Landon and raccoons and much sentimental backwoods inactivity*) makes me cry. I cry and *crah*. I'm always crying at the soppiest things. Mick makes me cry when he does sweet things. He does so many sweet things. You know, he's gone off for three days with his father hiking in Cornwall. Isn't that sweet? He's so nahce. He does such sweet things. He's so sweet and nahce and caring and . . .'

Not having a sickbag to hand, I feel it necessary to interrupt quickly with a brusque query. If Jerry is *not* a woman of artifice, is she then, *really* dumb?

'Oh, well, that woman of artifice stuff could come from something I said. I said when men were being patronising to me in business or something I just sort of smile sweetly and think, Beneath this peroxide lies a smart brunette, haha. And then L'Oréal, the hair people, liked it and so they used that line in their campaign that I did for them, but I said, Beneath this blonde lies a smart brunette. So you would presume I was faking dumb, but I don't think I have to *fake* dumb. I'm so uneducated on so many things, I *am* dumb. I've been trying to read Proust for a while but I haven't got through it. And I hang out with lots of people who are very intelligent, writers and different things, and I feel quite lost sometimes in their conversation so I try to read all the great classics, Proust and stuff, and a lot of them change my life because they're fascinating but it's a lifelong job. And I'm dumb. But I'm not stupid. I trust my instincts so I don't think I'm stupid . . .'

I ask Jerry Hall if she believes in God and she looks wide-eyed, *amazed* at the question.

'Why, of *course* I do. Don't *you*? I was brought up to believe in God and I always have. It gives me great joy to believe in God. I enjoy gardening and being with my children and being with God and I hope to continue all those lovely things. I think God is nahce.'

I ask her where she stands on The Rolling Stones. Does she sort of *dig* the elderly R&B ragamuffins?

'Oh, *yeah* I *lerve* The Rolling Stones. But I was brought up on country and western music. It's my roots. Have you ever listened to Nanci Griffith? She's great.'

So what's her favourite Rolling Stones song?

'Um . . . um . . .' She pauses and withdraws another cigarette from the emptying packet. 'Um . . . I think Miss You is the best.'

Miss You? That rather fearful disco thing rather than Gimme Shelter or similar 'golden great'?

'I like Miss You. And I *lerve* the new album. You know, *'You're not the only ship adrift on the ocean'* – I think that's so sweet. Every time I ask Mick, he says, All my songs are about you, honey. Hahaha. Actually, I guess I'm not a good judge of music.'

Jerry Hall suddenly swoops to her feet crying, 'What *tahme* is it?' It is a quarter to seven and the stage is calling. 'Quarter to seven? You're *kidding*! Ah got to get ready!!'

And in her hurried panic, she lets fly a curse that sounds more Mick than Southern belle. 'Shit!' she says. But then she remembers

DAVID ICKE

SCREAMIN' LORD SUTCH

JIMMY SAVILE

STATUS QUO

THE CHIPPENDALES

PAUL GASCOIGNE

BENNY HILL

DAVID MELLOR

MR BLOBBY

ROLF HARRIS

RINGO STARR

WILLIAM ROACHE

JEFFREY ARCHER

DENNIS POTTER

FREDDIE STARR

CLIFF RICHARD

herself, corrects the word with a coy Texan smile and a flutter of eyelids.

'Aw, shoot! And we were getting on so wayull . . .!'

Screamin' Lord Sutch

A point of order, Mr Speaker: the opposition leader is an exhaustingly tedious, staunchly unribtickling, lecherous old goat. And have we forgotten his unsavoury pop discs of yester-year? Or his claim to have invented punk rock? Or his unquenchable appetite for self-publicity?

A CRUELLY WIZENED figure in leopardskin coat and familiar top hat hobbles about the diminutive stage of the West London social club wheezing an old rock'n'roll tune into a microphone. Around his neck hangs a pink lavatory seat. On his face there's a grotesque rubber mask with a huge porcine snout. 'I'm a hog for you, baby!' goes the preposterously attired 'vocalist', while a workman-like backing band behind attempt to grind up some kind of frenzy. On the dancefloor, a few gathered here tonight at the social headquarters of Landis & Gyr Ltd (manufacturers of electricity meters and electro-mechanical components), frug discon-solately to the gruesome noise; rather more simply gaze upon this most undignified of stage spectacles, expressions of some bemuse-ment on their faces.

Screamin' Lord Sutch has been doing his rock review – ancient rock'n'roll standards like Good Golly Miss Molly and Johnny B. Goode, his own unsavoury 'horror' non-hits of yesteryear (Jack The Ripper, Monster In Black Tights etc), with the added dash of silly facial grimaces and gooning it up in general – for more than 30 years now. The 'big time', unsurprisingly, has eluded him, and his current backing band Some Like It Hot – who have pretensions to being a 'proper' group in their own right – evidently find sup-porting duties for the ageing showman something of a chore.

This tireless self-publicist, whose election antics, ever there grin-ning on the town hall stages whilst the returning officers do their perfunctory stuff, this founder of The Monster Raving Loony Party whose 'zany' (or, if you prefer, 'frivolous') 'political' activity has made him a household name, comes stalking through the Landis canteen area that serves as dressing room, bearing down upon the journalist with determination. He doffs the topper. He waggles the giant Vote Lord Sutch rosette on his lapel and cackles. He hands me a badge that bears the legend 'Give Masochists A Fair Crack Of The Whip'. And another that says 'Haven't I Fucked You Before Without A Condom?' 'Haw!' he goes. 'Cor! They're good laughs, them, ain't they?' Fresh from 'success' in the mid-Staffs by-election (he got 374 votes and 'I come seventh out of 14 and I beat the National Front candidate, you know, and I got cartoons out of it because there's a current cartoon in the new edition of Punch'), he seems in a state of some excitement, radically slurred of speech though he's drinking only lager shandies, ranting tomfoolery with no prompting whatsoever.

Trying on another topper from his case full of comical stage props, while a young girl whom he introduces as Samantha, Page 3 model and official Monster Raving Loony Party dancer, flutters about his person, he launches into the following party political broadcast-styled stream of old tosh:

'In the Monster Raving Loony Party we're still out there even in the dark with torches looking for the Heavy Plant Crossing. Has anybody ever *seen* this plant? And we're trying to get our new invention off the ground which is when you feed your dog tinned food it's got to have an ingredient in there that makes the mess illuminated so it saves you treading in it in the dark and then the traffic wardens can scoop up the mess and also we should plant a tree every day in these concrete jungles so we'll have trees and grass and that'll stop all these people in housing estates committing suicide and getting depressed and I want to stop the Channel Tunnel because it's stupid so my monster plan is to link up with Jersey and Guernsey and then we can declare ourselves a tax haven and turn the Isle of Wight into Loony Island or something and we wouldn't be in the mess we are now if we had enforced birth control. Look at China. Bring back the old money: LSD! Har har...'

And so it continues. '... and I'd put 5p on a gallon of petrol so that all these bands and lorries that come over from America can pay for the roads they're destroying'. Little Samantha looks on agog. Good evening, Screamin'. Or do we call you Lord?

'Oh, uh, well, you can call me David. That'll be alright.'

David Sutch was born in West Kilburn during the war. His father was a policeman who was killed in an air raid shelter in West Hampstead, 'but it's probably for the best because maybe he wouldn't have allowed me to go into rock'n'roll because my mum's still waiting for me to get a proper job.'

A Middlesex Boys' Boxing Champion, a plumber's mate, a garage mechanic, Sutch 'got into early '50s rock'n'roll through Radio Luxembourg because they had all these classics by the Bill Haleys and the Chuck Berrys and the Little Richards and Carl Perkins's Blue Suede Shoes and my favourite was Bill Haley except for Elvis Presley because he was rock'n'roll and sex and everything rolled into one so I wanted to be Elvis.'

Screamin' Lord Sutch – 'Screamin' was my nickname because I would scream and shout and then there was Lord because I wore a top hat' – began performing at The Clay Pigeon pub in Harrow in 1957 and auditioned to play at the 2 I's coffee bar in Soho where Cliff and Tommy Steele and Marty Wilde and Adam Faith got their early breaks. 'I was doing horror rock'n'roll because I liked the old black-and-white movies of Boris Karloff and Bela Lugosi films and those were my favourites so I thought I'd put that to rock'n'roll.'

Was this a notion 'borrowed', perchance, from Screamin' Jay Hawkins?

'Oh, no!' the Lord protests. 'He was more into blues but he was there doing his horror stuff and I admire Screamin' Jay but mine was a different sort of person because it was more like a Dracula sort of figure coming out of a coffin with long hair and buffalo horns and dressed up in a leopardskin suit and I went down the 2 I's with that get-up and I was mad and crazy and over the top and they thought it was quite good because I wasn't copying Elvis all the time and the guy who ran the 2 I's rang up the Sunday papers and they come down and took a lot of pictures of me and then it said, 'Newcomer Screamin' Lord Sutch Horns In On Rock And Roll . . .' because I had the buffalo horns on, you see.'

Sutch and his band, The Savages, went on to headline at the Star Club in Hamburg – 'The Beatles were just like a support band in those days along with The Searchers and Gerry And The Pacemakers. They were just the follow-up bands when I was head-lining and next week it was Chuck Berry and the next week it was Jerry Lee or Fats Domino and I shared a stage with Ray Charles' – and to tour constantly with this 'rock'n'roll horror show'. It was all this Jack The Ripper stuff and I did a whole show out of that which would last 20 minutes where I'd have girls dressed up as prostitutes who would run around the stage and Jack would be after them with a carving knife, har har!'

This all sounds in excessively poor taste, scarcely ideologically sound. Sutch, with shaking hand, raises lager shandy to his lips and takes on a puzzled look.

'What do you mean? It was just a laugh. It was like a mini-opera before its time and even David Bowie said that on Parkinson or one of them shows where they said, Were you the first to dress up and put theatrics into pop music? and he said, No, Screamin' Lord Sutch did it way before I did – and this was way previous to the Rocky Horror Show and that. And The Cramps are fans of mine, too, but these people like The Cramps are only catering for so long and then they die out of favour and then they've gone but I'm a survivor.'

Sutch is keen to inform you that he's a survivor, an innovator, a living legend. He refers to the early Savages as 'my famous school of rock'n'roll musicians' – and the number of sparkling names who passed through the Savages' ranks in the 1960s is, indeed, impressive: Ritchie Blackmore, Nicky Hopkins, Albert Lee, Mitch Mitchell, Jimmy Page (who appeared on the 1964 flop single She's Fallen In Love With The Monster Man), Jeff Beck (on the 1964 flop single Dracula's Daughter). Even Mick Abrahams of Blodwyn Pig.

'All these people were attracted to my band and I was the top guvnor because we had the only band that was wild and I didn't restrict musicians because the more guitarists go mad the more I go mad and I hand-picked musicians like Ritchie Blackmore and he went on to be at the height of Deep Purple and he said that was all down to his training in The Savages because I used to drag him round the stage by the end of his guitar with a leopardskin and Pagey was into none of that black magic stuff – I don't mean chocolates, har har – when he was with me because he was too frightened of the crowd because The Savages used to be dressed up in leopardskins like caveman savages, you see, and the band had to run through a crowded hall screaming and pick up their stuff and start with Shazam! or Peter Gunn or something. So all my band was always scared of the crowd because they had to run through with white skinny legs in front of everyone and they were embarrassed. Ritchie Blackmore used to hate the leopardskin . . .'

Sutch even appears willing to take the credit for the invention of punk rock, because, it seems, Malcolm McLaren and Vivienne Westwood once made him a leopardskin jacket and then 'McLaren phoned me up and said he was managing a new band and he said he was launching them on my style of publicity and my sort of image where I couldn't care less about anything, wild and scary and anti-social and whatever because I upset the parents and McLaren said there hadn't been anything to upset the parents in rock'n'roll for a long time so he asked if these Sex Pistols could be my support band and I took them round my college circuit but I had to kick them off because they smashed up all my PA because they stuck the mike stands through the speakers at Brunel College and I did a duff show because of them fuckers and we had a fight backstage, actually, because they were getting a bit heavy. McLaren stills owes me money for my PA but he just grunts every time I see him. When I see Johnny Rotten, I knock his green teeth in.'

Screamin' Lord Sutch's first single, produced by Joe Meek in 1961, was originally titled Knocking On My Coffin Lid. 'But they said it was too hard for EMI because they were frightened stiff to have a thing that mentioned coffins and death so they called it 'Til The Following Night' so they watered it down but it was barred by the BBC and then there was Jack The Ripper and there was Falling In Love With A Monster Man and Monster In Black Tights but all these horror songs were barred by the BBC which I thought was very narrow-minded.'

Sutch's singles were flops, each and all. 'I was very stupid on that because I never got in a studio proper because I only thought of doing gigs and entertaining people but that's rock'n'roll.' Doesn't he feel at all resentful, still scratching out a living in social clubs when so many of his former sidemen are now so very rich indeed? He looks at me, mouth open, for many seconds, as if he's never contemplated such a question before.

'Oh, well, no because I've still got a cult following and I'm coming up for 30 years and there's a lot of my colleagues that were massive stars driving round in limousines and stuff like Jimi Hendrix and people like that who've all died by the wayside and they're all dead, half of them, which is the case with Keith Moon and Jimi Hendrix and Jim Morrison that I knocked about a lot with in Los Angeles.'

Sutch was a duffer when it came to making and selling records.

His one talent was, and has been, a bent for self-promotion. Riches never flowed but column inches did. In 1964 he established Radio Sutch on a disused defence fort off Whitstable and tried to outrage the nation by reading out extracts from Lady Chatterley's Lover over the air. In 1972, he marched through London accompanied by five naked women to publicise a rock'n'roll show at Wembley Stadium at which he was appearing along with Bill Haley, Chuck Berry and Bo Diddley – 'We ended up down Downing Street with these naked women following me giving out leaflets. Unfortunately, they got arrested and they got fined. But I was let off because I had a leopardskin on so I was quite alright.' But his greatest prank was standing for Parliament, which he did for the first time, representing his National Teenage Party (although he was already 21), in 1963 at Stratford and South Warwickshire, a seat made vacant by the resignation of John Profumo. His 'manifesto' at the time included votes at 18 and the legislation of commercial radio – measures that have since passed into being, he's proud to tell you, as if this puts some gloss of respectability on all the political games.

Sutch remembers '63. 'I was known as a nutter, a rock'n'roller who couldn't string two words together, and I objected to this because I could string *three* words together so I went to Stratford amongst the Profumo scandal and he was a disgraced War Minister that was supposed to be setting an example and I thought I could do better than that.' Vote For The Ghoul: He's No Fool was Sutch's campaign. He received 209 votes.

Since then, Sutch has stood against Harold Wilson (who gave him a light for his cigar) at Huyton, against Margaret Thatcher (who complimented him on his leopardskin outfit) at Finchley, and in 25 other election contests. His Monster Raving Loony Party now has 8,000 members who pay £3 a head for the privilege of joining (which helps towards the lost deposits). The Party has many 'amusing' platforms – Sutch rattles on, less than coherently, about turning butter mountains into ski slopes, throwing fish into wine lakes 'so they come out ready pickled', about abolishing jogging and 'We say things like, Why is there only one Monopolies Commission? Har har!' But isn't the jape wearing a little thin by now? We see Sutch on the Heineken ad standing outside Number 10 – only Heineken can do this – and we find ourselves thinking this joke's not funny any more. Too much Sutch can become a trifle irritating, no?

'Course it's funny!' snorts the Lord. 'It's a laugh. But it's serious, too, you know. I'm really very serious and the politics has become a second hat because I believe that in entertainment if you're a singer you shouldn't do it 24 hours because it can be very dangerous and the politics is recreation and it broadens my horizons and is an escape and it's all got a lot of sense because if I don't get a thousand votes I get a thousand smiles and I'm happy.'

Is it the 'smiles' though, or is it all the acres of cheap publicity that spur this rather creaking individual on? On stage tonight, whenever the Q camera is pointed in his direction, he forgets rock'n'roll performance and poses quite *desperately*, unlovely teeth bared for the lens. Publicity, he thrives on it. He reels off the names of all the rather awful TV programmes on which he has appeared as if he's reading some scroll of honour.

'I've done Terry Wogan twice and I've done things like Through The Keyhole and I've done Russell Harty and I've done The Six O'Clock Show and The James Whale Show and Pebble Mill At One and I keep getting involved with these programmes where they say things like 'The best of English eccentrics' and I end up with people like Spike Milligan and all these weird characters like the guy that does The Sky At Night (Patrick Moore) and Bellamy and all these people and Cyril Smith and . . .'

Does it never grow tiresome being the Great British Loony, playing the fool, acting the goat?

'Well, I wouldn't say I was a goat, so to speak, because I try to be normal,' he says without a glimmer of humour in the tone, 'and I *am* quite normal and I don't *try* and be eccentric because I'm just getting through life the best way I can. It's just a question of surviving and making people smile. See, my ambition was to become known as a rock'n'roll singer and to become a household name and to meet Elvis Presley and I done all that because I met Elvis Presley in 1969 at the International Hotel in Las Vegas and he looked like a Greek statue and he was absolutely marvellous and he sort of vaguely knew who I was, I think, which was quite good but look at him now because he got killed through the bad trip of blowing himself up with uppers and downers and they chopped him up and they said he had the insides of a man of over 80 and he was only 42 which is silly because he had the whole world in his hand and he put it in the lavatory pan. So I'm doing better than Elvis. I'm bigger and more popular and playing to more people. I'm bigger than Elvis and that's all I ever wanted, really . . .

Back on stage, this befuddled entertainer who lays strange claim to Elvis's throne, this would-be maestro of the bizarre and the macabre, dawdles across the stage clutching in his hand, by the 'hair', a papier mâché model of a woman's severed head. 'I'm Jack The Ripper!' he tells us. He strikes a somewhat pathetic figure.

The social club's hall is not alight with smiles, nor with chilled screams. Nor with anything very much at all.

Nigel Kennedy

He's the man who made classical music mass-market. And this he achieved by reinventing himself into a lager-handed, spike-topped pseudo-lout, complete with textbook rock star accessories, an embarrassing line in pot-head verbiage and a rented Cockernee accent.

'**D**O YOU WANT me to get my ******** out, man?'
I beg your pardon?
Nigel Kennedy, fiddling person, laughs the coarse laugh of a 'barrow boy' and repeats his crude inquiry. He opens his violin case, swathed in the colours and insignia of his beloved Aston Villa football team, and picks up an instrument, not the Stradivarius (which is locked away in a safe somewhere) but . . . he flourishes the fiddle in the air . . . 'Haha! It's short for *Contr*eras who's the guy who made it, a Spanish bloke . . .'

On the pavement outside a pub in London's George Street (just behind the headquarters of EMI Records, Kennedy's company), Nigel seems thrilled to be drawing the attention of passers-by with his usage of the language of a fish-husband. A miniskirted girl totters by on the other, sunny side of the street and 'Nige' is away. 'Cor, check that, mate! Animal! Monster animalette, man!' Leers and sexist banter more suited to an oikish adolescent than to a respected classical musician in his mid-thirties, but then Kennedy does so love to exhibit himself as a man – or Jackass-The-Lad – of the 'people', what with his Aston Villa underpants, his 'cheeky' and overdone Cockernee accent, his somewhat retrograde slang ('mate, man, monster, animal, cool, groovy, cat, baby'). He took the last month off work to go to Italy and the World Cup where he 'hung out' with England's erstwhile premier folk hero Gary Lineker ('a real fun cat'), and got up to pie-tossing-styled naughty tricks, apparently, with England's *new* folk hero Paul Gascoigne

('Someone called me The Gazza Of The Violin; that's a very flatter-
ing description 'cos Gazza's out of his head, man!').

And to go with the beer and the footer and the matey chatter,
there's the look of the 'rock star', purple pebble sunspecs that he
refuses, this afternoon, to remove, bristled hair and bristled chin,
ripped jeans with a lump of quartz safety-pinned to the thigh in a
clash of punk/new age cultures ('I hate new age. I hate that shit.
But I just like the stone 'cos it's got a good vibe.')

Would you care for another glass of beer, Nigel?

'No, ta, mate,' he says, grasping my hand, for some reason not
in the polite English fashion but in American 'street' thumb-grip
style, 'I was up till five last night doing it (*i.e. drinking, one
presumes*), man. It was a bastard.' Nigel Kennedy, the man who
BBC announcers are wont to describe as 'the wacky violin virtuoso'
whenever he's about to pop up on Wogan, plays the rock geezer/
regular bloke role with panache.

When people stop outside the pub to gawp at the famous personage and his fiddle, when young girls request an autograph, 'Nige'
leaps to his feet and cries things like, 'Are you a muso, then? Cool,
baby!' (sounding, in his more hysterical moments, disconcertingly
like John Otway going 'Cor baby that's really free!'). Nigel Kennedy, it is thoroughly evident, is far from dissatisfied with his
position and his fame. 'Monster, animal!' he cries, as his attendant
make-up artist (!) takes his leave. 'Be *bad*!'

Nigel Kennedy wasn't always like this. He was born in 1956
(within the sound of neither Bow bells nor Villa Park's roar, but
in a Regency house in Brighton overlooking the sea) into a musical
family: his mother was a piano teacher and his father (who went
off to Australia before the boy was born) was at one time principal
cellist with the Royal Philharmonic Orchestra. And Nigel – as that
name would suggest – was a *quiet* little fellow. 'Yeah, I was. I
was overpampered and liked everything very easy and my mum was
looking after me on her own so she gave me everything I wanted
when I wanted it. I was a spoiled brat. Worse than that, I was a
spoiled classical music-playing brat.'

When he was seven, he was awarded a scholarship by the Yehudi
Menuhin School of Music, Surrey, where he remained until he was
16. He toured with Stephane Grappelli when still in his teens ('I
tell you, monster, I was up there like a shot. Anything for a jam!'),
moved to New York at 17 to study at the Juilliard School of Music

(earning extra money by busking outside Tiffany's on Fifth Avenue: 'They used to come out after buying their diamonds and they'd dump their loose change in the violin case. 'Cos they were rich bastards, their loose change was 50 dollar bills so it was a really good deal, man'). He left without a diploma after two years to take up the many offers of concert work he'd been receiving; and in 1984 his first proper LP, a recording of the Elgar Violin Concerto, became Gramophone magazine's prestigious Record Of The Year.

Look at photographs of Kennedy six years ago and you see a straight-laced young chap with awfully sensible hair and polite shoes (none of the brothel creepers or cowboy boots he favours today). He may be wearing a tie, he may be sporting an old-hat blazer. He's, ahem, *straight*, man. It was not until Kennedy changed this image, reinvented himself as the saucy boy in a sober world, the lad in the outré togs whilst all around him sport tails, that he began to become *famous*. It is the image as much as, if not more than, fiddling prowess that has helped him to sell half a million copies of his Vivaldi's The Four Seasons LP (and, they say, brought classical music in general to a wider and younger audience). But Kennedy – or 'old Nige', as he would have you call him – claims that there was no premeditation behind the transformation, no master plan to achieve (inter)national recognition. It all happened, so the story goes, by accident.

'I'd never liked wearing tails because I didn't feel like myself in them and I felt, like, trapped, but I was trying to wear them and do a decent job. But then I turned up in London after doing a gig in New York and it was a Sunday gig what I had in London and I opened my case and there was no tails in there and there was no shops open and so I had to go to Camden Market and buy a whole lot of weird stuff and I thought, Shit, am I going to get away with this? And I went on and done my stuff at the gig and a load of people came back afterwards and they were saying, Nige, it's wonderful what you're doing for the image of classical music. Like you normally get a great Brahms Concerto, Nige, but they were saying all this stuff about how great the image was.'

And so the proverbial light-bulb lit up brightly above the young man's head. Aha!

'I thought if people *like* it then I can wear clothes which are *me*. I can be myself instead of looking like everybody else. I don't really know why all these musicians in classical music try and look like each other because they're all individual people. My criticism of classical music would be that all the classical musicians I know, they are vastly differing personalities so why do they do this dishonest thing of trying to look like all the other classical musicians? It makes a ridicule of the profession I'm in. It's like pretending you're not a person and I'm not ashamed of being a person.'

But what kind of person is Nigel Kennedy? Hasn't he rearranged himself, made drastic alterations to the persona, to boost the career? Isn't that accent, in fact, adopted? Didn't he once speak more like a toff?

'Yeah,' he confesses, sipping on beer and pushing the groovy shades on to the bridge of his nose, 'but I did that when I was about 12 years old. I sort of changed my persona, as you put it, because I was uncomfortable with who I was. It wasn't a conscious thing. I was 12 years old so if people say that I did it as some career move, I just think it's very complimentary, 'cos if I was sorting out some sort of media exercise at the age of 12, then obviously I'm a bigger genius at manipulating the media than Malcolm McLaren. So if people say that, it's a great tribute to my intellect.

'I don't reckon I've manipulated the media at all. I have changed but people do change. You can't expect everyone to carry on needing their nappies changed or carry on looking like a foetus. So I would never deny that I've changed. I'm very conscious of how I project myself to the public, but that's hardly new. It's not new in show business . . .'

But it is relatively new in classical music.

'Yeah, I think it's new in classical music and that's why I think I'm doing good stuff for classical music. People look at me and people are on my side. People don't come up to me in the street and say, Oh fuck off, Nige. I'm glad that more people are listening to classical music 'cos of me.'

And where, pray did the argot come from 'Nige'; all the mans and monsters and cats and cools?

'Shit, I don't know. I must have heard people say it.'

You're not a 'pot head' are you, 'Nige'?

'No, man, I'm a very, very clean Perrier boy just like every other lovely musician, hahaha. Cool, man . . .'

A Nigel Kennedy Concert – ahem, 'gig' – is not as other classical recitals. Our fun-loving hero has been known to play amusing pranks on fellow musicians, such as sticking Playboy centrefolds into the sheet music of others or pinning small cuddly toys to the tails of a conductor.

'That's all lies, hahaha,' he says, beaming like some child at mischief. 'No, I'll do something like that if the show needs livening up, or something. Things like that loosen people up and stop them working in a premeditated, programmed way. I'll do *anything* to freshen things up so that we can make a new vibe instead of repeating what's gone before. It's cool.'

'Live,' he might have a microphone before him, to which he will skip forward betwixt passages and issue crowd-pleasing utterances like: ''Ello, 'ello, the maestro has just got you in a cool Mozart mood!'; or (before the Autumn movement of Four Seasons): 'This next one's about shooting hares and foxes and stuff but I hope you don't mind'; or, when tackling some preposterously fast and flashy passage, in a display of technique over content: 'Heavy duty, too much trying to break the speed record!' ('I hate all the technical things about music,' he tells me. 'I only do that fast, flash stuff as a piss take . . .'); or (accompanied by the English Chamber Orchestra): 'While we've been doing these gigs I've been a bad influence on these cats. None of that muesli stuff . . . have a brandy before you go on!' One wonders how long it will be before 'Nige' – who has played with Paul McCartney (who he calls 'Macca') and Kate Bush (who he calls 'Bush Baby' . . . in 'Nige's' world, as in soccer and, indeed, heavy metal, everybody must have their nickname) – will be saying 'Awright, Carnegie Hall! Are you ready to rawk?!?' or some such.

'It just loosens things up, stuff like that, you know?'

You don't think you're in some danger of not paying due respect to, of trivilaising, this, 'important' music – Brahms, Beethoven, Vivaldi, Elgar, what have you?

'Well, I reckon that people that only notice, like, my image and what I say are probably listening on a very trivial level themselves. It's not like I'm considered the worst fiddle player ever born, so people can listen on a *deep* level if they want to. I spend like four hours a day trying to get closer to what the dead composer was into, so I reckon that's paying it respect. And I'm giving the music respect by the fact that I'm communicating it to far more people than any other fiddle player in the world.'

You don't think you are doing a disservice to those who *like* to have their rock stars badly behaved, their classical musicians smart and mannerly, and never the twain shall meet? (Let us not forget Deep Purple's Concerto For Group And Orchestra: what a fiasco of indignity . . .) For the first time in our meeting, Kennedy drops the affable chap of cheekiness stance and becomes, almost, hot under the collar (though he is not, of course, wearing anything you could properly call a collar).

'Look, man, if I'm breaking down barriers between rock stuff and classical, I think that's very healthy. Barriers are bigotry. It's like, would you apply that kind of bigotry to racial discrimination? Do you think it's nice to have black guys living in one place and white guys in another? I just view it all as music and I think that any other way is kind of a bigoted way of looking at it. And also that kind of bigotry could be dangerous to me making a living, so I don't like it. Just as a white guy might not like it if somebody says only black guys play jazz well. Or a black guy might not like it if somebody says white guys are the only ones that do maths well. To have things compartmentalised, to have all classical musicians in tails and that, only asks for misunderstanding and bad feeling. I'm not on some fucking crusade to break down the barriers between rock and classical stuff, but I think the barriers are hypocritical and evil and it's a pisser and a downer. I just want to be myself.'

So. Does 'Nige' really encourage the English Chamber Orchestra, and other illustrious musical combinations, to hit the sauce before accompanying him in a 'gig' situation?

'Do I *encourage* them? Hahaha! I'm sure there's quite enough voluntary drinkers, man. Classical musicians aren't half as straight as the portaphone, calculator-carrying rock musicians who are going round the world at the moment, adding up all their royalties and making sure that they're seen to be at aerobics and I've-got-my-own-healthy-body-and-I'm-looking-after-myself-very-nicely-thank-you-very-much-I'm-a-vegetarian-and-I-do-nice-things-for-the-world-where's-the-next-benefit?-oh-how-we-all-suffer. What a lot of shit, man. Classical musicians are not like that at all. Classical musicians are pretty heathen compared with that kind of mentality. Classical musicians are monster animals, believe me, man.'

Nigel Kennedy, monster, animal, far too unbecalmed to be anything so ordinary as a rock star. Nonetheless, in rock star cliché fashion, he's recently done to Mark E. Smith of The Fall what Eric Clapton did to George Harrison and lots of other rock persons have done to lots of other rock persons since rock time immemorial – i.e.

nick the wife. Inside 'Nige's' violin case are two black-and-white photographs of Brix Smith, rock 'chick' extraordinaire, not many clothes and a group of her own (The Adult Net). Brix, to 'Nige', is (here comes the 'diminutive') Brixy. 'Brixy' held hands with 'Nige' when he, the celebrity, was on This Is Your Life. 'Nige' returns the favour by playing fiddle on his paramour's The Adult Net's forthcoming LP. 'Brixy' is, needless to say, a monster animalette'.

'She's a monster animalette, Brixy,' says the bloke, 'and she's making an album and I think I've done some of the best fiddle playing of my life on that. She said it sounds like Jimi Hendrix if he was still alive or something. Brixy's a great cat to be around. She likes music by dead people, too . . .'

Does Nigel Kennedy ever worry that he's more famous for being Nigel Kennedy, Aston Villa scarf-waving, rock 'chick'-toting, chat-show gooning, matey-bloking, general all-round celebrity geezer, than for being what he really is and ought to be . . . accomplished, nay brilliant, violin player. He ponders – this is unlike him – the question. 'Well, I'm communicating music with millions of people, aren't I?' Yes. 'But, yeah, I know what you mean, man. This Is Your Life, and shit like that, it's a laugh, isn't it? But . . .' But? 'But, you know, like, how it is to see somebody on the telly all the time and you start to hate them?' Yes. 'Well, it's dangerously close to that with me. If I was not me and I saw me on the telly, I would be thinking, Oh no, not that twat again, The vibes aren't that good, celebrity-wise, man. At the moment everyone thinks I'm lovely, but . . .'

But, indeed.

'But, like Pavarotti, he might be very popular as a personality now but in 20 years or so, he'll be remembered as the greatest tenor of his generation, and James Galway you can criticise for being a celebrity and some of the music he's done (*Annie's Song?*), but there's still the records there to prove that he is the greatest flute player of his generation. So I'm not really worried about being a celebrity 'cos I think my reputation will survive.'

And with that, the greatest violin player of his generation gets the distastefully nicknamed instrument out. He sits back in a chair outside the pub in the sweaty London sunshine and treats us to a private concert, er, 'gig'. He grins and twinkles and he does Rock-A-Bye-Baby and he does William Tell and I make a request for some bluegrass which he improvises impressively. The boy done good, as they say, and then there is Match Of The Day and a girl who is passing says, 'Busking again, Nige?' and tosses a somewhat superfluous 50 pence coin in to his open case.

'Monster!' cries Kennedy and carries on scraping . . .

Bernard Manning

Fat, foul-mouthed and rude? The roly-poly jokester accepts such titles proudly, for they are the credentials that have made him comedyland's 'Mr Nasty'. A word of warning: the following article contains material that many people will find offensive.

S OME WAY UP Rochdale Road, Manchester – a thoroughfare littered by the sides with unkempt 'public' spaces, gone-out-of-business 'Discount Centres' that once did a roaring trade in tacky and flammable three-piece suites, dilapidated council estates in need of much exterior refurbishment (though dotted proudly with shiny new satellite dishes) – one comes to a one-time warehouse cheerily decorated on the outer wall with the words 'Bernard Manning's World Famous Embassy Club'.

You recognise that it is, indeed, Bernard Manning's club by the huge photographic portrait of the man, the stout teller of sordid tales of sex and haemorrhoids and black men and more sex, that grins down from above. And you recognise that it is, indeed, 'world famous' (or renowned in local parts, anyway) by the number of coaches – some from as far afield as Sheffield! – that have drawn up outside its portals. Yes, this must be the place.

A tattooed minion at the door leads us, past many a framed photograph on the walls – old black-and-white snaps of Bernard beaming in pose with the dinner jacketed famous . . . snooker players, footballers of old (Bobby Charlton, Derek Dougan, the curly-locked Kevin Keegan), cabaret acts that time forgot, etc., plus a particularly *large* photo of Bernard, in 1970s suit and sideburns bowing as he shakes the gracious hand of the Queen of England – to the lair of the fat master. He sits, our portly purveyor of comical filth, in his dressing room (an airless, confined space where yet more pictures of him in conference with minor celebrities attest to

his status), slumped in a comfy foam-filled chair (evidently pur-
chased once from a nearby 'Discount Centre') and sweating profusely on the hottest day Manchester has encountered since records
were conceived.

He neither smiles nor turns his gaze away from the TV set, that's
showing an episode of the Australian soap Home And Away, as
he 'greets' us. He just grunts, in thick Mancunian, 'Want anything
to eat, lads, pie or owt?' And then, in a tone not dissimilar, he
cracks the first 'gag' of the meeting – an obscene conundrum
concerning a cricket ball and a well-known female athlete. Oh, my
aching sides. Call me a liberal, call me a prude, but I do not find
the wisecrack remotely rib-tickling. Perhaps it's the way he tells
'em – joylessly, as if reading from a telephone directory.

Here comes another: 'A bloke dashes in the house, he says, Come
on, love, pack yer bags, I've won the pools. She says. What should
I pack? Where are we goin'? He says, Just pack 'em. And fuck
off.' It's only when he turns away from the TV screen to wink at
you that you realise the punchline has arrived . . . I make a remark
along the lines of 'I cannot help noticing, Mr Manning, that you
are a very saucy fellow'. This is not, it turns out, quite the right
thing to say. With much effort, prompting a hacking cough to go
off like some chemical mortar, the mass rises up in the seat and
glares.

'*Saucy*? I'm not a bit fuckin' saucy! I'm fuckin' blue, son!' he
goes. 'Swear words come into my gags because I believe in telling
a joke as it is. If you drop a hammer on your foot at work, you
don't say, Oh dear, you say, Fuckin' hell! that's what you say. If
you miss a ball at snooker, you say, What a fuck up, what a
bastard! Don't you? I fuckin' hate clean jokes. They're childish,
aren't they? They're not funny. Why does a chicken cross the road?
Who gives a *fuck* about a chicken crossing the road? Bollocks. I
mean, I have got some clean gags – but they're only funny 'cos it's
me that's tellin' 'em. I'm not a clean comic.'

Bernard Manning, 60, has been in the entertainment business for
more than 40 years. He left school at 14 – 'I was a fuckin' thickhead
at school, but I can tell a story, I can time a gag, and that's what
people want. I'm a self-made man, me' – to work in his father's
greengrocer's business. And, because he was able to sing a bit, he
joined Oscar Rabin's Dance Band, performing at places like the
Lyceum, London, the Oldham Empire, the Glasgow Empire. He

started working a bit of 'comedy' into his act, then some 'more comedy and now I can do a couple of hours without repeating a gag and it's just gone from strength to strength and I've been to Las Vegas and I've done the London Palladium, Royal Command Performances, you name it, I've done it, son.'

Who were the fat chap's main 'influences'? Max Miller? Charlie Chester? Tommy Trinder?

'Fuck that. I wasn't influenced by nobody, son. Those old comedians, they wouldn't earn two shillings today. They used to do about 15 minutes, all the same gags. Those old comedians, Frankie Howerd, Arthur Askey, those sort of comedians, they couldn't live with me today. They couldn't compete. They were bollocks. They would never last.'

(Er, Arthur Askey's dead but Frankie Howerd's doing quite nicely, thank you. Er, let it pass . . .)

'Bollocks, they were. Still are, most of them.' Get the vast one discussing comedy rivals and modesty scuttles out the door. 'Jimmy Tarbuck doesn't tell gags, he just refreshes your memory. And this alternative comedy – it's like watching paint dry. Alexei Sayles (*sic*), the man will never make a carrot. He'll die skint. In three years you'll say, Who was Alexei Scayle (*sic*)? Forty-three years I've been in this job and they still know who *I* am. Alexei Scayles (*sic*), he hasn't got a fucking clue. He's about as funny as rabies in a guide dog's home. Rowan Atkinson and Ben Elton. Bollocks. About as funny as woodworm in a cripple's crutch. Foolish stuff, childish stuff, same as all these college educated people, these people that go to university, they don't know what a gag is.

'I go on stage an hour and a half and people are rolling about but this Rowan Atkinson, he's got to get dressed up like King Arthur with a sword in his hand pissing about and hoping to get one laugh. Bollocks. You want a quick-fire gag man, never stuck for a word, like me if you want to laugh. You'll see me go on there tonight, son, and tear the bollocks off the place, the fucking place will be falling about with laughter and you'll say, How does he fuckin' do it? Happens everywhere. Las Vegas, Jewish gags, gags about coons, the fucking place is falling apart . . .'

Bernard Manning, with the financial assistance of his father, bought up these disused premises on Rochdale Road and opened his 'World Famous' Embassy Club 30 years ago. He wanted his own club because 'this business is very precarious, like. One day you're drinking the wine, next day you're treading the grapes.' The Embassy has made the large one a millionaire. In the olden days all sorts of stars did support for Manning's crude patter. 'The Beatles, Freddie And The Dreamers, Jimmy Tarbuck, Mike Yarwood, anybody who was anybody, Matt Monro, Vince Hill, they've all passed through these doors at ridiculous prices. Fourteen quid for The Beatles. Seven quid for Freddie And The Dreamers, 30 quid for Matt Monro. The Beatles were fantastic. Good price, wasn't it? Fourteen quid. All nice boys. We used to bill our shows as Where You See The Stars Of Tomorrow Today. I was quite happy with that, I was. We all got on well 'cos I'll do anything for a laugh. People come here and they fall about . . .'

Thirty years ago, when he was starting, the stout raconteur never used the word 'fuck' on stage. That was just a bit too 'blue' for the times. But, he is proud to tell you, he said 'bollocks' and he said 'bastard' and he said 'tits' and he said 'arseholes'. And all that carry on. And nowadays there are no limits. He is happy to be comedy's most 'disgusting' performer. Mr 'Blue'. He tells jokes about sordid sex with ugly women, most amusing, jokes about 'queers' and 'coons', titter ye not. He's been banned by many a left-wing council concerned about the racist content of his act. 'Burly Bernard, the King-Six Comic' (copyright News Of The World) quite relishes this reputation as comedyland's 'Mr Nasty'.

'It makes me laugh me bollocks off, all that. As long as I'm funny and people laugh, why should I care? You can't get a seat in here any night. I'm like the Muhammad Ali of show business, plenty of mouth and plenty of bottle to back it up. But some people are so narrow-minded. I'm there to make people laugh and black people laugh and Pakis laugh so you've got no bloody problem, have you?'

So you are not then, contrary to common perception, a teeny weeny bit of a racist, Mr Manning?

'No, I'm not a racist, am I? That is ridiculous. I don't even know what a racist is. I tell jokes about Irish, coons, Pakis, Australians, Americans, fat people, thin people, people with thick glasses, er . . .' He leans forward to cough a spectacularly horrid cough. '. . . er, thin people, er, Russians, Germans, you name it. I have black people in this club and they're falling about with laughter. I have an Indian doctor lives next door to me and we get on like a house on fire. We'll have blacks in here tonight. You'll see them. You'll see them laughing . . . especially when we lynch them . . .' This hilarious aside/afterthought is accompanied by a conspiratorial wink . . .

Funnily enough, later, when Manning is on stage before a packed house, I inspect the audience and, amongst the post-adolescent lads in their casual best, shirts open to just below the chest, and their be-permed 'birds', tottering in tight stone-washed jeans upon high white heels, there is not a single coloured face to be seen. Bernard, waddling and sweating on the stage, confirms this. 'Not a bad act on the bill,' he barks into his microphone, 'not a coon in the fucking place either.' This draws a large cheer from his public. Suitably encouraged, he proceeds to tell the one about the professor in Alabama who crossed a 'nigger' with an octopus and got 'an ugly bastard, but what a fuckin' cotton picker!' and one about 'Pakis' in Bradford – 'You can't fuckin' move for 'em' – and one about a 'Chink' in a fish and chip shop – 'I've never seen a fuckin' Chinese in here. (*Cheers*). Those Chinks give me the elbow . . . Slant-eyed, yellow-faced bastards . . .'

So, quite clearly, Bernard Manning doesn't have a racist bone in his body. Why, he's even told witty stories about Johnny Foreigner in front of the Queen of England (Bernard's a staunch patriot, of course, and, like all self-respecting bleary-eyed celebs, does loads for charity, especially 'the kiddies').

'Yeah, son, I told a joke on the Royal Command Performance. I said, there was a Paki came over from India (*some geographical confusion here?*) and he wanted to be a conductor so they took him up and nailed him to a factory chimney.' Bernard winks. 'The Queen laughed at that. And there was other jokes I told. One Paki came over to this country and wanted to be converted so they kicked him over the posts at Wembley. She laughed. (*Really? Then so much for Her Majesty's Commonwealth concern . . .*) It's a joke. It's not serious. People must not take jokes seriously. It might be serious if I stood up with a swastika on me arm with loads of thugs around me and started spouting about coons and Jews and they shouldn't be here. But it's a joke. I laugh, they laugh, we all laugh and have a smoke and a drink.'

Grand. Would you consider that you are a trifle on the 'sexist' side, Mr Manning?

'I don't know what sexist is. I *tell* jokes about women, of course. There's millions of jokes about women, isn't there? She's got a face like a bulldog chewing a wasp. She's got a face like a blistered pisspot. I bet you've flattened a bit of grass in your time, love. I bet you've seen more ceilings than Michelangelo. I was giving a bird a fuck the other night and she was 36 stone – I was burning my arse on the electric light-bulb . . . It's wonderful to see people laugh.'

Ah, the healing nature of humour.

And, Mr Manning, what of your attitude to homosexuals? Five years ago, he caused a bit of a tabloid fuss when he was reported as saying 'Gays should not be allowed on television, on stage, in clubs or pubs. They should keep to themselves. They have a corrupting influence on the young . . . etc.,' roly-poly Manning 'stormed'. Homophobic, or what?

'I don't know what that is,' he says. 'I'm not college-educated, I'm a fuckin' thickhead, me. But, with queers, well, I've mellowed in that because when it first started, all the queer nonsense, we didn't really understand it. It's an illness, anyway, really. It's . . . it's I don't know what it is. But it's frightening. I mean, people like my mother, she doesn't understand it; she's 90 years of age but she's very intelligent, you know, and she says, what's this? A man importuning in a toilet? What is it, importuning? I don't know what fuckin' importuning means myself so how do I tell her what importuning is?' (Manning proceeds, here, to recite a catalogue of celebrities whose names he can never quite recall – 'What was that fucker's name with the horse?' – who have been 'caught' in homosexual liaisons, doing things that Manning doesn't think are very 'nice' because they set a bad example to the 'kiddies'.)

'If you're buggering some fellow, I think that's a very, very sick thing. But it's not their fault, is it? It's a freak of nature, isn't it? I'm mature now. Each to his own . . .'

Mature. But still the 'queers' come in for a pasting whenever the fat man takes the stage.

The nearest that the corpulent comic of the unsavoury sallies has ever got to being anywhere near 'hip', is his recent lampoon crooning of some Smiths songs on Jonathan Ross's show. But he only did it, it seems, because he was asked and he doesn't really understand why it was supposed to be funny, anyway. And sadly, he appears never to have heard of Morrissey. 'Morrissey? Well, everyone's heard of Bernard Manning, but Morrissey? Flash in the pan, son. I liked Elvis, me. He seemed a nice boy . . .' then comes that wink. 'Elvis is making a comeback. Only the feet to go.'

Is there anything Manning *wouldn't* tell a 'gag' about? Are there any lines drawn? Indeed. Bernard takes on a sincere aspect and, puffing, leans forward in the dressing room armchair.

'I *never* tell sick gags,' he says, coming over like some scoutmaster of high church moral principles. 'They're not nice at all. I tell blue stories about arses and tits and pricks but I don't tell jokes about handicapped people.' Excuse me, wasn't there some jocular utterance earlier about woodworm and a cripple's *crutch*? 'No, son, I don't make jokes about cripples, I make jokes about a cripple's crutch. It's nothing to do with the cripple. Like, a fellow's carrying Houdini's coffin and he says, I bet the bastard's not in it. See?' Um, not exactly, nasty fat person, no. 'Well, I don't tell jokes about cripples or handicapped people or people with one eye or people with bad legs or something like that because I might offend somebody (*Heaven forbid*!), and because I'm fat and horrible myself, really. I'm no oil painting, am I?'

To be brutally frank, no, you are not.

'Well, you see, I used to be *beautiful*,' he says, small eyes a-quiver with remembrance (for this is meant as no jape . . . he's entirely serious). 'If you saw photographs of me when I was a young man, you wouldn't believe how I looked. I looked like the young Errol Flynn. Slim, plenty of hair, beautiful blue eyes, lovely soft cheeks, velvet skin . . .'

'. . . 'Ello, love!' The perspiring hulk of Bernard Manning leans forward precariously at the front of his Embassy Club stage and leers down upon a young woman at a nearby table. 'You know, every time you laugh, your tits go up and down like that!' The girl giggles and covers her face in embarrassment; her male companions hoot in appreciation and applaud the ribald 'quip'. Soon, the girl is party to further humiliation as Manning drags her up for a bit of a singsong. She blushes and squeaks. 'Cor, I hope you fuck better than you sing, love,' goes our jolly jester. 'I like big women like you. I could pull you on like a gumboot. Where you from, love?' Rochdale. 'You call a spade a fuckin' nigger in Yorkshire, don't you?' Oh ho ho.

How much of this mirth and merriment can the audience possibly take? Lots. Bernard is right. The place *is* falling about. All these folk, swilling lager and sipping Ponies, are rolling with some species of laughter. They are, of course, all completely mad. And so I slink off into the night, the punchline, an ugly afterthought from the great man – 'Cor, what a fuckin' ugly woman, bet she's got bollocks instead of a ****' – and raucous, mirthless cackles ringing in my ears.

'How does he fuckin' do it?'

Sir Jimmy Savile

There's something unsettling about the tireless benevolence, something irksome about the infantile banter and spangly self-satisfaction, something eerie about this strange old uncle patting the heads of the young and unfortunate.

'**N**OW THEN NOW THEN as it 'appens 10 out of 10 yes indeed guys 'n' gals yes indeed young sir Swinging Blue Jeans The from the good good year indeed of nineteen hundred and sixty three not bad for to be certain as it 'appens says Jim to all his good friends very good now then indeed ow-ooo ow-ooo . . .' Etcetera.

Somehow one expects Jimmy Savile – the newly-anointed Sir James – to speak in this infantile and irritating manner, the annoying banter he never refrains from using on radio or TV, all the time. And sure enough, as he greets me at the front door of his London flat (his 'gaff', his 'bed'), a stone's throw from BBC Radio and from Regent's Park, he seizes me roughly by the hand, tugs me inside, almost causing me a mischief as my forehead nearly brushes against his gargantuan cigar, and then whoops unconcerned into the annoying lingo.

'Hullo my friends from Q Magazine here that great much-purchased magazine indeed and now welcome to the house of Jim good sirs 10 out of 10,' he goes, in the much-imitated but never quite captured Yorkshire accent. 'Now then a seat most comfortable for sitting on young journalist mister sir.'

The interview has yet to commence and one feels exhausted already . . .

Puffing on a smelly stogie, exuding essence of self-assurance, Sir Jim (we used to call him 'Sir' Jim, but, sadly, our 'amusing' inverted commas are redundant now) sits, swivelling in his swivel chair, in

'Green' T-shirt and blue track suit trousers. Track suits are all he ever wears: the days of the '60s when he'd sport outlandish jackets and dye his hair funny shades are gone. No more Mister Wacky, our Jim is now Mister Charity, the unfortunates' friend, one or more money-raising fun runs, half or full marathons per week, plys voluntary work at Stoke Mandeville Hospital, Leeds Infirmary, Broadmoor and elsewhere.

On his left wrist, Saville sports a most ostentatious and jewel-encrusted watch. The flat is not so gaudy. In fact, apart from a photograph featuring sheep (presumably Yorkshire sheep) on the wall, and a monstrously unsightly 'trophy' perched atop the television set in the corner (male Jewellery Wearer Of The Year Award, apparently), you wouldn't believe anyone at all actually *lived* here. If Loyd Grossman were to visit with the Through The Keyhole camera team, Frostie's panel (Chris Tarrant, Eve Pollard, Willie Rushton, assorted ghastlies) would be stumped. The fact is that Sir James Savile has nowhere he can call home. 'England. England – she is my home, lovely lady England,' he says. He just has 'beds'. In Peterborough and Leeds and Scarborough and here, in Broadmoor, Stoke Mandeville, and a couple of caravans. Never married, never settled down, rich beyond the dreams of avarice (the £10,000 and upwards he charged for each of the frequent personal appearances of his career have been invested wisely). A bachelor gay, as they used to say. A psychiatrist might conclude that there's something awry with the old fruit's nopper, that he could be considered a trifle mad . . .

The trouble (or one of them) with interviewing Jimmy Savile is not the imbecile speech patterns, *nowthennowthenowsaboutthat-thenowooetctenoutoftenswingingbluejeansthe* . . . , by which he seems so possessed – these appear, strangely, to almost disappear once you have engaged him in 'proper' conversation – but the huge cigar. I pose the psychiatrist-styled question and I get, in response, this:

'*Mmmphph* shrinks *puff puff ppp pppp humph*, you see *mmmph* what I'm *phhh* saying?' No, Sir James. He puts the cigar aside. 'We should *burn* shrinks! *Burn* the bastards. If a psychiatrist would think that I was strange, it would take me absolutely no effort at all to completely unsettle him and maybe show that he himself needed some treatment. The disarming thing about me is what you see is what there is. That knackers people. Because people like your good self are always looking for the behind the scenes. You're looking for a defence or a this or a that or a blah blah blah yi-yi-yi or a skeleton in the closet . . .'

Jimmy Savile was born in Leeds in 1926, the son of a 'skint' bookmaker's clerk. What was childhood like? I ask. Something of a mistake, here. The trouble (or one of them) with interviewing Jimmy Savile is that should you set him a poser he is wont to go on at length, at tangents, to include spurts of individual and barely comprehensible 'philosophy' and anecdotes that seem to have no bearing on the subject in hand. Jimmy Savile, *mmmphph puff*, waffles and blathers. Often he makes no sense at all. 'I'm a good raconteur. I can tell a story without verbal padding,' he says, proudly. 'I can deliver the goods, yes, good sir.' This is deceit . . .

Childhood?: 'Give yourself a mental exercise. First of all you are born into a war. In 1939, I would be 13 or so then, there's the war with the air raids and the whistling bombs and getting blown up by Adolf Hitler, cowering under a familiar table that you eat your food off, with this peculiar whistling bomb coming down like a flute, thinking, Fuck me, I don't know what death is but I'm not too far away, and all that sort of stuff and the excitement of coming out and smelling all the burning and picking up all the souvenirs and all the exciting things and then you go down the pits, into the blackness, and . . .'

He goes on at interminable length about the deprivations and bleakness of his youth, concealing the 'flow' of the account with *mmmph puffs* on the stogie, imitating the sound of falling bombs with a faulty whistle, talking about the Duchess (that's what he called his mum) and pals in random fashion. Suffice it to say, when he was down the mines as a Bevin Boy, he got injured in a pit explosion that left him with a wonky back. He had to walk on sticks and one day saw a reflection in a shop-window of a young person on crutches and was horrified to realise it was himself.

'Fucking 'ell! But – this is very, very applicable to the readers of your magazine – it does people good to see themselves as they really are.'

Does he mean that seeing himself as he 'really was' invested him with a social conscience, turned him into a tireless charity worker? It is hard to say just *what* is the significance of the shop-window anecdote, for my phrase 'tireless charity worker' has diverted the man more than somewhat.

'No, you see your phrase tireless charity worker, I don't think it's tireless charity work. It was like an acorn that grew and grew and grew and grew into this lovely big bloom. I just think it stemmed down from two main factors. One was my mother and father were skint but they had this great social thing where they would take on isms and schisms and do this and whist drives, but number two was in the early '60s I was earning about a grand a week because I used to turn up at Radio Luxembourg and record five programmes in one day so I had six days off, so I reversed the Bible. Thou shalt labour for six days and rest on the seventh. I laboured on one and ligged about for six. And the alternative to charity is going loopy doing nothing, you see. Or, conversely, chasing happiness. It's always a bad thing to chase, is happiness. Without being yucky, it is much nicer to cheer up a little kid who won't walk again than to say I will go and walk around Harrods. Happiness is not a thing I want to chase. It's of no interest, you see.'

Once he had recovered from his pit injury. Savile threw himself into a variety of unorthodox careers. He claims to have single-handedly invented the discotheque – the concept of dancing to records – spinning 78s in primitive amplified equipment in a room above a café in Otley, Yorkshire for £2.10s. 'That was the point I knew I was a millionaire. There. Was. No. Question. At all. All I needed, then, was £999,997 and ten bob. And I knew I'd get it. I had the Rollers lined up in my mind.'

He managed dancehalls in Leeds – and claims to have single-handedly invented the concept of twin-turntables. He became a professional cyclist and a professional wrestler ('I fought for eight years, top of the bill every bout, not because I was a good wrestler, but because I was a larger-than-life personality.' Were the fights fixed, Sir James? 'Ooh, I wish they were! My fights were fucking blood baths, fucking hell, not many, ooh ooh ooh, you don't think any self-respecting grappler is going to go and lay down to a bleeding fucking blond-haired fucking wise-cracking boy, do you, ooh ooh!?). And then, as a disc jockey with Radio Luxembourg, as a TV pop personality (it was Jim who hosted the first Top Of The Pops on New Year's Day, 1964), the man became a celebrity, peculiar linguistic approach, preposterous baubles, exotic hair-styles, wacky, zany Jim, guys'n'gals.

'I invented guys'n'gals, all the flash patter, all out of my head. I was the only one, you see. I was larger-than-life. I was king of the disc jockeys. Nobody could compete with all that.'

Jim sort of misses the 1960s . . .

'Oh, yi yi yi yi! I'd been through the valley of shadows, I'd been through getting blown up by Adolf Hitler, and then you get to the '60s and there's girls showing their bottoms off with miniskirts and their bristols hanging out and they're very permissive and they're chasing me . . . Do me a favour! Yi yi yi! Mama mia! What *more* can you want? I had all the money and I could have all the saucy young ladies I wanted and, yi yi yi yi yi, I'm in a disco with 600 birds in Plymouth and one of them says, Listen, you don't have to go back to the hotel, and you say, Phew, yeah! and that is the stuff Heaven is made of.

'But having all that money and the ladies after you and you've got all the ingredients of going well round the bend and you've got all the ingredients of dying very quickly, which a lot of my people did because the '60s were far more dangerous than fucking wartime . . .'

'My people' says Jim – he is about to expose himself as confidant to the stars – 'My people' are people like Jimi Hendrix . . .

'Well, The Jim, you see, the Jim was a lovely feller, he was a super guy, he was the loveliest guy in the world, he was like my brother-in-law and he'd ask me for advice. Then there were The Stones. They were considered dirty and filthy and pissing on the petrol forecourts but they were anything other than that. Brian (Jones) was the loveliest lad. His fan mail used to upset him because he couldn't get around to reading it and answering it so he used to leave it with me. I finished up with three sacks of his mail and when he died, I just had it all shredded. And The Mick (Mick Jagger) he used to say, What do you think, Jim? Many of them came to me looking for like the meaning of life and all that business. And I had a considerable effect on a lot of them. So many people would beat a path to my door and I've given them the facts of life. Some of them have won. And some of them, like The Jim, have chosen to ignore what I said to their cost.'

Could we have some further examples of Savile-inspired 'winners'?

'Er, Tom Jones, for instance. I resolved all his problems when he was Tommy Scott And The Senators. That's a known fact. And there was this feller who wanted to sing the blues and I said, You've got as much chance of singing the blues as I've got of flying to the moon, pal, you're a little boy so you're going to sing little boy songs, pom-ti-pom-ti-pom, and I was laid out on my kip and he sat on the kip and I rubbed his tooth for luck . . . That was Peter Noone out of Herman's Hermits . . .'

Gracious!

People are loath to speak ill of Sir James. The man is a saint, millions raised for charity; he is the kiddies' friend, ever on the telly placing a Jim'll Fix It gong around the neck of some abashed youngster who's just been a hovercraft skipper for a day. It is churlish, cynical beyond belief, to suggest there might be anything untoward about the benevolent one. But *isn't* there, perhaps, some oddness afoot? You hear tales, entirely uncorroborated, of course, whispered in sniggers at dinner parties . . . I'm looking for a defence or a this or a that or a blah blah blah yi-yi-yi or a skeleton in the closet. But . . .

'As far as skeletons are concerned, I must be the most boring punter in the world because I haven't got any. I'm totally boring. It knackers everybody. There are no skeletons and I got knighted so that proves it, doesn't it? Because look at the amount of good work this fiercesome lad has done and all the money he's raised and you'd have expected some kind of recognition before now and what people, the tabloids, were constantly saying to me was, Jim, how come you've got a knighthood? What have you got to hide? Bollocks. So it was a relief to be recognised. And then they say, Well then, why aren't you married and, now, it's very, very simple because I escaped marriage and that lemming route. I'm the wise owl that sits in the tree watching those lemmings going over the cliff – over we go, carry on, whee, splat, splat. Fucking hell. But I look down from my wise owl perch and see some lady and go, Eh, there's a nice one, so I hoist it up on the branch, keep it for 24 hours, and then say, You really have to go now. It's comfortable on my perch and marvellous. Everybody thinks you're a bit strange, but yi yi yi yi yi! You can't be in a disco with 600 birds in Aberdeen and stopping overnight and faithful to one fuck in Leeds . . .'

Ahem, Sir *James*! Didn't he, the man who sits in the plump chair on the telly playing the strange old uncle to the 'kiddies', ever want to have children of his own? No, he did not.

'I'm not a lover of children. I don't *like* children. They have to earn my respect. My sisters and brothers all had kids but all I could hear was moaning and groaning. I never had any paternal feeling. *I don't like children.*'

This might come as something of a blow to the eight-year-old in Kettering who, even as I write, sits with crayon poised to ask Jim to fix it for her to play footie with Gazza or be Torvill and Dean for a day, or whatever.

'Jim'll Fix It is a different atmosphere. They get sandwiches and they get orangeade and they get *me*. It's a freak-out for them.'

I bet it is. But to return to the non-existent skeleton . . . Not true, the rumour that Savile is rather fascinated with dead bodies?

'I'm not fascinated with dead bodies,' he replies plainly. 'It is very simple. Last night at Stoke Mandeville, I was hanging around in the porter's lodge until about half past two this morning. I am a voluntary helper. Therefore, one of my jobs is to take away the lately deceased and I personally consider that task to be a considerable honour. You can look after somebody, be alone with somebody, who has lived a whole lifetime and he might have been a potter or something quite lovely and I'm just saying goodbye and looking after him. That is a privilege and an honour, you see. Some people are most dis-chuffed with cadavers that freak them out and put their hair on end. Some people get hold of the fact that Jim likes looking after cadavers and say, Aha, Jim's a necrophiliac! I'm not a necrophiliac.'

In the garage below the London flat is housed a Jimmy Savile Rolls-Royce. He is proud to be the owner of a Rolls, a self-made millionaire from the Yorkshire working classes. He is proud to be 'physically in brilliant nick', to possess 'a photo-memory', to have a friend in the Prime Minister. ('Maggie's a pal. But I don't give her much advice because I'm not in the Prime Minister business,' he says. 'I couldn't stand the drop in wages.') He's proud of many things, Sir James – but not *that* proud because, after all, he owes it all to God.

'God is my pal,' he says, gripping the fat cigar in the sturdy teeth and gazing up at the ceiling where, presumably, God lurks. 'He's my pal. My special pal. He does things for me, makes life easy, gives me a bit of luck, and if it ain't going too well I give him a bollocking, say, Oi! Are you akip, or what? Do me a fucking favour! See? I'm always having words with the governor upstairs. So I've got a Roller outside, cigars in the pocket, cup of tea, very nice, no need to worry about nothing, worrying's not Jim's game.'

One could be forgiven for thinking that Jim, Sir James, now then, is a trifle on the self-satisfied side . . .

As I take my leave, plumes of stogie smoke are wafting up toward the 'governor' above and Savile is conducting 'conversation' on his telephone. 'Lucky lucky lucky lucky lucky indeed yes sir now now now yi yi you and Jim your pal. J.S. 10 out of 10 OK be it not . . .' I close the door on the gibberish that has made the man so famous, the gibberish that has made Sir James, well, unique . . .

'Gazza' Gascoigne

It's all so inevitable, Brian. When the chubby striker with the watery eye returned from Italy, a modern folk hero was born. But the publicity machine rolls inexorably onward, rapidly reducing him to an over-fêted mini-industry and – God help us – 'rap' recording artiste.

'**E**R, I'M OPENING A BOUTIQUE, Brian.' This was the answer that Monty Python's befuddled, inarticulate footballing star would give to any query in an interview situation. 'Er, I'm opening a boutique, Brian,' he'd say in his confusion.

Paul Gascoigne – 'Gazza' to the universe, Britain's biggest footballing star since the 1960s when the nation was told what to eat for breakfast by the TV commercial rallying cry of 'E for B and Georgie Best' – has a fresh variation on the theme. 'Hur,' he begins in his almost impenetrable Geordie accent. 'Hur, I go fishing. I find fishing a very good thing to relax.'

You haven't asked him a question about his relaxation techniques. You haven't asked him anything connected in any way with fish. You haven't asked him where he goes. You've probably asked him something about the 'Gazzamania' publicity machine and whether it's all getting a trifle out of hand, and he says 'Hur, I find fishing a very good thing to relax.' Brian.

Thus has Gazza sold you another of his child-like dummies . . .

Paul 'Gazza' Gascoigne is not fishing today. (Does he ever, really? How does he find the time, what with all that training, all that footer to play, pizza parlours to open, Best-Dressed Man Of The Year ceremonies to attend, tabloid photo opportunities etc., etc. as the 'Gazzamania' machine rolls inexorably onward?) No, today the chubby midfield general in the exciting Holsten-sponsored Tottenham Hotspur shirt, England's cheeky prankster who single-handedly won the World Cup for Blighty (except for the Germans, damn 'em), the star with the greased-back hair and the amusingly poking tongue, is in the offices of a record company, RCA, doing promotional chores for . . . oh, God, how inevitable it all is . . . his forthcoming pop waxings. Paul Gascoigne, admired by 'kids' and their mums (drawn to the infant features and baby-face grin: at 23, Gascoigne resembles a pram-based tot, a major factor in his appeal and 'profile', surely) all over, has made a single, a rap version of Fog On The Tyne recorded with those veteran Newcastle strumstrels Lindisfarne. And he's made a long player, called – it's good, this – Let's Have A Party.

Gazza talks music. What are your primary musical influences, Gazza, if I may call you that?

'Yur. Gazza,' he goes. 'Hur . . .' And he starts to sing. 'I've got a brand-new combine harvester and I'll give you the key . . . Dee deedle dee deedle dee. D'you remember it? It was really good. It was by The Wurzels, weren't it? That's right. And I love Elvis. I like Elvis. Jailhouse Rock. But I've just really got into GI Blues. He's got, you know, with GI Blues like, he's got . . .' And he starts to sing again. 'You ever you ever get you ever get one you ever get one of them days you ever get one of those days boys . . . I can't remember the words. Dum-di-dum-di-dum. Two two. Er . . .'

Isn't he a little bit on the young side to be an Elvis devotee? Wasn't he an 'Antperson' or a 'Numanoid' or something like that in his 'formative' teenage years?

'Oh, yeah, I like songs,' he replies. 'I like a load of songs. Loads of groups. So that's good. I like Phil Collins. I like Billy Ocean. You know? Hur, it's good for us to make a record, isn't it? It's good, it's different, it's really different, like. But with songs it's, you know, I go training every day and I go back, go fishing. I find fishing a very good thing to relax.'

And to prove his 'point', he picks up an inflatable plastic 'electric' guitar, pretends to reel off a number of irrefutably 'tasty licks' – tongue protruding, Gazza trademark – and then says, 'See that. It's good that, weren't it?' He is pointing to the words 'Elvis' daubed upon the fake guitar in black felt tip pen. 'I wrote that on the guitar meself.'

Paul Gascoigne, dressed in the kind of casual togs that earned him that much-coveted Best-Dressed Man award, is sitting there with his plastic guitar, thumbing through a pile of Paul Gascoigne publicity photos. Beside him sits some kind of minder, a long-haired bloke, sporting a grubby 'Elvis' T-shirt, (who, when I ask him who, exactly, he might be, replies, somewhat mysteriously, 'I'm, er, I'm here to look after Gazza,' to which 'Gazza' adds: 'Aye, that's right. Hur. So you can't ask the horrible, bad questions.' I see . . .). Gazza's publicity photographs are all identical – they show the fellow with greased-back hair and playful grin in sensible jacket over what looks suspiciously like the kind of shirt worn by members of Brotherhood of Man circa 1970 – but he studies each one intently, possibly looking for imperfections in the prints, whilst all but ignoring the interviewer's presence.

How does it feel to be the nation's most fêted and famous young rascal, me boy? I enquire.

'Ur. Dum-di-dum,' he replies. 'What's yer name?'

Tom. Tom Hibbert.

'Oh,' he says and proceeds to scrawl 'To Tom. Good Luck. Gazza.' on one of the photos, which he hands over to me as he smiles a beamy grin. I thank him for the unsolicited gift. Where were we? How does it feel to be so very famous, Paul, Gazza?

'I'm, I'm, well,' he shuffles his photo pile, 'I'm . . . everyone says that I'm famous. Everyone says that. Nay. I just try and keep being meself, that's all I do. I don't think that I'm famous. I know for a fact that I am famous in a certain way, that people think I am, you know. I know that people think I'm famous because of what I've done in the World Coop but I don't look at it that way and I don't go round being a big, flash bastard saying, I'm Paul Gascoigne, me. I will never change. People say, Yeah, he'll change and I won't change. I won't change, no way. I will go and relax, I will go fishing because that's a very good thing to relax, and I'm not doing bad for that, am I? I'm doing very well, aren't I?'

Paul Gascoigne is doing very well. Prior to the World Cup finals in Italy, July 1990, Paul Gascoigne – born in a rented room in Pitt Street, Gateshead, Tyne and Wear, on May 27, 1967; kicked his first football at nine months old before he could even walk (or so the tabloid yarn ever goes) – was just a highly-talented footballer with a reputation for acting the goat on and off the field. He was called an arrogant, overweight under-achiever; England manager Bobby Robson described him as being 'daft as a brush' (a remark which inspired the 1989 Christmas non-book Gazza: Daft As A

Brush, a supposedly humorous tome, supposedly written by Gazza himself).

Tell us, Gazza, are you or are you not 'daft as a brush'?

'Yeah, of course I'm daft. I'm really, really daft. But I wouldn't say I'm daft as brush. Bobby Robson said that. And look at us. I went to the World Coop and done him a favour, see. I did. I'm the same guy now sitting here with yous, I'm the same guy as Bobby Robson called me daft as a brush. I don't think he'll call us daft as a brush again. If he does, I'll play better if he calls me that again. My lads, the lads on the team, they call me Fat Bastard sometimes, but I don't mind. I just play better, me, and be meself like I always am.' . . .

It was England 'skipper' Bryan Robson that all the newspapers were waxing hysterical about before the World Cup tournament began. Captain Courageous. Captain Marvel. That sort of thing. But Robson crocked himself, as per usual, and had to retreat from Sardinia to the doctor's. Cometh the hour, cometh the man. A new hero for brave little England (who managed, somehow, to fluke a win over Cameroon). His name was Paul Gascoigne. Twinkling feet and toddler's attitude.

Cue GAZZA'S TEARS. When the boy broke down in floods before the penalty shoot-out in the semi-final against West Germany (he was blubbing because he'd been booked by a crafty referee and thus wouldn't be allowed to play in the final if England got there), the nation wept with him, or so we were told. He had expressed emotion – fine foil for more typical footballing macho 'virtues' – and shown himself to be some kind of 'New Man'. With the droplets streaming down the baby-face, he had bared his heart and a modern folk hero had been born. (Diego Maradona blubbed too, after Argentina lost the final, but Maradona's just a jumped-up Johnny Foreigner dago and a cheating pigeon-chested swine to boot, so his tears didn't count.)

Gazza was the toast of Greavsie and all other 'pundits' on the telly, he was the main topic of dinner party conversation, he was on the front page of the Sun and similar journals for days and weeks on end. Except there wasn't much to say about him apart from the fact that he blubbed once, was a bit of a clown (when the England party returned home to national approval and the waiting, adoring crowds aching for a glimpse of the great tubby, Gazza was seen to be sporting fake ladies' bosoms: what a wag, what a sport), and was rather good at football. And so we were treated to half-baked 'sex stories'. Why I Gave The Boot To My Gazza . . . World Cup has ruined our love (i.e. he had split up with 'childhood sweetheart' Gail Pringle) . . . Gazza's New Bird (i.e. he had, supposedly, got a new girlfriend, Heidi Shepherd, who was pictured on the front of the Sun with rather a lot of her clothes curiously absent). And nonsensical boozy tales: Beer Battles Rage As Gazza Makes Merry (i.e. Gazza once went to a pub and whilst he was there somebody else got thrown out) . . .

But flimsy as it all was, 'Gazzamania' still managed to hold the public attention . . . and just look at the value of contracts and endorsements a man can get through blubbing in public before viewing millions. Crying can get you places, can't it, Paul?

'Ur, it was just something I couldn't stop meself from doing,' he says. 'The fans were brilliant. I was leaving them. And I don't regret it one bit what I did.'

I didn't suppose for a moment that he did regret it.

'No, I cried because the fact is because the fans had been with me throughout all the shit that was wrote saying they were wrecking bars and all that but you've got to realise that the press was going up to fans offering them 50 quid to take photos if they were having a fight or smashing up a bar and all that and that's the English press. They want us to get beaten up and it was the biggest disgrace ever at the World Coop ever, probably we were the only country that done it, we were the only bastard.'

But doesn't he need the press? Haven't they helped to fuel the so-called 'mania', to put him in a position where he'll be a huge millionaire before you can say Jack 'Jazza' Robinson?

'No, no,' he says, putting aside his beloved publicity snaps and looking me, for once, in the eye. His mouth is agape. 'No, the press they're cowardly bastards. There's stupid stories of girls and all that, this girl I never really took out or nothing and the poor lass must have went through hell all because of these horrible, some of them really are cowards, cowardly bastards is all they are. Who needs press? Because of the World Coop people didn't know me because they read the papers, people seen it on the telly, didn't they? And that's where I really done well is because now this Paul Gascoigne, whatever they call it, Gazzamania, is because of the World Coop and they watched the World Coop on the telly, didn't they? So I don't need the press because they are all shit bastards, all of them. The fans are brilliant. They know theirselves that it's all shit what's written about us.'

When Georgie Best made his instantly infamous appearance on the Wogan show, insupportably drunk, using unpleasant words like 'screw' and being unkind about Paul Gascoigne, there was an outbreak of indignation around the country. How dare the dissipated Irishman be rude about our national hero? And then there was an outbreak of concern. Not about Georgie, poor old fool, but about Gazza. Perhaps, vexed citizens ringing up countless radio phone-in programmes thought, perhaps Gazza might go the Best route: overfêted, famous too suddenly and too soon, squandering his talent. It seems, however, less than likely that Paul Gascoigne will end up as a George Best for the 21st century. After all, in George's day footballing stars weren't turned overnight into mini-industries: George didn't have an army of accountants and lawyers, as Gazza does, looking after the star business. What George did was open a club, Brian, and proceed to drink the profits. Gazza is protected from such shenanigans by men in suits. I ask the young man about the George Best syndrome and he gets really quite interested in the 'debate'.

'Yeah, I heard about that and Gazza is going to be like George Best. Yeah, no problem. I would never do that, hopefully, touch wood.' (He raps his knuckles on the wooden table: superstitious breed, footer players.) 'I don't have to be like George Best and go to a newspaper or on Wogan and slaughter a young lad like me who's trying to earn a living and who's enjoying hisself just for a bit of cash, because George Best has let hisself down so bad it's unbelievable. He's let hisself down bad, cor, eh mon, well, and I mean the thing is people say, Cor, that George Best, you see him on Wogan and he's a footballer, him, and then us footballers get embarrassed. We think Ooh, shit, people think us all footballers is like that drunken fat man and we isn't. Let's think . . .' Gazza pauses to consider the drift of his argument. 'Yur, and you see the fat man's got jealous of me. George Best, the drunken fat man is jealous. He absolutely slaughtered us for a bit of cash and that's a scum bastard.'

At this point we find Gazza's minder in the grimy Elvis T-shirt making untoward throat-clearing noises and looking pointedly at his charge. Sir Gazwell is not here to discuss tears, Georgie Best, his 'psyche' or anything like that. He is here to plug his fabulous pop disc and the minder is reminding him of the fact. And so, in mid-stream of consciousness concerning the relative merits of 'scum bastard' Bestie and 'cheekie chappie' Gascie . . . 'I always been cheeky with me tongue out and relaxed like fishing and that which maybe George Best needs, like' . . . he takes the minder's cue and goes, *non sequitur* fashion, 'That's right and the record's going quite well as well.'

Oh, alright, then, tell us about your dreary record.

'I didn't want it to be released if it sounded shit. If it were sounding like shit, me record, people might think, This sounds like shit and that wouldn't be much good, like. But people say, Yeah, it'll do well, so I released it and I done an 80-minute mix with 20 great singers on, fantastic, and I've got Gilbert O'Sullivan on and it's called Let's Have A Party and . . .'

Gilbert O'Sullivan? Gracious! And who are the other 19 'greats', pray?

'Yur, wait a minute, and it's called Gazza And Friends and Danny Baker's on it and me sister's on it and her friend and some of the lads but they're only singing like not a song but just at the end (Gazza proceeds to sing once more) All you need is love ba ba ba ba ba and whatever it is and it's the first album with Elvis on.'

Pardon? Could you clarify this peculiar statement, Gazz? His 'minder' does it for him by saying, 'Er, ah, you see, it's the Elvis medley that was out some years ago and it's been re-edited and it's the first time it's available on CD.' 'Hur, that's reet,' says Paul Gascoigne, footballer, 23.

I ask Gascoigne, pop hopeful, what he thought of his Tottenham team mate (and new England 'skipper') Gary Lineker's choice (Dire Straits, Simply Red, etc.) when, recently, Lineker was purred at by Sue Lawley on Desert Island Discs.

'Desert Island Discs? What's that?' he responds. I try to explain the concept of the celebrated radio programme. 'Oh, I see. I didn't see it. What, do you want me to go on there?'

Er, no it's not really in my power to select Ms Lawley's guests.

'Oh, I'm sorry, yeah, yeah, that programme's on telly, isn't it?'

'It's a radio programme, on Radio 4,' hisses the 'minder', losing patience with his charge.

'Oh, it's a radio programme?' says Gazza. 'Oh, I just put a compact disc on all the time. It's sort of snobby, radio, isn't it? If you want me on your Desert Island Discs, it's got to be a lot of tracks off Elvis.'

No Dire Straits? All footballers adore Dire Straits.

'Who's that? No, hang on, hold on. On the bus to the Hungary game in the World Coop, I give 'em, I put on Elvis and the lads really sang along to it so I'm not doing too bad, am I?'

Ignoring the fact that England didn't play Hungary in the World Coop, the history of footballers making pop records is a sad and grim one, indeed, from Kevin Keegan's It Ain't Easy (major flop) and Head Over Heels In Love (on which the be-permed supremo was backed by the super Smokie and got into the Top 40 in 1979), to the relatively recent chart-storming efforts of Glenn (Hoddle) and Chris (Waddle), it's a catalogue of aural indignity. Gascoigne seems unaware of footballing solo singer history.

'Hur, Kevin Keegan made a record? I'm trying to think . . .'

'Minder' butts in. 'The trouble with Keegan was he was trying to sing.'

Gazza: 'Oh, I see, yeah, he was trying to sing. I can't sing. I can rap, uh hur. Now I just enjoy it. I go training and I go fishing to relax. It's a very good thing.'

And with that he rises from his seat and says, 'Cheers, mate. I didn't think there were any more questions because I got to go . . .'

Go? Go fishing? Brian?

'I got to go to Luton.'

And so to Luton, beaming like the child who scoffed all the Mars bars, he goes . . .

Benny Hill

Waddling after over-nourished women, slapping small, bald men on the head and saluting in the manner of an intellectually-underprivileged person has made him incalculably famous and unaccountably wealthy. Throughout his career he has shrewdly avoided journalists' nosey questions. Until now that is.

'GO ON, BENNY, do the spectacles gag, ha ha.'
Standing at the bar of the South London 'theme' pub (theme: many, many photographs of the hostelry's most celebrated customer, i.e. Benny Hill, upon the walls . . . Benny chats with Jack Lemmon, Benny pretends to ogle a large-bosomed lass, Benny pulls a goony 'Fred Scuttle' face, Benny ogles another large-bosomed lass, etc.) a TV producer, Dennis Kirkland, is egging on the elderly, moon-faced comic to perform a party piece.

'Oh, go on, Benny, do the spectacles gag. It's funny,' goes Dennis. 'You'll like this,' Dennis says to me with a conspiratorial wink. 'Benny's my hero, you know,' he whispers . . . And so, under some protest, the plump comedian deigns to perform said 'spectacles gag'. Dennis supplies the feed line: 'Where are your spectacles, Benny?' and Benny tugs at the back of his jacket, runs his hand around the sides and up towards the breast pocket from out of which appear, yes, a pair of spectacles. This is the 'gag'. The specs, we were supposed to imagine, were trapped in a broken lining – except they weren't! Boom boom!.

'Ha ha, that's a *great* gag, isn't it?' guffaws Dennis, chucking me with some violence in the ribs. I offer a chuckle which, I fear, is by no means convincing. Benny Hill, meanwhile, looks somewhat embarrassed at being called upon to play the clown for my benefit. 'It's a potty old world, isn't it?' he mutters softly into his glass of wine. 'Ha ha ha!' goes Dennis. 'Ha ha ha!' goes a TV executive

producer, Adrian Hilliard, also accompanying Benny to this pub
lunch this day. 'Golly,' goes Benny, gloomily . . .

It has long been suggested that Benny Hill, never much one for
appearing on the Wogan sofa, let alone as a guest on Mr Matthew
Kelly's You Bet! or stuff like that, is an intensely shy individual.
And this suggestion is rather borne out by the number of acolytes
he has chosen to surround himself with at this simple pub lunch/
interview today: there's the cheery Dennis, here to crack jokes, to
answer questions directed at Benny whenever Benny is lost for
words, to bolster Benny's confidence by saying things like 'The
unfortunate thing about my hero here is he's too damn famous.
He's part of the legend of British show business and he's terribly,
terribly famous'; there's young Adrian, there to laugh in all the
correct places; there's Art Wood, brother of Ronnie, who used to
be a rock musician of sorts himself (he was in the Artwoods –
hence the name) but is now a graphic designer working on Benny's
latest record sleeve. And so we all sit down at a table in the corner
and Benny peruses the menu in silence, declining to meet my eye.

'It's a potty old world,' whispers Benny Hill to (I take it) himself.
'It's a *mad* world.' A waitress appears, Benny pats the podge of
his impressive stomach and addresses her in prime polite manner.
'Ooh, I'll have cod, chips and mushy peas, please. You're very
kind. Thank you very much. You're very nice.' It is refreshing to
note that he refrains from leering at the 'serving wench', pinching
her bottom or indulging in any of those high jinks for which, in
his television persona, he is so renowned. He just says 'You're very
nice,' peers sullenly at the tablecloth, clears his throat and quaffs
some wine. 'It's a potty old world,' he says again. I do not know
why he says this . . .

Benny Hill, 66, was born Alfred Hawthorne Hill in Southampton.
At the age of eight or nine or 10, he tells me, he used to stand in
the corner of the living room doing impressions of Jack Hulbert
and Cicely Courtneidge and Janet Gaynor and lots of people
nobody's ever heard of while his dad played a one-string fiddle.
How traditional and showbiz it all sounds. At the age of 12 or 13
he joined something called Bobby's Concert Party which performed
at working men's clubs and Southampton variety shows with titles
like Saucy Gals. *Le plus ça change*, as they say. He remembers
fondly one of his earliest jokes: he'd dress up as an enthusiastic
vicar and say, 'The young mothers' club now seems to have a

shortage of young mothers, in spite of all the efforts of myself and the bishop'. Boom, ahem, boom.

By 1953 he had his own show on the telly. He's never looked back or felt much need to alter a brand of 'humour' that relies on vulgarity, innuendo, the oh so saucy fare of knickers, bottoms, bosoms, sexually feeble husbands and stupid yokels with straw in their hair who go, 'Cor, 'er dumplin's are boilin' over!' in an annoyingly wanton manner whenver a country lass in a low-cut blouse traipses by (i.e. quite often). It's the stuff of Donald McGill seaside postcards – bawdy, unsophisticated, some would say simple-minded. Silly, silly horseplay. Benny Hill, as half-wit, lusty cowboy, propositions the dance hall queen thus: 'I'll show you my 38s if you'll show me yours'. Collapse of audience in cackling and stitches. It's all terribly, terribly low-brow – with Hill's Angels, 'bimbos' to a woman, rattling the old lounge sex-o-meter not much – but it rarely fails, does it?

And it is a form of humour so lacking in subtlety that it translates easily to foreign parts: Benny Hill's shows are seen, and seemingly enjoyed, all around the world. The man who lives all alone in Teddington, South London, who is sometimes snapped by the tabloids walking down the high street carrying nothing but a mournful expression and an old carrier bag, the man who they sometimes call Scrooge (or 'Mr Mean' if it's the Star because none of their readers has ever heard of Dickens) because he seems to do nothing extravagant with all the money he earns apart from splashing out on the odd cod, chips and mushy peas in the local pub (except it's Q magazine that is paying for this feast today), has done his bit for the trade deficit. You could say that . . .

'Ha ha ha,' roars Dennis as I broach the subject of Benny Hill's trans-global humour and the miracle of it all. 'We're seen in 100 countries! That's Benny you see. Benny is my hero. I hate to flatter him but he *is*. Do you know that Greta Garbo in her dying days said, What I like to do is have a bottle of vodka and a bottle of scotch and I like to sit and watch reruns of the Benny Hill show? She did!'

Delicately, with some deliberation, Benny Hill cuts one of his French fried potatoes in half and places the segment within his plump face. He is not laughing. He is thinking. Thinking . . .

'Well, yes,' he says, thoughtfully, speaking for himself for the very first, reluctant, time. 'Our humour translates to between 90 and 100 countries. They've just sold 30 Benny Hill shows to Iceland and 45 to Angola. You can't get a much broader spread than that. I've had fan letters from Poland, from Russia, I get them a lot from Ecuador, Venezuela, Colombia. I get them from Mexico. I believe I have been on in the Lebanon and I was on the front cover of Argentina's version of the TV Times right in the middle of the Falklands War, which just goes to show how stupid it all is. And the mayor of the drug capital of Colombia went on TV and said, This is a dangerous city so don't go out after 10 o'clock. Stay in instead and watch the Benny Hill show. So that shows you journalists, doesn't it? You don't know which is *worse*, do you?: drug wars or that great, fat, sexist, ugly, hypocritical, would-be so-called crap comedian Benny Hill.'

It is as if I have been issued a minor warning: Benny Hill is not one to warm to the prod-nose journalist. But it is *he* who has brought up the sexist (dread word!) topic so I carry on regardless.

Ben Elton, speaking to Q in 1986, had this to say: 'You have Benny Hill in the late '80s chasing half-naked women around a park when we know in Britain women can't even walk safe in a park anymore. That for me is worrying.' In the late 1980s the British public noticed that Benny Hill's style of humour was possibly less than ideologically sound. Sexist in fact. Benny bridles.

'Oh, it's all silly nonsense, all that, isn't it? Ben Elton's got all the tit gags under the sun so what is sexist about me? Everybody says, At the end of Benny Hill's show he strips the girls and chases them. I don't chase *anybody*. At the end of the show when they play Yakkety Sax, *I'm* the one who's chased – that's c-h-a-s-e-d. not c-h-a-s-t-e . . . but maybe c-h-a-s-t-e as well, the way things are going at the moment.'

Boom boom.

'It's silly when you hear somebody say, All he does is pinch girl's bottoms. It's just not so and it really is hypocritical of people because I don't like putting fellow performers down, which is why I don't mention names, but you can do all sorts of intricate stuff and then get the biggest laugh just by using the word 'wankers'. I saw someone doing that on the telly just the other night. It's all rather sad. And there was a comic, mentioning no names, on the television the other day and he had 17 f-words in his act and there were 74 *mother* f-words. Nothing in the paper the next day. And then there's the word I can't bring myself ever to say, the dirty female c-word – I heard that 11 times in five weeks and I was only watching what the average person watches. Nothing in the paper about that. But I look at a girl and all I say is, Oh, her dumplings are boiling over . . . and that's labelled *filth*!

'You've got calendar girls, wall to wall swollen chest pimples, they look like they're following you around the room non-stop, and there's people that say Benny Hill is sexist. I don't understand it. We have girls in long dresses doing a pretty dance routine and the next day's write-up is all about girls in minuscule bikinis writhing. What show do people like you *see*?'

Benny Hill seems to be denying here that his show could be in any way deemed offensive – what with all the other 'filth' flying about the screens. Attack is the best form of defence and good-hearted family fare with girls in pretty frocks is the Benny Hill show, he would have you know. Never a sly quip appertaining to a bosom?

'What?' he rasps in some irritation as he dismembers his cod. 'Big tits don't get a laugh. On my show? Tell me when, tell me when!'

Are you denying that scantily-clad girls play a major part in the B. Hill repertoire of hilarity?

'What? Scantily clad girls don't get a laugh on my show. *I* do. We haven't had a scantily clad girl on there for about eight or nine years! It's quite bizarre that you should think that. There was a girl not so long ago on some programme or other with the lights up totally naked in close-up and you saw *everything*, but you're not complaining about *that*, are you? You see, a lot of my comedy is based on observation. Before now, perhaps, a young lady has come to see me and she is, maybe, a tiny bit edgy about being with me and once this *particular* lady was there and I put on the music from Streetcar Named Desire, great bluesy music and she changed there and then. Suddenly, she was in the mood . . .'

Benny has totally lost me here. One minute he is defending accusations of 'sexism', the next he is, I suppose, describing his seduction techniques. It's a potty old world . . . And then the next minute, such is his way, he is on the defensive once more with this:

'Yes, but, all these people call me sexist but one of my favourite forms of comedy is changing the sexes over. Reverse the roles and you see how silly all this silly nonsense is. If a man looks through a window at the sensuous and exciting body of a naked woman undressing, he's a Peeping Tom, but if a woman sees a *man* undressing, it's indecent exposure, isn't it?'

Dennis can't resist it: 'I was had up for indecent exposure once. I was let off because of the lack of evidence!'

And Benny can't resist the comic challenge laid down by his producer: 'I was done for gross indecency once. But I hadn't been indecent 144 times!'

'Ha ha ha,' goes Dennis. 'You see, you don't have to be filthy to get laughs.'

Benny Hill is now settling into the ice cream course – three scoops; vanilla, chocolate, butterscotch . . . plus a large cognac on the side. 'Je suis au club de pudding,' he has said to a-tittering all around. And yet he is still riled at my 'sexism' enquiries.

'It's a nonsense what you have been saying, really,' he says. 'I think we're getting on to something that's a bit heavy. Let's talk about something else. I must say, it's nice to talk to an admirer, somebody who really wants to talk about your success.' The sarcastic, slightly irritated tone does not go unnoticed by Dennis.

'Yes,' says Dennis. 'How about lightening this conversation. Get on about the record. Plug Benny Hill!'

Right. Benny Hill – no 'stranger to the charts' because he had some hits once with Transistor Radio and Ernie (as in 'he drove the fastest milk cart in the west') has been in the studios. Abbey Road, no less. There's a single called Screen Stars which contains lines like 'I met Kim Basinger, I knew I'd end up chasing her' and 'If I could see more of Jane Seymour, I'd let Jane see more of me'. 'It's very, very funny,' says Benny Hill. There might be an LP, too, and Benny's even been doing some television work with Vanilla Ice who is, it appears, 'a jolly nice chap'. Benny is trying to impress me with his musical credentials. He can play the trumpet and even the pan pipes. 'I'm very musical,' he says with great sincerity. 'I was telling Phil Collins about this. I made a video a couple of years ago with Phil Collins, you see, and he said, I'm going out for a paradiddle, so I said, No, it's a *piddle* you're going out for.

'But as for the pop stuff, like Ernie, you see I was once a milkman, and they say you only write about what you know about and Ernie is really based on truth. Though I suppose *you* would say, like so many have, that Ernie simply perpetuates the myth of the milkman being the stud, the rapist, you know, when it was just a *funny* song.'

I would say nothing of the sort. I'd just say that Ernie wasn't very amusing and that The Ladybirds' backing vocals were hugely hopeless . . . but let it pass. Let me ask, instead, why Benny Hill is such a private person, shunning all invitations to appear on Wogan and suchlike celebrity jaunts.

'It's difficult, you see, because I'm supposed to be funny, and when you're put on the spot like that you don't know if you're going to be funny. I'm not funny all the time, you see.'

Are you the sad old misery guts with the windswept carrier bag that the tabloids like to make you out to be?

'Pardon?' says Benny, sipping on the cognac.

What I am getting at is: are you a miserable person?

'Miserable? Do you think I'm a miserable person?'

'Benny's not miserable,' says Dennis, helpfully.

Oh, that's alright, then.

'I know, I know, I know, what you're talking about. The papers don't know what to do. I'm Mr Mean one week and then the next week it's Big Hearted Benny helps crippled girl. They say the same about Michael Jackson. He's a big fan of mine, by the way, and so is Randy Travis. And all the people that count. Frank Sinatra. I've worked with Liberace, Sammy Davis Jr, Maurice Chevalier, people like that. But I'm not a money person. I don't live by money.'

What does he *do* with all the money, one wonders? We shall never know for Dennis interrupts with an amusing quip about Benny owing him a fiver. Controversy cunningly diverted. So, I ask, does Benny Hill actually *enjoy* being 'terribly, terribly famous'? From the evidence before me this day, it would appear not.

'Show him the pictures of Daytona Beach,' Benny orders Dennis and Dennis shows me these photographs of Benny on Daytona Beach with girls in bikinis. Girls grin; Benny ogles.

'Look at these pictures,' says Dennis. 'All these gorgeous girls with Benny. Look at that! What Benny is trying to say is that that is a bloody good reason for being famous.'

'Look at the little girl kissing me there,' says Benny. And I look at a bronzed girl in a swimsuit kissing the fat cheek of a leering Benny Hill. It is all rather odd.

Lots of people imagine that you might in some way be gay, Benny, I croak, and he looks into his cognac and slaps his ample tum and says '*This* is my only problem. I'm fat but . . . Oh dear, it's a potty old world, isn't it?'

Dennis and Adrian go 'ha ha ha'. Benny Hill doesn't.

Cliff Richard

He is a National Monument like Stonehenge or the Queen Mother, the Saviour of Mankind to whom all our thoughts turn during the Holy Season of mistletoe and wine. Crumbs! He was even present at the birth of rock'n'roll.

THIS IS a tricky question, I said, but tell me, Cliff: what is it in your half-a-century bound on earth, in your illustrious career, that makes you most proud?

'Crumbs,' said Cliff. 'That question's not so tricky at all. Because I have a really nice home and there's a swimming pool area and there's a pool house with a bar and I've got all my memorabilia up on the walls. And one of my fans has done this quote in stained glass. It says, God And Rock'n'Roll Work Well Together In The Hands Of Someone Who Loves Them Both. I'm proudest of that.'

He could have chosen the fact that, single-handedly, he invented rock'n'roll (give or take an Elvis or two).

He could have chosen the fact that his fabulous discs have spent more time in the Hit Parade than anyone else's.

He could have chosen his OBE, his pair of valiant attempts (failed, alas) to win the Eurovision Song Contest for brave little Grande-Bretagne, his sparky Technicolor romps with double-decker buses and Una Stubbs and Susan Hampshire, or the many times he's defeated Mike Read at tennis.

Or the fact that he is a National Monument like Stonehenge or the Queen Mother, and the Saviour of Mankind to whom all our thoughts turn during the Holy Season of mistletoe and wine.

But Cliff is a humble man. He chose a bit of glass, a gift from a fan. Cliff feels a great responsibility for his fans, he told me. 'I wish I could say the same of all artists,' he added with clicking tongue . . .

Cliff (Richard – the surname is redundant: he's as famous as Elvis or Jesus) is at a hotel-cum-health-centre retreat in South Wales warming up for an Australian tour with rehearsals and some 'secret' shows. He sits all alone in the heart of a large and bare conference room; autumnal sun is filtering through the skylight alighting, halo-like, upon the head of the Peter Pan of Pop. Layers of photographic make-up lend a timeless duality to the celebrated bespectacled visage. How old, would you say? 17? Methuselah? Dorian Gray or the grotesque portrait? 51? Yes, that seems about right.

But what does it matter? Gee, whizz, it's Cliff! I greet the legend and ask him about the old days, three decades ago when Harry Webb was reborn as Cliff and curled a lip and twitched a hip and the young folks squawked to the moody beat.

'I say night after night that if there hadn't been an Elvis, there couldn't have been a Cliff Richard.' Heaven forfend. If Cliff hadn't existed, we'd have had to invent him. 'I nearly met Elvis in 1976. I was offered the opportunity but he was going through a very fat period and I thought, I don't want to meet a great big fat guy. But obesity is something we've all dealt with in our time and I regret it now. I'd rather have met him even in a fat state.'

As Britain's principal teen sensation, Cliff reigned supreme, through the rock'n'roll of Move It to the hey-kids-let's-put-the-show-on-right-here-in-the-youth-club cinematic frolics of The Young Ones and Summer Holiday, for five years. Then came The Beatles to knock him off his perch. Did Cliff give in to the human failing of jealousy at this point, one wonders?

'There was a certain amount of jealousy. I suppose,' he confesses. 'It was hurtful to be overlooked so dramatically by the media. But I still sold records by the million, so what the heck? And look at me now. The Beatles don't exist any more and I was going five years before The Beatles so no-one's ever going to catch me up. I'll always be ahead of everybody. I've just done my 1,000th week in the chart and my nearest competitor hasn't reached 500 weeks in the chart which means that if that person is to catch me up, I would have to stop recording now and they'd have to have a record in the charts every week for the next five years. It's not possible. I'm well ahead.'

Cliff, OBE ('I've sold 250 million plus units so I've done something for the economy'), contrary to what I wrote up there some time before, is not such a humble man.

'And another thing: when it came to rebellion, we were far more the rebellious crowd. The Beatles were accepted by Royalty, they were accepted by all the high society. The Shadows and I never were. So we had one up on them.'

To picture Cliff as a rebel seems as hard, somehow, to imagine as, say, Esther Rantzen as axe murderer of tiny children. The saintly warbler protests:

'Oh, but I *was* a rebel, you see. They said I was too sexy for TV. And what I do nowadays is I communicate the positive factor; I communicate Jesus rather than Hitler and that's far more radical than being airy-fairy and wafting around saying, Drugs, yeah, take drugs. That negative approach is so easy. It would be really easy for me to become a massive thing overnight by doing a video that was vulgar, that was sexual. I see Madonna videos and I think, crumbs, I could get good-looking girls and film them. We all know how to behave sexually and sexily but I find that all a cop-out. To present what I'm saying in a positive way is far more difficult and radical. It's like I used to swear like mad but I got myself out of it with the help of The Shadows and it's much more demanding not to swear. I feel far greater for not swearing than I did for swearing. Swearing is really easy.'

Crumbs! You'd think that Britain's original rocker (if you don't count Tommy Steele) fails to understand, or has forgotten, what rock'n'roll is supposed to be about: i.e. being noisy and vulgar and sexual and sweary and annoying the squares. Cliff does not agree with this astute sociological analysis.

'That's not the rock'n'roll that I know and love,' he says. 'Negativity is not what rock'n'roll is about to me. A band like Guns N'Roses create something that I personally would rather be rid of. Guns N'Roses create a violent atmosphere and they try to paint that on to rock'n'roll and that's when it comes into my world because I was there at the conception of rock'n'roll. I was there. So it annoys me that people like Guns N'Roses come along and purvey the fake rock'n'roll lifestyle, the one that kills people like Janis Joplin, and the public are to blame because they allow themselves to be manipulated by some 20-year-old who doesn't know anything about life anyway. Why do people accept this trash? People like Guns N'Roses have simply got to grow up rather fast!'

Cliff goes on railing away at the iniquities of rock'n'roll abuse.

'You're smiling but I think this is actually more serious than you think. There again we'll get over it. We got over The Sex Pistols.

The Sex Pistols couldn't play and he couldn't sing. Who would dare say that that is a part of rock'n'roll? Who bought those dreadful records?'

Well, dare I risk divine wrath and confess that, er, I did, actually. I dig Cliff's Apron Strings but I like Pretty Vacant, too; what is wrong with me? Perhaps it would be wiser to pass on before the fellow blows a gasket.

Cliff has been speaking out like this for 25 years, of course. In 1966 he was converted to Christianity. Within moments he was blasting away, having a go at The Beatles for their flirtation with the Maharishi.

'I didn't have a go at The Beatles,' he corrects me. 'I was having a go at anybody who was presenting the drug life, the LSDs and the trips and things, as though it was normal. And that included The Beatles. I thought, crumbs, this is very dangerous for the fans, for the people who we rely on for a living. I mean, of course there were drugs when I first started: that was that funny smell in the dressing room that I didn't understand what it was – that was pot, I learned much, much later. But it wasn't upfront in those days, so our fans were shaded and protected from all that. But nowadays, because of certain stupid exponents of rock'n'roll, there are many young people who are no longer alive. We cannot shrug that blame away from rock'n'roll.'

He was in bed when it happened.

'I spent three years discussing it with friends and reading books, but it wasn't until that moment that I lay on my bed and said, OK, I give in, Jesus. I want you in my life, that I became a Christian. And I felt a release.'

Wasn't he ever concerned that making the conversion public might affect his popularity, that youngsters would sneer, Pooh, daddio, religion's for the straight cats? Well, by 1966, Cliff seemed pretty old-hat anyway, but it seems the possibility did give him some cause for thought.

'Oh, I thought about that, yeah, but I felt that if my faith meant anything to me, then surely it was worth losing 50 per cent of my fans or even 100 per cent of my fans. Either God was all-important or he didn't matter that much. If God had to play second fiddle to my career, then that's not a particularly great God. So I got up on stage with Billy Graham and I did my thing and the press were going, Cliff's Got Religion – and that year we did pantomime at the Palladium and we broke all the box office records! So obviously people didn't mind my beliefs. And why should they? We Christians can be pretty proud, you know, because even if it turned out that Christianity was wrong, what would we have done bad? We would have started 90 per cent of the hospitals in India, we would have spread a lot of love and kindness, so we'd have done pretty well in life and spread something in the world that it needs.'

'We' would also have started a few trillion wars and spread a lot of persecution, but let it pass. Cliff is 'proud of the fact that I was able to say to people, Look, you can be a Christian, it's not cissy, it's not fuddy-duddy, you can be a contemporary person and have a spiritual life. Crumbs, it would be great to be remembered as that kind of person.'

Over the years, it has become part of our National Heritage, great sport, to Mock Cliff; his faith, his 'cleanliness', his age, his occasionally weedy records (from Congratulations to the Xmas-toddlers-around-ye-olde-yuletide-log offerings of the recent past) make splendid targets for the odd fun-poke. How does he take it, the Cliff foolery?

'Oh, I combat mockery by continuing to be me and winning more and more people over to my way of thinking. It's easy to counteract because the simple, right-minded person sees what I am saying and can see that I'm not a person to mock. I'm not a nasty, bad person. I'm basically a nice guy.'

And what of the sniggering speculations concerning his private life. Cliff's never married and, apart from that brief and unlikely fling around the tennis court with Sue Barker, has never looked likely to. He must be a 'queer'.

'Oh, I learned to live with that years ago. It's my mum that can't live with that. It's me that's having this rubbish thrown at him so I can stand there and go, Up Yours!' Cliff blows a raspberry with some gusto. 'You can think what you like. I'm not going to change my life to prove anything to you. If you think I'm going to get married just to prove that I'm heterosexual, well, that's absolutely up the spout. Think what you . . . er, like.'

Crumbs! I think he almost said a rude word, there.

Nonetheless, he is not averse to taking legal action if the abuse steps over the mark. He sued the NME once:

'I can turn the cheek time after time, but the minute you hit libel, I'll hit back. And this girl wrote this review and she said, "If they drop a bomb on London, I hope it drops on you, Cliff, and catches you with your leather pants down". And she called me a little Hitler. Well, that really got to me, so I sued for £5,000 and gave the money to my Christian Arts Centre group. But it's not me that I worry about, it's my fans – but my fans don't give two hoots about what the critics think. If you were to write something nasty about one of my concerts, the people that came to see me would just say, What a funny bloke.'

And Cliff can turn frosty if career moves do not go quite according to plan. After all these years, he is still cross that he didn't win the Eurovision Song Contest.

'I didn't get swizzed so much the second time because I was beaten by two people, but the girl that won should never have won and what's interesting is that Anne-Marie David, no-one even remembers her name, and Power To All Our Friends sold 1.7 million, so that was a swizz. And Congratulations was just bad luck because if Yugoslavia had given us two votes instead of none, we would have won the Eurovision.'

He feels a fury that he's never made it in America: 'To think that I started the whole thing off. I mean, I meet people like Elton and Eric Clapton and they're bemused that I haven't made it in the States. The potential market is there: Devil Woman sold 1.4 million copies so I don't understand it. Do you know, I was in America a couple of years back and I decided to have my hair cut and you know how barbers talk: this guy said, What do you do for a living? and I said, I'm a singer and he said, Oh, really, do you make any money at it? So I told him my name . . . and he'd never heard of me at all! It's quite fantastic! It's quite impossible to understand my lack of success. I have to blame my record company. I can't blame anyone else.' (And so he continues, reeling out a series of figures – 'I've had nine Top 30 singles there; the I'm No Hero album had three Top 30 singles and the album didn't break the hundred, which is an impossibility and Miss You Nights blah blah' – to prove the extent of the swindle; it is a trifle unsettling how he has all the minute statistics of a career – chart positions, sales returns, Yugoslavian jury voting figures – so firmly lodged in his memory.)

He feels slighted at the poor critical reception afforded to Time, the stage musical extravaganza featuring Laurence Olivier as a hologram, Cliff with a hair extension, and some rather dismal tunes: 'The critics didn't like Time but 750,000 people came to see it, and these days if you go to any show in the West End it's high technology up to here with things moving and revolving and lasers. Well, it was we rock'n'rollers who showed them how to do that. We did it in Time, five years ago!'

But what really gets Cliff's goat most is when the positive spirit of his beloved rock'n'roll is debased, brought into disrepute. Who else would go so far as to ban one of his own records because he found it offensive?

'You're talking about Honky Tonk Angels, but I didn't ban it, I just refused to sing it or promote it because I made that record in good faith and the week it was released I was doing a Christian gig and sometimes at these Christian gigs I have open questions and this girl in the audience said, Did you know that your latest record is about prostitutes? Crumbs, I nearly fell over! I didn't realise that "honky tonk angels" are women who frequent bars. I thought, golly, this might upset people, so I've never sung it since.' (But, he confesses subsequently: 'I've still got my record of Honky Tonk Angels on my jukebox. I'd never sing it but I do like listening to it.' A puzzling moral conundrum, indeed.)

And who else would deliver the speech that Cliff delivered at the BRIT Awards in 1989. The audience had greeted special guest Kenneth Baker, then Education Minister, with boos and catcalls and, boy, was Cliff hopping mad! 'The rest of us have just got to grow up!' he snapped.

'When the audience booed him, it was reflecting on us, on rock'n'roll. We in the musical world invite people to be our guests of honour in boxes and then we permit people to boo them? Not in my philosophy. So I thought, well, as the elder statesman of rock'n'roll, it was up to me to say something. Because nobody else said a thing. There were all these Bros fans in the audience and they needed a spanking – so I gave them one.

Oh, it's not easy being Cliff, protecting and defending 'rock'n'roll' – the wholesome entertainment he helped to found – from the vulgarities of a Madonna, the depravities of a Guns N'Roses and general impudence from all sides. It's a lonely crusade requiring the patience of a saint. 'Sometimes I get so frustrated,' our elder statesman sighs. 'I think, Am I the only person in the world that wants to grow up? Am I the only person that wants to be an adult?'

David Icke

It's the strangest CV of modern time: goalkeeper, snooker commentator, Green Party activist... Son of God. Cue all manner of laughably lofty pronouncements and strenuously non-specific predictions. But there was something he didn't see coming.

I N A LARGE London bookshop, I was searching for a copy of The Truth Vibrations by David Icke. No easy task, for what on earth would the peculiar volume be filed under? New Age? Astrology? *Fiction*? Feeling like the flush-faced teenager in the chemist's shop croaking his awkward request for Durex, I sidled up to an assistant to enlist help. 'Oh, David Icke!' she said, her voice rather too loud for my liking. 'You'll probably find that in the basement under Hysterical Madmen!' At which we both had a jolly good laugh . . .

Poor David Icke. It was a year ago that he became the butt of the latest Grand National jokes as, in turquoise shell suits, he wandered among us casting portents of doom, forecasting apocalypse for New Zealand and assorted calamities. He was (apparently) a messenger from God, a Messiah – Hallelujah! – a prophet despatched upon a mission, beseeching the peoples to be as one with the vibrations of the cosmos and to pull their socks up sharpish because, lo, the 'transformation of humankind' was upon us (or something). He was (obviously) exotically crazed. Oh, how we roared at this global village idiot! New Zealand failed to disappear off the face of the planet as predicted and we all had a jolly good laugh . . .

'And so we rejoin the match in the sixth frame. Dennis Taylor trailing four–one, Jimmy White at the table . . .' That was his catchphrase. He had been a professional footballer, a goalkeeper for Coventry City and Hereford United, until rheumatoid arthritis ended his career. He turned to sports journalism and a job as gabbling head, wide-of-tie and permed-of-coiffure, at all the thrilling snooker fests from the Sheffield Crucible to the Reading Hexagon. Then, in the late 1980s, he forsook the green baize for the Green Party for whom he became a national spokesperson. Guarding the goal-mouth in the mud of the lower divisions, using the words 'temperamental' and 'genius' and 'Alex Higgins' in the same sentence on telly, delivering speeches in empty halls on the subject of The Poll Tax Is Horrible And So Are Motorcars And Everything Else for a squabbling minority political group . . . a 'chequered' career, many might say. Icke would disagree: 'What a life it had been,' he wrote in The Truth Vibrations. 'I would go for something, achieve it, leave it, and move on to the next goal. There was a definite pattern emerging. I became convinced that I was led by forces beyond my understanding. Something strange was going on.'

Golly. On March 29, 1990, the 'emerging pattern' finally, well, emerged. Hoping to relieve his arthritis, Icke had consulted a medium and spiritualist healer called Betty Shine who, in mid-therapy, had one of her 'turns' and told her patient that he had a cat with diarrhoea – which, extraordinary as it may seem, he *did!* And then Betty went yet *more* curious, receiving a 'visitation' from a Chinaman called Wang Yee Lee who was millions of years old and flitting about in the ether with Socrates. Wang and the antique Greek had something frightfully important to tell Betty about David Icke: 'He is a healer who is here to heal the earth. He will be world famous. He will face enormous opposition.' That was the gist of the message from beyond.

Unearthly forces will not be gainsaid and soon after this uncommon experience, Icke 'was seeing eyes wherever I looked,' he says. (Not *real* eyes, you understand, but the wobbly sort that people often complain about when they've been at the sherry trifle or the LSD). These eyes were significant, Betty Shine told him, because they indicated a surging development of psychic powers, so he left the Green Party and began to write The Truth Vibrations. Through communications delivered by 'master souls' and 'extraterrestials', the Chinaman and the Greek and some bloke called Rakorczy (the, um, Ascended Master and the Lord of Civilisation), Icke told of many things: of what became of Atlantis and its inhabitants; of Icke's previous lives as a General in Napoleon's army and a Red

Indian called Chief Eagle Tail; of how UFOs work; of how Icke *originally* came from a planet called Oereal – and, by lucky coincidence, so did his wife Linda; of why there's no mention in the Bible of what Jesus was up to between the ages of 12 to 30 (he was on his hols in the Isle of Wight, apparently). Armed with all this Knowledge – the Truth about corn circles and the Holy Grail and Noah's Ark and reincarnation (did you know that cot death babies 'are spiritual teachers who leave the body soon after birth to present the parents with a challenge to overcome' or that disabled people are usually disabled because 'they have treated a disabled person badly in the past and need to understand what it feels like'? – Icke would heal the Earth. But Wang and Socrates had been right in one respect: when David Icke began to pass on this essential information in the spring of 1991, he *did* face enormous opposition.

At press conferences he sat alongside his wife Linda and his daughter Kerry and a woman called Deborah Shaw, Icke's chief spiritual guide and 'channeller' (who the unenlightened blockheads of the press took for Icke's mistress – and who later changed her name to Mari Shawsun for some, no doubt very significant, reason). They all wore turquoise, because it 'vibrates' with the earth really well, and Icke issued his Truths. And the journalists mocked. Icke straightened his hair and it was long and he went on the Wogan show and the audience tittered and Terry said, 'Look, they're *laughing* at you,' and Icke said, 'Oh, yes, but they laughed at *Jesus* didn't they?' How we *hooted*. New Zealand still hadn't blown up. The earth remained unhealed . . .

Either Icke is improbably thick-skinned or he is possessed of gigantic determination. The brouhaha has died down only recently but here comes another madcap book. In Love Changes Everything (a title which, by the mysteries of symbiosis, is exactly the same as that of the moving song by Mr Music himself i.e. Andrew Lloyd Webber who is, probably, the reincarnation of Beethoven or someone) Icke tells his readers the Truth about Planet Earth and Reincarnation and Creation and Everything – 'with particular emphasis on the last 12,000 years'. (Crikey, 12,000 years in 160 pages. Why, that's 75 years per page!) The underlying 'message' ('Be nice to each other', as Ms Jackie Trent – reincarnation of Voltaire? – so sweetly put in the theme song of Mr & Mrs) is undeniably sound. The book, with its nigh incomprehensible passages about Muans (ancient earth civilisation with telepathic powers) and Rakorczy (who's changed his name to *Rakorski* in this volume) and planets called things like Ur (which the Hubble telescope would be unable to detect even if it worked properly) and the author as the reincarnation of King Arthur, et cetera, is undeniably barmy . . .

So it was with some trepidation that, having made a crossing on a Southampton–Isle of Wight ferry, I climbed the stairs to a first-floor flat in Ryde and knocked upon the door. David Icke/King Arthur/Chief Eagle Tail/the man from Oereal opened it. To the naked eye, he didn't appear deranged at all. Dressed not in turquoise, but sporting cream jacket and stripy tie instead, he looked more a chartered accountant (or, indeed, a sports presenter: his curls are back) than a Redeemer Divine. His wife Linda (reincarnation of Gabriel, an Angel of the Godhead) seemed entirely rational too, providing normal tea and normal biscuits in a normal way. The son Gareth's Oerealian connections were undetectable as he played Subbuteo on the floor. Then Icke began to speak.

There was nothing untoward about the tone of voice – this was muted and reasonable. It was the words that were rum. 'Everything around us here is not a vacuum,' he said. 'It's *energy*. It's energy all *around* us.' His hand made a sweeping motion around the room but I saw only drab furniture. 'This is not a vacuum flask,' he said. 'It's *energy*. We can't see it because it's vibrating quicker than our eyes can see but it's there. We *live* in a sea of energy.' Outside the window, seagulls flew with energy over a sea of, er, sea. This is called the English Channel. It is not a vacuum flask.

I had yet to ask a question and already Icke was into a hectic stride. 'What I am saying is *not* a load of baloney,' he insisted. 'Reincarnation is the only sane explanation of life because we are all made up of negative and positive energies and what we are doing with experiences through reincarnation is seeking a balance point between the two and it's called karma; well, it's called karma on *this* planet but goodness knows what it's called *elsewhere*, call it what you bloody like, call it Jimmy Tarbuck for all I care, but in seeking the balance point, how do you know where the balance point *is*?'

This last, it transpired, was a rhetorical question: before I could reply 'I don't know, where *is* the balance point?' he was off and prattling again, sprawled back in the armchair, face turned to the ceiling, fingertips together, the pose of a dull and pompous academic banging on about some pet theory.

'You see, once we get this perfect balance on one frequency of negative and positive energies you're going like *that* all the time (*his fingers twiddled to indicate the direction of "that"*) but you probably start like *that* (*twiddle*) and then you start going like *that* (*major twiddle*) and once you're *there* (*extravagant twiddle*) this generates a *third* energy which makes the real us which are energy fields vibrate quicker like *that* (*twiddle-di-dee*) and then, you see . . .' My eyes and my mind were glazing over. Still he rambled on. 'And then you can actually change the rate of the vibrations and tune into other frequencies but . . . er . . . all this is not worth going into now, actually.'

What? The claptrap had come to such an abrupt halt, with this unlikely conclusion to the address, that I was taken quite by surprise and thus forgot the question I had been attempting to ask for what seemed one hundred years. This was a shame because, after the briefest of silences, he simply started up again. 'Let me try to explain this. Part of the energies of the soul come into a physical body and that is known as the lower soul and the rest of the soul stays on the non-physical frequency but once you lose touch with your higher self, you become delinked and . . .'

Enough. I snapped. I barged in. 'Do you, excuse me, but do you think that people who make fun of you are "delinked"?' David Icke looked quite taken aback at this interruption.

'Um,' he said, sniffing at the air for inspiration. 'Um. Dunno. But those that just dismiss everything I say, such people, as time passes, as it will, they will think My *God*, what have I *done*? People who ridicule me will realise that I am basically right. They will *see*. And they will learn from that experience.' Was this a warning? Surely you *understand* why people make fun of you, what with all the turquoise track suits and . . .

'Yes!' he broke in. 'People fear the unknown. But I've *never* claimed to be the Messiah or the Son of God. I've never claimed to be *anything*. I am a communicator. My lifeplan is to communicate information to people and I have been chosen for that. It's not *me* that's going to change the world, it's my *information* that's going to change the world. Even the people who mock, even the people in the Wogan audience, something within them has been triggered because they know it's *true*. *Everybody* knows what I say is true.'

Do they really? Anyway, just what *is* this communicator saying?

He says that reincarnation is a *fact* which is possible, I suppose (though he also makes it sound like a complete swizz: 'If you want to see some of the most evolved souls incarnated on this earth today, don't go to the President of the United States, go to a beggar in India,' he tells me). He's saying (or was a while ago) that New Zealand is going to go all wonky, which it didn't. And he's also saying a lot of things that are not only implausible but also have no bearing on man's fate anyway so why did he mention them in the first place? Shakespeare, for example, didn't write those plays. Francis Bacon did. This amazing 'fact' is a tired old chestnut but Icke gives the wonky theory a new twist by explaining that Bacon was, actually, our multifaceted friend Rakorski in disguise. Blimey!

Icke supplies a slippery answer to the Shakespeare 'riddle': 'I don't know for sure whether Shakespeare wrote the plays or *not*. All I can do is pass on the information that says he *didn't*. I am challenging the whole basis of the bloody system. I'm not saying that every last detail of what I say is correct, but everything I say is *basically* correct. I'm trying to get people to *think* because what they've all been *programmed* to think is nonsense. Once they *start* to think, they'll see that what I'm saying is the only sane explanation of life. But *now* people are so concerned with the twigs that they don't see the forest.'

This casual saunter down Contradiction Lane is making my head all a-teeter. Icke's argument – which seems to go, Yes, what I say *is* rubbish but that's because it's *true*, as one day you shall recognise – makes any exchange of views fruitless. And renders me near inarticulate: Look here, look, excuse me but I really don't understand how, when you say . . . But he's not listening to my splutterings anyway. He has something vital of his own to impart: 'I have now started to be able to see situations more clearly. From the basis of how karma works, I can see what is coming.'

Exclamation! Is this a prelude to a melting-ice-caps-engulf-globe-and-everyone-drowns-(not-counting-New-Zealanders) premonition? No.

'For instance, there's football and I *knew* Paul Gascoigne was in for a big blow. He'd reached such a peak and I knew something was going to happen to give that guy an experience on the other side of the balance point. And that's *exactly* what happened.'

This 'prediction' is so *singularly* non-astonishing that I request another one from our hopeless soothsayer. He pays no attention.

Perhaps his mention of football has brought forth reveries of a previous life in a goalie's jersey, but suddenly Icke drops his defences, replacing the hogwash with a form of sad sense.

'Let's be honest,' he murmurs. 'Let's be *honest* – a part of me *wants* to go out there to make people think. But there's another part of me that just wants to run a tea shop in Ventnor and disappear. Just imagine what it was like for me last year. When they laughed at me on the Wogan show, yes, I *did* understand it to a certain extent because there's a prat sitting there in a turquoise track suit, you know. And when I was doing that, the part of me that was *not* doing the interview was saying, David, would you *please* stand up and walk off the set so I just slowly *die*. I thought, What am I *saying*! This is ridiculous! I'd have *loved* not to have gone through all that, I can assure you. My *God*!'

So why did he go through it? I should have kept my mouth shut. A resigned sigh suggests he considers the question stupid and his mood swings back to 'normal' again. 'Why? Because I was *meant* to. I have been orchestrated and my lifeplan has been to bring this and information to people. Being a television presenter was all part of the plan because you need to have a name to make people listen and snooker was getting *phenomenal* audiences so I was in the public eye . . . So this was all part of the plan; but the person I was before last March would have said, Bugger *this* for a game of soldiers. So I was orchestrated to tune into powerful frequencies – and when you do *that* it can blow you away. I got blown to an extreme of what I call the Hey Man Syndrome where you slip away on a spiritual dream and lose touch with the practical side of life. But I started to come back, to find the balancing point. You need to keep your feet on the ground. And *I* need 10-inch nails through my bloody feet, me.'

So what Icke seems to be saying here is that last year, during the turquoise crisis . . .

'That was me going beyond the tolerance point,' he snips my question. 'The power took me over. Turquoise *is* important because it generates an important energy. But it don't mean you have to go round in it all the bloody time!'

So what Icke is *saying* is that last year he went all biffy in the head but he's not a loony anymore. Yes? The 'loony' word strikes a chord. He sits up, lunges forward in the chair, rasps:

'Hold on! I'm a loony, right? I accept that. It said it in the Sun so it *must* be true. But I'm *glad* I'm a loony because when I see what goes for *sanity* in this world, I don't *want* to be sane. I don't *want* the system's thought controllers *challenging* the system. I'm CHALLENGING the bugger! Challenging with everything I've *got*. And I haven't even started yet!'

One may have not a clue what I said Icke is going on about half the time but one must admire his passion. At the conclusion of his inflamed speech, he smiled. It's the first time he has granted himself the earthly pleasure since we met. It's a *funny* sort of smile . . .

Ringo Starr

He was The Lovable One who cracked his daft mop-top jokes for The Queen. The Fab With The Big Nose who you could take home to meet yer mum and yer dad. But no more.

RINGO, WHY DO you wear two rings on each hand?

'Because I can't fit them through my nose.'

Beethoven figures in one of your songs. What do you think of Beethoven?

'He's great. Especially his poetry.'

How did you find America?

'We went to Greenland and made a left turn.'

But that was nearly 30 years ago, innocent times when the small one – Ringo, how tall are you? 'Two feet, nine inches' – with the extended nose sat with the other three before the press of the world and cracked his mop-top jokes, playing the clown and acting the goat, The Lovable One, the one you could take home to meet yer mum and yer dad. In The Great Throne Room at Buckingham Palace, October 26, 1965, the Queen asked the 'Fabs' how long they had been together and, quick as a flash, came Starkey's reply. 'Forty years!' The wag.

It is now much later, April 1992, but that 'natural' Scouse 'wit' of olden times remains intact: The Lovable One clambers aboard a podium at London's Dorchester Hotel and drily announces: 'My name is Ringo Starr.' The assembled members of the press laugh loudly at the pithy sally; a female reporter from Belgium, in the excitement of the moment, squeaks 'Yah!' It is quite like old times . . .

We are gathered here today to hear exciting news. Ringo is about to release a new LP and it is called Time Takes Time. Furthermore, his new amusingly-named All-Starr Band – featuring Dave Edmunds and Joe Walsh and Todd Rundgren and diminutive trampoline champion Nils Lofgren – is touring Europe in the summer. Cameras clack and the PR woman sternly warns us to limit our questions to 'the present and the future' (i.e. nothing about *them* – The Beatles – and nothing about alcoholism, if you please). And so the probing begins as a girl from Sweden asks the occasional drummer why he is starting his tour in Sweden: 'Why not?' Uproarious laughter. And a girl from Italy asks him why he is finishing his tour in Italy: 'Crazy question. It may be a surprise to you, lady, but I am a musician.' Hoots. And a girl from somewhere equally foreign asks him if he is 'reaching out to the new generation' – 'You had zis Thomas Ze Tank Engine, no?' – and he says he's just playing his kit now because he is a musician and he likes to feel the 'love' flowing from an audience because it's in his blood. Somewhere along the way we learn that Ringo has absolutely no intention whatsoever of playing with George Harrison at tonight's Albert Hall concert in aid of The Natural Law Party because what Ringo's doing now is promoting his album which is really jolly good and everything so everybody should buy it . . .

Two hours later, upstairs in a hotel suite, Ringo Starr is staring at me through his darkened spectacles. The expression on his somewhat wizened face is somewhat sour. 'This record deserves to be a Number 1,' he is saying. 'It's a fine album.' The ready quips are not dropping from the lips of The Lovable One this afternoon. His impressive nose is twitching in irritation. I have made a dreadful mistake. I have dared to ask him about . . . them.

He had entered the room in seemingly stony mood. He had thrust himself down upon a sofa and had glowered. 'Is this yer first time?' he had muttered. Er, come again, Mr Starkey? 'Is this yer first time?' My first time what? My first time in a posh suite at The Dorchester Hotel or what? 'Just joking,' he had muttered bemusingly. My opening question had been designed to be one of the most psychologically challenging – nay, disturbing – ever to be posed within the context of a rock interview. It was this: Have you, Mr Starr, or have you not, felt a twinge of pity ever for Pete Best (The Good-Looking One who was booted out in favour of Ringo, of whom John Lennon was once heard to remark, 'When I feel my head start to swell, I look at Ringo and know perfectly well we're not supermen')? There was a pause containing the faintest twist of menace. 'Crazy question,' The Nice One murmured, adding a withering stare for good measure.

'Did. I. Ever. Feel. Sorry. For. Pete. Best?' Yes, that was the enquiry. 'No. Why should I? I was a better player than him. That's how I got the job. It wasn't on no personality. It was that I was a better drummer and I got the phone call. I never felt sorry for him. A lot of people have made careers out of knowing, er . . . The Beatles.'

He has said it. He has uttered that word, that thing that we are not supposed to mention because Ringo has 'moved on' and is living for today and for tomorrow and not for, in the word of his old mucker in the rhythm section, yesterday. He has said 'Beatles'. So can we talk about The Beatles, then? Ringo shrugs his shoulders. 'Sure,' he grunts. So tell me about your image. You were The Goofy One. Was this an imposed personality or was it the real Starkey or what?

'That's not how I am. That was how we were in the movie, in Help! And A Hard Day's Night. That was what people felt we were like.'

But didn't you mind always being given the goony songs to sing, Octopus's Garden and Yellow Submarine and that awful one about 'the greatest fool who ever made the big time'?

'They were writing a lot heavier songs than I was and the ones they wrote for me were never that heavy, either. That's what made the combination that we were. All completely different but together we were a mighty force.'

Presumably this 'difference' in personalities was what made the breakup of The Beatles particularly acrimonious and acid. Discuss.

'That's stupid. We'd changed. We didn't have the time to put in all that energy. We were all married then. Most of us were married. I had children. John had a kid. George got married. So it was a natural end to it. We finished. That's it.'

At the morning's press conference, Ringo had been banging on about how you can't beat the feeling of playing live, of how he's 'addicted' to it, the love teeming from the audience, the 'buzz', the 'vibe' et cetera. But if we examine the history (and leave out the Ringo Starr and his All-Star Band jaunt of '89), we see that since '66, he has played on stage hardly at all. This is not a criticism, I was just wondering whether . . .

'Look, playing live is how I started,' he snaps. 'That's where my blood is. We played live for four years as The Beatles but in the end it was impossible because the reaction we used to get was so loud that I was turning into a bad musician because I could only keep the off-beat, so we were deteriorating. How often do you want to play stadiums? We as The Beatles lost the contact. I want to feel the love from the audience and you don't get that in a stadium. Bruce Springsteen loses the love and the audience contact and Guns N' Roses and the Stones and Paul McCartney, they all lose the love and the contact. They just forget that it's a great privilege to play to an audience, so on my tour I'm playing Liverpool and I'm playing Hammersmith and . . .'

And so he goes on for several weeks about all the intimate sheds he's going to bash his drums and sing that one about 'You're sixteen and you're beautiful and your mii-iine, or whatever it is, in.

So stadiums are useless. I had always imagined, in my simplicity, that The Beatles at Shea Stadium was just one of the most thrilling moments in all of popular music history. Am I entirely incorrect?

Ringo tuts and he crosses his arms, a huff-orientated posture.

'Shea Stadium was *brilliant,*' he goes. 'We were breaking new ground. Of course it was brilliant. But if you see the video on Shea Stadium, you see how crazy we all were, anyway. John wasn't playing it note-for-note. John went mad. It was a thrill.'

Did Ringo go mad all those years ago, what with all those American girls saying he should be President and swooning at his shaking fringe?

'It wasn't only American girls, you know,' he points out, helpfully. 'It was English girls and Swedish girls. So, yeah, I went absolutely mad round about 1964. My head was just so swollen. I thought I was a God, a living God. And the other three looked at me and said, Excuse me, *I* am the God. We all went through a period of going mad.'

Presumably drugs made a major contribution to the mental mayhem.

'The drugs came later. Well, there was always some element of alcohol and amphetamine and then several other substances came into play and then The Beatles was over.'

And in '68, you all went to India to 'groove' with Mr Maharishi Mahesh Yogi. That was mad . . .

'Well, I was in hospital with my ex-wife (Maureen) delivering Jason, my second son, and I got back and there was two messages on the answerphone, a message from John and a message from George, and they were saying, We've been to see this Maharishi guy. So I said, What's that all about? So they told me how great it all was and I met Maharishi and I fell in love with Transcendental Meditation and I got to India and I took two suitcases, one full of clothes and one full of baked beans because I don't eat curry, and it was high for a while and then I thought, That's the end of it for me, thank you very much. . . '

By this time, the drummer of the Perky Personality had embarked upon his unlikely career as a screen actor, playing a gardener who has love on billiard tables in the hippy sex romp Candy (which featured Marlon Brando as a guru personage not a billion miles removed from Mr Maharishi), and then a foil for Peter Sellers in the simply awful The Magic Christian (and then being actually quite good as a Teddy boy drummer in That'll Be The Day). Ringo doesn't think that talking about his thespian pursuits is very interesting at all because he's moved on and music's the thing, like . . .

'We just decided we wanted to be an actor. I'm not interested in that acting anymore . . .'

In the mid '70s, Starr made (along with some really dud LPs) a couple of splendid pop singles: Photograph and It Don't Come Easy. The man who, in 1963, said 'whenever I hear another drummer I know I'm no good' (and who sits here today peering at me with a certain chill and insisting 'I am the best rock drummer on earth and it's not just me saying that, many fine musicians say that' when I have never even questioned his capabilities) comes over refreshingly modest for once when I say I liked those tunes.

'Well, I just decided to make some singles because The Beatles always took so long to make albums and so I started to write but I could never finish a song. I was great for two verses and a chorus but I could never finish a song so I'd have to ask George to finish it and we'd just have rows because George would always put in the "God verse" and I don't sing about God, so after a few smashes it all went downhill because, er, well, yer know . . .'

I do know. It all went downhill because Ringo was hitting the sauce with alarming abandon.

'It was my addictive personality. Suddenly you're starting to drink at nine in the morning and I was procrastinating me balls off and I was just trapped as an alcoholic, a drunk.'

He was too drunk even to pay any great attention to the shooting of John Lennon, he says.

'I wasn't well when he got murdered and I wasn't well after it. I was in such great pain that I hardly noticed . . .'

The voice of Thomas The Tank Engine and The Fat Controller was killing itself with booze. But then – hey presto! – Ringo booked into De-Tox Mansions, USA, and everything was alright again.

'One day I had a second, maybe half-a-second, of clarity and I was in so much pain and I knew that Barbara (Bach, second wife who he met on the set of the dismal Caveman film in '81) had mentioned a sort of re-hab situation. She had a problem, too. She found this place in Arizona. I haven't had a drink or a drug since and that was October '88 and I've given up smoking cigarettes, too.'

Ringo was cured of his urges by the power of love.

'It was love. It's love. And the proof of the difference in my lifestyle is that I've put a band together, I've made this album and . . .'

Ringo takes this opportunity to tell me what a great musician he is and how his new LP is really jolly good and everything until I interrupt to suggest that however good his new LP is, it can hardly hope to top Abbey Road, can it? He looks at me as if I am deranged:

'What, as an album? My album can't beat the Abbey Road album as an album?' That is, in a nutshell, what I was driving at.

'Well, the so-called B-side of Abbey Road is one of my favourite sides, the one with Bathroom Window and Polythene Pam but just by chance I was re-listening to Sgt Pepper the other day and that's a fine album too and it's a bloody marvellous album, it's a bloody fine album and The White Album was great because we were like a band after Pepper and all the craziness and Rubber Soul was great and the first album which took 12 hours to put down was an achievement . . . So I don't know what you're talking about. That was 30 years ago, man. I'm still making records and you can hear that I'm a great musician on the new record, Time Takes Time, if you can ever be bothered to mention it. This is an actually bloody *legend* in front of you. I'm not expecting you to comb the bloody legend's hair but you could mention the new LP and these other fine musicians I'm still playing with.'

Ringo Starr is close to rage and I don't know quite why. I decided to placate him by talking about his All-Starr Band. This ploy is not a success. What is it like working with Todd Rundgren, I enquire? Todd Rundgren's a bit mad, isn't he?

Ringo lunges forward in the sofa, almost doing himself a mischief.

'What? *What*? Have you met him? Why would you say shit like that? You don't even know the man. How dare you say shit like that about a friend?'

I meant 'mad' as in 'genius'. It is a compliment.

'You're talking shit. That's like saying Frank Zappa's mad. Frank Zappa's probably the nicest man I ever met in this business. I've been in the game too long for this shit! I've done my bit. I've made a record, I've made the thing and I hope it's a Number 1 because I've done my bit, I'm promoting the thing . . . or I am trying to promote the thing . . .'

What manner of umbrage is this? Ringo Starr seems to feel – and strongly – that my failure to spend this interview discussing his new LP and the brilliance of Tom Petty and Jeff 'Skunk' Baxter and Harry 'Schmilsson' Nilsson and everybody else who played on it – is impudence of the first order. But wouldn't such an interview be a trifle limiting and boring and . . .? I am unable to make this suggestion because The Clown, The Lovable One, seen here in his updated role of Pop's Mister Crosspatch, continues to rant away . . .

'If you bothered to listen to the single Weight Of The World you'd hear this line in it which goes . . . er, er . . . well, it says that you can't live in the past and that sums it up. Because you're living in the *past*. As far as this interview has been going on, it's *shit* because it's been The Beatles interview and you haven't even mentioned Time Takes Time or Weight Of The World. But that's OK. You've got the time. That's what you asked. I've answered your questions. And . . .' Ringo rises from the sofa, two feet nine inches of unbridled anger . . . 'That is *it*!' And it is. He flounces from the room, a cry of 'Thanks a lot!' that oozes with sarcasm, his cheery farewell. What this man needs, in my estimation, is a stiff drink, or a cig, or both . . .

That night, on stage at the Albert Hall, George Harrison played Taxman and a lot of other aged songs and then announced 'a blast from all our pasts' and on bounded Ringo. How could this be? Had not the man assured us earlier in the day that he would most definitely not be gracing this political rally thing with his presence? Well, there he was, anyway, and he played drums on While My Guitar Gently Weeps and Roll Over Beethoven, no doubt feeling all the love wafting up from the auditorium. Then, at the conclusion of this horrid old rock'n'roll novelty, up strode some representatives of the peculiar Natural Law Party to talk embarrassingly about this 'night of magic' that the crowd had been privileged to witness. And as the spiritual oration continued, a lone cry of protest rang out from the back of the stage, a bellow of annoyance, a sharp 'Shut up!' The culprit of this ill-mannered intrusion was identified only as a man with drumsticks and a great big nose . . .

The Chippendales

Who is this pneumatically-muscled man-thing, devoid of body hair and basted in baby oil with a pound and a half of large root vegetables crammed into his tiny cycling shorts?

B ETWIXT THE UNDERSIZED T-shirt and the outsized shorts resides Arthur's midriff. It is a magnificent midriff. A remarkable specimen: taut and glossy, full and firm, tanned and immaculate, marinated in the finest cosmetic oils of the Western World. Glistening and wondrous, a sight to behold. And somewhere above that finely-hewn navel there are the locks. Blond. Supreme. Challenging, almost. Splendid stiff-yet-flowing creation, courtesy of Nettle And Rosemary Conditioner (for 'problem' hair) and the finest LA stylist money can buy, teased to perfection through hours avec la blow-dryer.

Arthur, bronzed Adonis of the polished pectorals, is in a phone booth backstage at a Nottingham theatre. Arthur turns toward me, his eyes two blue chips of ice set amongst the squarely-chiselled facial sculpture. Arthur speaks.

'Duh . . .' is what he says.

'Duh . . .'

Sorry, come again.

'Duh . . .' says Arthur and then, warming to this theme, he elaborates. 'Duh . . . uh, ya got a, uh, pen?'

So I place a biro into the hand of Arthur and he gazes at the implement, twists it around in fingers shaped like Wall's Pork Sausages, seemingly at a loss as to what to do with it.

'Duh . . . thank you, 'ppreciate it.'

Lifting the telephone receiver, Arthur drops the pen and this calamity throws him into a state of some confusion. He sighs, he grunts, he exits the booth. 'Duh . . . the call can wait,' he decides – and with that he moves on to more urgent matters. Matters like pulling up his T-shirt to examine his nipples and adjusting his hair. Grooming and fine tuning as he goes. Arthur, you see, is a Chippendale . . .

In all my born days – and there have been several of these – I have witnessed no more pitiful spectacle than this: the Nottingham stage is athrong with blokes, 'guys' with puffy shoulders and gigantic thighs, all clad in bulgy and revealing Linford Christie-styled shorts. They are pumping their arms up and yonder, thrusting their pelvic regions in suggestive motions, as they lip-sync to a terrifying awful 'song'. 'Give me your BODY, give me your soul,' it goes (and then comes the hopeless rap bit). Yes, The Chippendales, muscle-bound gentlemen from the US of A who entertain our UK ladies with their chests and their bow-ties and their apologetic hints of genital action, are making a pop music video. They're useless. They can't dance for toffee and after each clumsily per-formed manoeuvre, they break to drink mineral water and/or gulp down a banana ('Hey! These guys are body-conscious!' the man-ager tells me with some pride. 'Bananas – hey! Bananas spell nutrition!'). The 'guys' have oily bosoms and it is a sad reflection on British society that The Chippendales – great big biceps and great big bollocks but no discernible talent whatever – have become a household name, a phenomenon of the 1990s.

Mark Smith disagrees. Mark is one of the few Chippendales I am permitted to encounter face-to-face for an interview. ('Some of the guys are more articulate than others,' says the publicity person. 'You should talk to Mark.' Because Mark knows some quite long words. Like 'motivation'.)

Mark, following video exertions, is sweating not a little; droplets trickle down his face wreaking havoc with the mascara and the browny-pink stuff upon his cheeks. He pants and he swigs Evian (water for the 'body-conscious') as I ask him this: Are The Chippen-dales completely poxy or have I got it all wrong? 'Oh, well, yeah, right, right,' goes this polite and mild-mannered 'sex object' from Tennessee. 'We get a whole lotta comments like that. They say The Chippendales is for the lower class. They say it's very crass. They say it's not very tasteful. Our show is very tasteful. The quality of talent and the quality of guys and the quality of men is very classy. So if you say The Chippendales is a crass thing, well – hey! –

Shakespeare in his time, the same thing was said about him by the established critics!'

Pardon me, modom, and blow me down with a feather. In my ignorance and in my prejudice, I had always believed that The Chippendales was simply a collection of body-building posing pouches whose public gyrations reduce audiences to raucous tipsy women on a hen night to a lather of lusty cackles. Stupidly enough, I had never realised that The Chippendales experience was, in fact, *art* . . .

In the back row of the stalls – as the video director high on enthusiasm ('There's so much oomph here, you guys!') frets on stage about camera angles and so forth – I speak to Victor Brookes, a second 'articulate' member of this chunky entourage. As he inflicts his rippling torso upon me (the entire front of his T-shirt has gone missing for some reason), Victor addresses himself to the topic 'Chippendales – crap or what?' He mulls over the question for some time. He drinks some Evian. He attends to his hair. He checks the muscles of his upper arms. Finally, he composes an answer of sorts:

'The Chippendales? Were you asking me about The Chippendales?'

Indeed.

'Yeah, see, The Chippendales . . . what you're saying here is The Chippendales is not of your kinda taste, right? You know what I say? I say I don't care what you think because the women come to The Chippendales and I take them away from their problems for an hour, maybe two hours. And those women, they're raising families and they're taking care of the husband so they need an escape and a release from their problems and I just provide that release and escape for those women whose lives are like not so nice. I give them a smile on their face before they go back to their kids and their jobs and their problems . . .'

The Chippendales: not only *art* but a *social necessity* to boot . . .

There are more than a hundred Chippendales in the world, different assemblies of giant-boned men putting on the same titillating show. They parade the beefcake and then their trousers fall off. Then if you fancy it, ladies, you can go up on stage and have a Polaroid picture taken of yourself with your fave shiny hunk! (That'll be five pounds please, Mrs and, by the by, can I interest you in a Chippendales calendar, saucy poses'n'all for a mere tenner?)

Mark: 'The Chippendales, we're the number one calendar sellers in the world. I'm sure I'm correct in saying that. The merchandise, er, they, er we sell a lot of merchandise.'

Here, 'ladies', is a Warning: 'The Chippendales is very provocative,' says Mark in hushed tones. 'Yeah, you might be a little shocked – like my mom loves the show but she has to close her eyes at some of the bits! But, see, what The Chippendales does is a high form of strip so you see the body but you don't see the *full* body, because The Chippendales like to leave an air of mystery about it.'

In other words The Chippendales keep their underpants, however scant, in place. (Swizz or blessing: discuss.)

And here, 'ladies', is a question: Why? The Chippendales, prancing buffoons, capering chests and utterly unqualified suspicions of steroid misdemeanours, make a killing, a fortune, through their pseudo-sexy antics. Why?

Mark has a (not entirely spectacular) stab at analysing the success. 'The Chippendales, we are a unique entertainment form and my theory is that Europe is a focus for these vibrant energies that we project. Hey! – the women that come to the shows, they just go crazy! It is amazing to see them in this environment. They scream, they yell, they jump up, they dance, they clap, they sing, they lose their minds and throw roses and, er, underwear. They throw knickers! I've got some bras and I've got some knickers. It's wonderful,man!'

I ask Arthur: what, pray, is the Chippendales philosophy? 'Duh . . .' he says and looks quite bemused so I rephrase the question: Why are The Chippendales such A Big Thing? He's stumped on this one too. I turn to Victor for enlightenment. Why are The Chippendales such A Big Thing, Vic?

'You are absolutely right, man! The Chippendales is a real big thing. Britain, your provincial towns, Europe. Wow!' Victor throws up his tree-trunk arms at the amazement of it all and I have to start again. The question was as follows: Why are The Chippendales such A Big Thing?

'The Chippendales? Yeah, well, I been a Chippendale for six years and The Chippendales is . . . is . . . is . . . it's life-steps, it's life-cycles, it's free enterprise, it's emphasis on health, it's working out in the gym and it's er . . . great because the whole world is becoming Americanised, er . . . you know, I preferably stay away from the married ladies because that's just a common male courtesy but . . . er . . . we're gorgeous guys, gorgeous beautiful men and who's gonna pay large sums of money to see a guy who ain't gorgeous?'

Victor forgets his self-obsession for a moment and casts his eyes on me – pallid, unshaven, shrivelled, eight-stone, crumby-teeth me. 'Shit!' he goes (then claps his hand over his mouth, presumably because he's uttered a bad word that a Chippendale is not supposed to utter). 'Er, I mean, look at you, man! There's no woman who'd pay to see you! I mean, man, don't you want to look attractive? You should go hiking, man. You should get a lifestyle!' Victor is from California and therefore has no manners. Victor, I enquire, do you never awake in a frosty sweat afore the dawn breaks thinking, 'Glitter and G-strings, what a derisory way to make a living'? Victor clearly thinks I'm potty.

'I wake up each day and I count my blessings, which is that I've got a body that women like and that I am courteous to women who are sweet girls in England except the ones who once or twice get a bit handy and grope you down there (Victor gestures towards the sensitive region of his shorts). I mean, I don't mind talking to these women, but – hey! – they should just keep their hands to themselves!'

The Chippendales were invented in 1979 in Los Angeles by a Bombay-born nightclub entrepreneur called Steve Banerjee. In the beginning all that happened was that these fellows pronged about and drunken women stuffed dollar bills into their nether-garments. But in California everybody is ridiculous so in no time at all the sleazy male strip-persons had become something of a cult. Banerjee (who has a taste for antique English furniture) gave the troupe a name, took them to New York, and then to Australia, South Africa, Hong Kong. The Chippendales became a business, a concept. Today there might be six different sets of The Chippendales cleaning up in six different countries at any time with their 'provocative' act. Imposing torsos wriggle, phallic items (here a truncheon! here a candle! here a snooker cue!) are wielded. The female spectators cry, 'Gerremoff' and raise the rafters with their salty titters and then squander the week's housekeeping on the unappealing produce in the foyer (a Chippendales clock or a Chippendales mug or a Chippendales tea towel or a Chippendales calendar) just to annoy their husbands.

'Bunch of bloody nancy boy poofters,' mutter the husbands

whenever The Chippendales are mentioned; but they, the hubbies, don't really mind about The Chippendales at all. The Chippendales are safe. The Chippendales are tame. The Chippendales retain their underpants and frequently appear on Bruce Forsyth's Generation Game. They are, in short, just a bunch of goons in a sideshow.

'Some of the guys, the husbands and the boyfriends of the women that came to see me, to see The Chippendales, feel threatened by us,' says modest Victor, shrugging his monster shoulders, 'but – hey! – I can't help it if women love us!'

The Chippendale Calendar of 1992, describes Victor thus: 'The gods of the volcano are pleased! Victor has an explosive personality and a rock hard body that give off more heat than a lava flow!'

Lumme! Jealous, gals? I am sitting right next to this rock hard human Vesuvius! 'You know,' he's saying, 'those husband guys can learn a lotta lessons from The Chippendales – like body-consciousness and eating healthy and working out in gyms. Right?' The personality is exploding all around me. Gingerly Victor pats his hair-strand-alignment and as he does so I find myself thinking God, what a bore to be a Chippendale, flexing your muscles in the looking glass and worrying about wrinkles and hair-loss possibilities every moment of the day. Preening, ever preening (not to mention talking in a fey New Age-fashioned accent).

Victor, don't you ever want to go out and get fantastically drunk, or something? Do the words 'massive-amounts-of-recreational-drugs' mean nothing to you?'

'Nah,' says Victor. 'You do drugs, man, you're not a Chippendale. You wanna see those guys, you know, one of those guys that does drugs, a drug guy who's like a rock'n'roll sorta music guy, one of those guys like . . . er . . . er . . . the drug guys in the groups, you know . . . er . . .' This sentence is causing Victor some discomfiture so I leap to his aid: What, you mean guys like Keith Richards?

'Yeah, guys like Keith Richards.'

Victor the Volcano pauses, studies his reflection in the clear plastic of his Evian bottle until I rather fear that he has mislaid the thrust of his 'argument'. Quite possibly he has forgotten my very existence. Yes? Well, what about guys like Keith Richards? I prompt. 'Yeah, right!' booms Victor. 'See, if you wanna have a great night and to be smiled at by gorgeous guys, that's The Chippendales. If you wanna see . . . er . . . Keith Richards, just go to the local supermarket or wherever it is they go.'

And now we hear the video director calling this muddle-headed Chippendale to the stage where he will engage in funky press-ups and pretend to sing the words 'Give me your BODY, give me your soul . . .' Before Victor can set about this professional task, however, he has to greet fellow Chippendales who he hasn't male-bonded with for at least 10 minutes: there's high-fives and upside-down handshakes, slapped backs and a lot of 'Hey!'s.

'You guys are beautiful!' gasps the video director. This is a most unnecessary remark: The Chippendales are very well aware of this fact already.

Mark: 'We are aware of our bodies, oh yeah, and that's a great thing to be. We are American guys, we're virile, we're young and we're exotic and we've found that your women are drawn to that. We have a lot of energy that Europeans connect to. We're American and we're good-looking so we have this starry-eyed kinda reality about things. And you British people find that charming and enchanting!'

Do we, really? Who wants to be a Chippendale? A Chippendale doesn't have much fun. A Chippendale doesn't even *drink*. 'Occasionally I go to the pub!' Mark whispers in my ear as if he's confessing to cooking human flesh thrice daily. But mustn't a Chippendale eat plenty of bananas and be an idiotic American. 'Hey, you've got an air of thinking Chippendales are dumb, right?' says Mark. 'I respect that. I understand that. But you'd be surprised because of a lot of us have degrees in many different fields, like, some in technical engineering and some in biochemistry!' (Which is all very well except that in America one only has to be able to count to 10 and tell the difference between Mickey Mouse and Goofy in a comic book to get a 'degree').

A Chippendale (if he's single and happens to be of the heterosexual persuasion) doesn't even get much backstage sex action: it's not allowed (and all the 'groupies' are out of their heads on Bailey's and Babycham anyway). A Chippendale gets no 'artistic' control, is answerable at all times to the management and its whims. 'See, The Chippendales is like working for a company,' says Mark, 'and it's a very conventional company. Like, there's a rigid diet. Like, you don't show up scruffy. Our owners try to keep us all in line.'

Our owners? This makes The Chippendales sound like a string of racehorses. Which, when one comes to think of it, is almost what they are (except that racehorses are, on the whole, better looking): the average life span of a Chippendale is three years;

when a Chippendale gets into his thirties, it's the knacker's yard. What does become of a Chippendale when his teeth no longer gleam and when his once-sturdy bosoms turn to flab, I ask Mark. 'We take them out and shoot them. When their looks go, they're useless . . .'

Up upon the stage, Arthur is attending to his shorts and fussing with his hair and attempting to master the tricky dance movements involved in The Chippendales' first ever pop video. Arthur is being called upon to wave his left arm in the air and then to wave his right arm in the air and then to stop waving his arms altogether whilst bending his knees. It's a simply baffling routine and Arthur can't get the hang of it at all.

'You see,' says Mark as he looks up at this choreographic catastrophe. 'What The Chippendales is, is we're, er . . . we're real.'

Status Quo

Their misguided denim trousers and under-inspired guitar tunes are as dependably English as fish'n'chips and the Queen Mum (gawd bless her!).

'She wears denim wherever she goes/Says she's gonna get some records by the Status Quo...'
The Concept, Teenage Fanclub, 1991.

EASING A HAND, cagily, carefully, into a pocket of the over-tight blue jeans, Francis Rossi extracts a blue plastic comb. He totters toward the dressing room mirror, pauses (comic timing), pats the head, drops the comb, delivers the punchline. 'Not fucking worth it, is it?' Get it? No? Well, you see, Francis Rossi (despite sporting the ponytail that time and fashion forgot) has scarcely any hair on top but this doesn't matter, because if you're in Status Quo you're supposed to be all creaky and grizzled; you're supposed to be of the balding tendency. If you're in Status Quo you're still playing your heads-down-no-nonsense-mindless-boogie-con-legs-splayed-in-trim-fit-denim even though you're over 40 and, consequently, old enough to know better. This is the quip. This is why all Britain holds the Quo in such affection. This is why when Rossi sits down upon a chair in his dressing room, he does it slowly and gingerly like a codger whilst (humorous bonus) making a farty sound with his lips (flatulent codger). And then, in case you'd forgotten that even though the Quo are ancient they're still 'lads' and, er, 'diamond geezers' all at the same time, comes an inevitable and negligible Knob Joke, at which everybody in the room – the management people and the equipment people and the sundries – endeavours to cackle as loudly as possible.

Crikey, 20,000 years at the top, I say, attempting to open an interview amidst dressing room japery. Er, 20,000 years at the top: this must make you feel all sort of, um, 20,000 years at the topish. Rick Parfitt – the other 'proper' Quo – looks at me all furrowed brow and gravity.

'I think,' he corrects me, 'I think you mean 26 years, don't you? Not 20,000.'

'Get down deeper and down/Down down deeper and down/Down down deeper and down/Get down deeper and down' Down Down, Status Quo, 1974.

At the ice-rink, Ryde, Isle of Wight, hard-core Status Quo fanciers – teenaged softies with wavy hair and wonky spectacles and distressed denim jackets festooned with sew-on patches that say Extreme and Bon Jovi: Slippery When Wet and Status Quo – are gathered by the foot of the stage. Behind these throng other examples of the Quo Public. It takes all sorts. There are women in white high-heels sipping yellowish cocktails out of plastic beakers, there are thick-necked bruisers with failed moustaches and shell suits eyeing said women up; there are kiddy-winks of the Nintendo generation hand-in-hand with grandmothers togged up in sequin-fronted jerseys for the beanfeast; there are couples of middle years in their Sunday Asda-shopping-expedition best. There are sorts who look like gangsters and sorts who look like wets. The appeal of Status Quo knows no barriers. Status Quo, they're the ones who strummed for Prince Charles in their waistcoats and for charity and they're 'down-to-earth' and 'just-like-us'.

And they don't even take drugs anymore, bless 'em . . .

Rick Parfitt is attempting to conjure up a memory but he's not doing very well, so he turns to Rossi for assistance.

'You remember. '78 or '79. The guy was called Brian and we were in LA and we got into coke. There was a party in the hills and he offered us a line. It was Brian whatsiname, remember?'

Rossi: 'Robertson?'

Parfitt: 'No. Brian. Him with the glasses, you know?'

Rossi: 'Brian?'

Parfitt: '*No*. Brian. Brian, you know, the one . . .'

Rossi: 'Oh, that Brian. Yeah. Ur, I don't know what you're talking about.'

In simple conversation they do make an acceptable double act. And Roy Hudd complains that music hall is dead.

Parfitt: 'Yeah, anyway, so Brian got some toot out and so we thought we'll have a go at this and we had a line each and then we went outside and sat in a car and said to each other, Is anything happening to you, yet? No, nothing's happening. So we thought, Well, we're not bothered with drugs, then, that's great! But then six months later . . .'

Six months later, the drug was sampled again and, alas, this time it seemed to do the trick. Hooked. While Rossi murmurs assent to a tale of woe, Parfitt, like reformed 'fiends' are wont to do, embarks upon a lengthy thesis called Drugs Aren't A Very Good Idea, On The Whole. 'Blah blah,' he goes. '. . . vicious circle . . . blah blah . . . horrible spiral . . . blah blah . . . vicious, er, spiral . . .' He was on the stuff for 10 years.

'I needed a toot just to get into the shower' – and, oh dear – '10 years is a lot of dough and it's a lot of brain cells and it's a lot of shit been talked. I spent four hours one night just trying to teach Francis how to shake hands with people properly. Remember?'

Rossi: 'Yeah . . . I'm going to tell Tom about the pen.'

Parfitt: 'No. No, don't tell him that . . . Er, Francis gave up on the coke before I did, though, didn't you?'

Rossi: 'Yeah . . . but I got a good party trick out of the coke. Because my septum's gone and my nose doesn't work properly anymore, I can put cotton bud up one nostril and it goes up and I pull it out the other side.'

If only I had a Q Tip about my person I could ask Rossi to demonstrate this remarkable nasal feat.

Status Quo in the early '80s were, says Parfitt, 'smashed on gear and booze. But the band just got bigger because, in all truth, we never did coke on stage.' Francis Rossi, with the gesture of a contrite schoolchild about to confess to mischief behind the bike sheds, puts his hand in the air and says, 'Ur, I did. I did coke on stage.'

Parfitt seems disappointed. 'What? You never told me! I knew you went out on booze – but not coked up. Did you?'

'Oh, yeah,' says Rossi. 'I did. I just thought, Fuck this. It's rock'n'roll. Rock'n'roll sounds marvellous when you're pissed and coked up. You think you're fucking wonderful. And nobody dares tell you that you're crap.'

I am longing to tell Status Quo that they're crap because they haven't made a decent record since Whatever You Want but I can't get a word in edgeways.

Rossi: 'I'm going to tell Tom about the pen. I am. Ha ha. I was staying at Rick's house and we'd been in the studio and doing a lot of coke and he came down one morning and he looked like death and he said, Oh man, my fucking nose, for fuck's sake, my nose hurts. And then – dunk! – out his nose comes the centre piece of the pen we'd been snorting through. It had been up his nose all night. Ha ha ha!'

This unseemly anecdote has sunk Parfitt into a dark frame. 'It wasn't the centre piece of the pen,' he grumbles. 'It was the bit on the end where the actual ball-point is.'

'When I look up to the sky I see your eyes a funny kind of yellow'
Pictures Of Matchstick Men, Status Quo, 1968.

In March 1968, Esther and Abi Ofarim were Number 1 in the British Hit Parade with the bewildering Cinderella Rockafella and Status Quo were at Number 7 with Pictures Of Matchstick Men, a grand example of English pop psychedelia. Pictures Of Matchstick Men – the best thing the group ever did (if you don't count We Ain't Got Nothin' Yet, recorded when they were still called The Spectres) – never features in a Status Quo live set. Just like Spinal Tap, who never like to be reminded of their 'flower power' period, Status Quo are ashamed of their flitty beginnings.

'We were a plastic-haired bunch of pop stars,' says Rossi, stressing 'pop stars' as if it were an alternative term for 'neo-Nazi-pederast-calamity-misfits' or something worse. 'We'd been on the telly so we were . . . pop stars.'

'We didn't know what we were, really,' says Parfitt. 'We didn't really know how to dress, so we dressed like everybody else did, with bell bottoms, flares that were about 14 feet across, and frilly shirts and the business. We must have looked like a couple of poofs.'

Rossi wrote that first hit sitting on his lavatory.

'I was on the bog because I couldn't get away from the wife at the time. I'd only just got married and I moved in with the mother-in-law and the wife – ex-wife now – in this prefab in East Dulwich and the best place to get away from them was in the bog. But it was tricky because those prefabs had narrow bogs. You had to sit like that. (There's a mincing-buttock-mime here to the accompaniment of appreciative laughter from Parfitt.) So I went to the bog and I sat like that and I started writing this song and then the mother-in-law and the wife went out so I went into the lounge and started on the lyrics and then they came back so I went back in the bog. It was my favourite room in the house. So I wrote all the lyrics in there and it was easy because it was just dream-sequency . . . anything that comes into your fucking head that sounds stupid.

'I just wrote this thing that sounded slightly "pissed-adelic": I didn't know what they were going on about when they were talking about "psychedelic", all those hippies and people back then. The closest I knew that "psychedelic" meant was when you went to gigs at college they'd put up coloured gels (*blobby "light shows"*) that moved around and made you sick all over the fucking place. And Marsha Hunt would always be there. So, anyway, I'm just in the bog going, *When I look up to the sky* – fine – *I see your eyes a funny kind of yellow* – that's fine. That'll do.'

One must give them this: Status Quo have a refreshingly honest approach to the art of lyric-writing. There will be no Bernie Taupin-styled coffee-table books of so-called 'poetry' from these geezers, no Lou Reed-type 'analyses' in the posh Sundays.

Rossi: 'When we got big and famous, there were all these critics saying Status Quo's lyrics are meaningless but I agreed because as far as I know our lyrics mean nothing. *Down down deeper and down.* What's that mean? Fuck knows. But then you hit Australia and they say, "Phwoarrr, down down, eh, I know what you mean, mate!" because they think it's all about sex. Same with Roll Over Lay Down: everybody thinks that's totally sex – "Woooargh, you crafty devil, you!" – but it's not sex at all, it's just the opposite because it comes from my ex-wife. I'd come home and if she had the hump, she'd be sleeping on my side of the bed so I'd have to wake her up to get in so I'd say, Roll over.'

This discursion upon The Imagery of The Quo Lyric proves so fascinating that I find myself asking Rick Parfitt how he came to 'pen' Mystery Song – the one that goes: *'The boys know what you're giving/You give the boys such a lot of fun/dum-di-dum-di-dum-something/You really got me going, baby/Baby can you give me a price?'*

'I've no idea,' he replies. 'All I remember about that was I was doing some sort of drugs at the time. I don't remember what sort of drugs they were.'

Rossi: 'Hang on, I'd given you some speed that morning, remember?'

Parfitt: 'Oh, that's right, yeah. We were in the studio and I was feeling a bit rough because I'd been out the night before so you said to me, Come to the toilet with me, and we went into the bog and I'd never done speed before but you gave me some speed.'

Rossi: 'Sulphate.'

Parfitt: 'Sulphate, yeah, and I thought, This is great!'

Rossi: 'We left you at midnight sat on a stool and we came back in the next morning and you were still on the stool with the guitar writing your fucking song. And the reason it's called Mystery Song is you couldn't remember what you'd called it in the fucking first place.'

Parfitt: 'Yeah. Right. But what happened was you spiked me, Francis, mate, and the speed was great so I put these chords together and done these lyrics about this girl I was supposed to have known who Francis knows who she is but I don't.'

Rossie: 'What the fuck are you talking about?'

Parfitt: 'Basically, the song is about a prostitute. I don't know who she was – but you don't when you're on drugs, do you?'

They are not very ideologically sound, the Quo, are they, readers? Their attitude to women (particularly ex-wives) is hardly New Man, they use words like 'poof' and 'wop' with no blink of realisation that it might give offence (though 'wop' is alright because Francis Rossi comes from an Italian ice-cream family).

They did their very first protest song only recently: In The Army Now. How did it go? *'Smiling faces as you wait to land/But once you get there no-one gives a damn/You're in the army now, oh-wow-oh . . .'* Brilliantly observed polemic or not, there is little point in being in Status Quo if you're of the protest persuasion: Quo and rebellion, just like oil and water and blood and bleach, simply do not mix.

Rossi: 'You're right. I'm 43 years old so I'd be pretending if I said I'm 20 years old and I'm an angry young man, wouldn't I?'

Parfitt: 'Yeah, that's right, because the other night there was this woman in the audience and she was amazing and she had a warm glow about her and she was really old, like 70 or 80, and I find it much easier to smile at people like that than I do at regular Quo fans. I find it a pleasure and a privilege smiling at an old lady like that.' Even a Jimmy Tarbuck-type, or one of Tarby's golfing-Sunshine-Variety-bus-chums, might wince at this onslaught of 'sincerity'. Rossi, at least, has the common decency to place his head in his hands and mutter, 'Christ . . .'

In the late '60s, they'd go on stage in their Carnaby Street kaftan togs – the 'poof' clobber – only to find that the dolly birds would 'scream a darn sight louder for Amen Corner or the Love Affair or Marmalade than they did for us.' So they discovered gym shoes and denim and long hair and a dumb method of nodding the head and a kind of boogie music that Rick Parfitt eloquently describes thus: 'Durm-durm-durm-durm-durm. It's a sort of shuffle rhythm. There's something horny about it. You can stand there all night going durm-durm-durm-durm-durm, can't you?' 'Yeah,' agrees Rossi, 'that's how we became boring.' Durm-durm-durm-durm-durm and they never looked back.

They pioneered the hard rock/HM denim look. (In 1975 there was even a Quo brand of denim clobber available in the shops. Rossi: 'There was Quo jeans and Quo jackets and it was all in C&A and Woolworths and places like that. It was stuff no-one would buy – wash it once and it went green. There's only one guy who ever bought it – a guy who's actually changed his name to Status Quo. He's got "Status Quo" tattooed on his neck and he's changed his name by deed poll. Status Quo. That's his name. He is Mr Quo and his friends call him Status . . .') They murdered John Fogerty's Rockin' All Over The World and popularised the lame boogie (durm-durm) and they became a National Institution. They are like Marmite and they are like the ravens at the Tower of London. Like the Queen Mum and Cliff. They are just there and not an ounce of harm in them . . . yes, they are rubbish, aren't they, Status Quo?

'I've always liked Jim Reeves,' says Rick Parfitt (apropos, seemingly, of nothing). 'What I mean is we've never been the world's most fashionable band and our image has gone boring over the years with the jeans and stuff like that but I think that's gone in our favour. That's why we are what you said – The Queen Mum.'

'When we did Live Aid,' says Francis Rossi (apropos, seemingly, of less), 'we were the only band on that bill not to have product out. Everybody else on that show had product to promote. And I thought Hang on, I thought we were doing this for charity! And that's Quo, right?'

Outside in the cold of the skating rink auditorium, the people shuffle to music rasping from the PA (Survivor's Eye Of The Tiger, mostly) as they wait for the evening's main feature. Any moment now there'll be these blokes up on the stage hopping about in plimsolls for an hour or so, shaking their manes to their pub-rock stuff. One of them (Rossi) will shout 'Shit!' very loudly into the microphone and the people will cheer the naughty slice of wit.

Durm-durm-durm-durm-durm. Status Quo: the band that became a parody of itself.

'Yeah, it's right what you said about Quo,' Francis Rossi is telling me minutes before showtime. 'We're the Queen Mum. That's fine. I like the Queen Mum, me, so what if people say we're boring and only do three chords? There's no point in getting hung up about it.'

Rossi and Parfitt nod their wise old heads in unison.

'But sometimes,' says Rossi, 'sometimes, like when Marguerita Time came out, I was really desperate for that song to prove a point, although I don't know what the point I wanted to prove was . . . but I was listening to Capital Radio and they had that comedian on, that Richard Digance, and he played Marguerita Time and he said, Great to hear from them again, same old bleeding three chords. But there's two or three minors there in that song. If you're going to be totally honest, Marguerita is actually a six-chord track.'

Rossi is becoming quite heated here. Gone is the tiresome tom-foolery of farty lips as he defends the National Heritage that is Quo. 'Like, I always used to get laughed at when I was young because I was brought up with Italians and every wop in the world sings opera. I grew up with that. I'm not ashamed of it. And take Nessun Dorma, the basis of the choral section of that has three chords, La Donna E Mobile, the basic section of it that everybody knows also has three chords. Verdi and Beethoven – quite a lot of that stuff is just three chords. So . . . so . . .'

'Um, yeah,' says Rick Parfitt, leaping to his colleague's crumbling defence. 'And . . . Whatever You Want has *five* chords.'

Rolf Harris

He single-handedly invented everything: world music! The synthesizer! The protest song! The Beatles! Mawkish ditties about little boys!

A FORKFUL OF what those of the Australian persuasion are pleased to call 'tucker' (in this case school-dinners-styled spaghetti bolognaise) is lurking close by the mouth of the Australian celebrity. But it can't go in. The mouth – can't you see? – it is all a-tremble. Perhaps it's the battle's noise. The lips and the greying beard of the most famous Antipodean that ever there was (until they invented Kylie) are quivering; the eyes, eyes so accustomed to twinkling and sprouting feigned delight behind the thick-framed spectacles on your telly, have gone faraway and moist and misty. With the 'tears of a clown'. Rolf Harris drops the fork, and with it the spaghetti. Rolf Harris is blubbing.

And all I ever said was Two Little Boys . . .

Two Little Boys, that extraordinary example of the pop musician's art, that mawkish thing of sentiment – 'Two litt-el boys had two litt-el toys, each had a wood-en *horse*' – a plodding nonsense to irk even the most idle of brains, the Rolf Harris superhit that spanned two decades (it was that last Number 1 of the 1960s and the first of the 1970s). All I ever said was Rolf, old thing, dear chap, let's face it, Two Little Boys is the worst record ever made, isn't it? And as he sat there in a record company conference suite, twiddling fork in a mound of pasta, his eyes, at first startled by the affront, went foggy.

First there is the scoundrel's defence: 'I don't know about the *worst* record ever made,' he went in that familiar Australian twang. 'It was one of the *best-selling* ever made. It sold 90,000 copies in seven bloody weeks, which by today's standards would be about a triple bloody platinum or bloody something.'

Then there's the mitigation: 'It was a song that got to so many different people on different levels. Little kids loved the story and they sort of quietened down when they heard the story. And women loved it because it made them cry and made them emotional. And men liked it because it was a good marching tune and it said a lot about companionship and comradeship between blokes. It's a marvellous yarn. When I first heard it, the writer sang it to me and at first I thought, Oh, shit, what am I going to say to him, it's such a namby-pamby bloody dreadful song? But then he got to the *Did you think I would leave you crying?* bit and all the bloody hair on the back of my neck went up and all the muscles in my scalp went *ooargh* and goose pimples went right up my arms and shoulders. It had that effect on me for months. Every time I sang it, I would be close to tears.'

Rolf Harris, the most famous Australian in the world (if you don't count tiny Kylie or the notorious heterosexual Jason Donovan) is close to tears.

And, finally, he throws himself on the mercy of the court: 'Much later, my auntie said to me that Two Little Boys was the story of my father and his brother, my uncle Carl, in the First World War . . .' There follows an interminable story about Rolf's father and Rolf's uncle on the battlefield years ago; the father was wounded and the uncle died. And Rolf Harris is blubbing.

But hold on a trice. Rolf Harris, as we have seen, comes from Australia, home of the funnel-web spider and the macho man, where Big Boys just *do not cry.*

'You're right,' says Rolf, removing his spectacles and rubbing the lenses with a paper serviette as he composes himself. 'You're right. If you cry in Australia, it's like, Is he poof or some bloody thing? That's why I never considered myself as a singer. I was embarrassed about showing any emotion. Coming from Australia it's like "Boys don't cry" and all that bloody crap. That's what you're brought up with in Australia. So when I hear American lyrics where the fella sings "I'm gonna cry" or some bloody thing like that, I go hot and cold with embarrassment. There's a man saying he's going to cry – you just shiver with embarrassment. It's a funny old hang-up that I've always had. That's why I've never had the courage to put myself forward as a singer. I'm just a novelty-type guy doing weirdo bloody comedy. I'm bloody sorry that I have done that, limited myself to being a weirdo weirdo comedy bloody bloke, you know?'

Indeed. It has been a mighty long way down rock'n'roll for this king of the didgeridoo (oversized wooden pipe that makes a ghastly drone when you puff down it) and the wobbleboard (annoying percussion 'instrument'), this purveyor of fine art and thick-paste doodles of Tweety Pie and sundry untoward cartoony fauna, this veritable 'weirdo weirdo', Rolf Harris OBE.

He was born in Perth 63 years ago. He was good at swimming, won the junior backstroke championship of Australia when he was 15 (the achievement of which he remains most proud, he tells me). In 1952 he arrived in Britain to attend art school; he auditioned for BBC TV, upon which he did drawings and told daft yarns for the kiddies. In 1960 he made his first record, Tie Me Kangaroo Down Sport. A hit! Then, in 1962, came the didgeridoo-driven, Aboriginal swerve of Sun Arise which, preposterously enough, reached Number 3 in 1962. Rolf Harris (despite unlikely beard) was a pop star and, single-handedly, he had invented World Music.

'I invented world music?' he replies, his eyebrows shooting up in the quizzical style familiar to all devotees of his fabulous television extravaganzas. 'Well, I don't know about that,' he says, eyebrows furrowing now as he tackles the impish suggestion with a certain gravitas and lack of humility. 'I suppose, in a way, I did. I pioneered world music, certainly. You see, I've been fascinated by the didgeridoo from the time I first heard it. I just find it a most haunting and primitive, primal thing which seems to go through your gut. It's a very safe, secure thing which all primitive people have that doooorrrmmmoorrrdrrrm (with pursed lips, he imitates the irksome hum of the didgeridoo). The Tibetans stand in a circle and do that powerful humming thing which becomes a trance-inducing thing where all these people go hurrrummmmmmmmm. They go off into another world and it's wonderful. Hurrrummmmmmmm.'

As he hurrrummmms, Rolf Harris goes off into another world. It is wonderful . . .

When Rolf Harris was a pop star in the early 1960s, he had this song called Someone's Pinched Me Winkles, a novel stupidity all about winklepicker shoes, a regular crowd-pleaser. I remember it well because my older brother thought it was really funny. I mention it, just as a side issue, for amusement value. Rolf takes the bait. Rolf is angry.

'Yeah, well I wrote that as a result of Charlie Drake (diminutive and irritating 'funnyman' of yesteryear upon whom Mick Hucknall out of Simply Red based his entire image) having a big hit with that song My Boomerang Won't Come Back. I was outraged that he should mock the Aborigines to such an extent with so many bloody false bits of information in the bloody song. I got really uptight about that and so I went away and wrote a Cockney song with as many bloody false bits of information in it as I could, as a sort of protest.'

Rolf Harris, Protest singer. Yet another feather in the already feather-festooned cap.

Rolf Harris. Pop star. Too old at 33 for such larks, and really too hirsute, he went on the road in those funny 1960s.

'It opened my eyes up!' he exclaims, opening his eyes up to show me what it looks like when someone has his eyes opened up. 'Jeez! Bloody hell. It opened my eyes up, I tell you that! I was on a Larry Parnes (wonky old manager/promoter) with Joe Brown And The Bruvvers and Eden Kane and, er, Telstar was on it, you know, The Tornados with Clem Cattini on drums and Heinz, the blond, er, and there was that bloody bloke who changed his name to Alvin Stardust. What was his name? Shane Fenton. His real name was Bernard Jewry. And so Shane was on it and I travelled with him all the time and he had this big driver called Eddie Falcoln and I'd never seen violence before, because my dad was the most pacifist guy, so when I did see violence I was appalled. We'd come into a town and all the local boys would be up in arms against all these pop stars because all the local girls would be flocking around them and this guy Eddie Falcoln used to travel with an iron bar down his coat sleeve and if there was any trouble, that bar would come out, I can bloody tell you! I was appalled! But I did have one funny experience on that tour because we were doing a bloody dance hall in Epsom and I did my spot and I came off the stage absolutely disgusted! And I said to the promoter, Never again! There were young kids out there drunk! Youngsters of 12-years-old drunk out of their heads and they were smoking cigars. This is absolutely disgusting. And the promoter said to me, What do you mean, young kids? They're jockeys! Cor, what a shock that was!'

Rolf Harris laughs at his winning joke. I feel sure that we have heard it before, from somebody else. Les Dawson perhaps. It doesn't matter.

Did Rolf ever 'do' drugs in his rockin' days, one wonders? Thought not.

'I never did. I still never have. I've seen marijuana smoked a couple of times. Had a row with one of my band for smoking marijuana, got really choked with him because marijuana doesn't seem to fit in with my image at all.'

Rolf's early singles were produced by George Martin and so he met The Beatles but The Beatles failed to 'turn him on'.

'Nah. They didn't have much to do with me, really.'

In 1963, Rolf was accorded the honour of compèring The Beatles' Christmas Show at the Finsbury Astoria. He even gets mentioned (sort of) in Albert Goldman's stupid book The Lives Of John Lennon: 'A helicopter descends upon the pad, and out climbs the MC, Ralph (*sic*) Harris . . . By now every seat would be soaking wet.'

Well!

'George Martin finished up having to drop me for The Beatles when they became famous,' recalls 'Ralph'. If not for that calamity, I say in jest, you could have been bigger than The Beatles, perhaps? Rolf fails to see the funny side, decides to answer the question in all seriousness.

'Well, er, no I don't think . . . er, I never had that common touch that The Beatles had. Like I mean, *It's been a hard day's night/ And I've been working like a dog*. Oh, shit, that's wonderful, that's magic and Yesterday. *Suddenly I'm not half the man I used to be/ Now a shadow's looming over me* or whatever the bloody words are. Exquisite. But The Beatles mucked about with me. At that Christmas show, they stood off in the wings with a microphone and made silly comments during one of my songs one night and I came storming off the stage and shouted, Get some bloody professionalism into you! Jesus! You don't muck around with somebody else's act! Don't ever bloody do that again! I was so angry. And after that they didn't bloody do it again, I can tell you!'

He ponders the memory, the wonder of it all.

'Cor,' he says, regarding the ceiling. 'Cor, just think of all the things I've done in my time.'

Indeed. Just think . . .

In 1967 on his BBC TV The Rolf Harris Show (a variety fest which introduced the amazing dancing legs of The New Generation to the world), he pioneered the vexatious new musical instrument known as the Stylophone (you played it with a knitting needle and it made a nasty buzzing noise: see David Bowie's Space Oddity for the aural proof).

'This guy invented the machine and brought it to my show's producer and said, I've got this great new electronic organ. It was the first of its kind. It was the forerunner of all the synthesizers and bloody keyboard things and we used it quite a bit on my show. I think (*Rolf twiddles his thumb and forefinger together to indicate the rustling of money*), I think there was a bit of that, you know.'

What? Payola? Surely not!

'Oh, I should think there must have been because we used the bloody thing all the time. But, er, don't say anything about that. I don't know anything about that. Actually, the Stylophone didn't have a very pleasing sound. It was likened by some bloke to a demented bee trapped in a bloody bottle.'

Rolf puts his lips together and goes buzz in imitation of a demented bee trapped in a bloody bottle.

In 1974, he saved lots of nippers from drowning through a series of jaunty, safety-conscious telly commercials set in a swimming pool.

'I nearly got drowned making that bloody commercial because all the bloody kids were mucking around and crawling all over me and they had me underwater and were holding me down and all of a sudden I thought, Oh, shit, I'm going to drown me bloody self so I'm going to have to thump one of these kids. I'm actually going to have to whack one of them really bloody hard. Scared the shit out of me.'

His speedily-executed works of art have been seen by millions upon the television screen. In a recent survey, when 1,000 Londoners were asked to name a painter, 38 per cent said 'Rolf Harris'. He was streets ahead of Goya or Turner or anybody good.

'It's amazing, isn't it? It's the power of television. I mean, did Rembrandt do any paintings on television? He probably didn't. But you see art galleries have got a little bit of an elitist feel about them, whereas people can look at me painting from scratch, from a blank canvas, and they go, Oh, wow! and it helps them to understand the finished process and it encourages them.'

His latest weirdo weirdo comedy wheeze is a peculiar version of Led Zeppelin's Stairway To Heaven, complete with wobbleboard and amusing asides like *Oh, and it makes me wonder. How does it grab you blokes?*

'I haven't met anybody who's said they hated it yet. I met a few Led Zeppelin fans who came to see my pantomime (Cinderella in Bath: Rolf as Buttons) and they said they liked my version. I don't feel good about heavy volume stuff but those blokes that wrote that song, well, they're probably laughing all the way to the bloody bank because they were the writers so they're copping bloody royalties on it.'

In the 1970s, after the horror of Two Little Boys, Rolf Harris became one of Britain's most derided public figures. He was the Jeremy Beadle of that decade. His was the name to mention if you wanted to score a cheap laugh. Rolf remembers.

'Yeah, well, I guess that's because I wasn't doing anything very new in the '70s. I stayed doing the same weirdie bloody things and there wasn't much new creativity happening there. I was a sort of bloody joke to a lot of people and some of those comments hurt. But what really hurt was Australian people saying, Oh, he's nothing more nor less than a professional Australian. That is regarded as being a really heavy knock in Australia. When I had that enormous hit with Kangaroo (i.e. Tie Me Kangaroo Down Sport), that was the first genuine Australian accent-type song that had ever happened. What's wrong with that? Seemed a bloody good thing to me.'

Nowadays, of course, Rolf, close to pensionable age, is someone we all love, is he not? Laugh and we all laugh with him, et cetera. The kind of student who had made a cult of ancient telly naff like Stingray and other puppet-y idiocies, simply revels in Rolf. And Rolf simply revels in this (misguided) admiration.

'The cult thing is amazing!' he says, an indulgent gash of toothy white splitting his greying beard. 'A couple of years ago I had a letter from Warwick University where these blokes had said that they didn't want their recreation room called after a political activist who had been jailed for life in South Africa for murder as an anti-apartheid provocateur so they wanted to change the name to The Rolf Harris Room. And they held a meeting to vote on it and 95 per cent of the students union voted for The Rolf Harris Room. That was magic! I went up there and presented a painting of me as a kangaroo and I entertained them with every song I'd ever thought of singing with no musical accompaniment and all these great big strapping youngsters were joining in because Two Little Boys was the first record they remembered. And then I signed autographs for about two and a half bloody hours. The queue was just going on forever. I was absolutely shattered but it's a lovely feeling. And there's a group in Harlow. Whenever I go within range of Harlow they turn up and they all wear beards and glasses and paintbrushes and pieces of hardboard . . .'

You don't suspect that such people might actually be taking the piss, Rolf?

'No way!' he rasps, horrified at the prospect. 'No, they're just ordinary youngsters, just real enthusiasts about what I do. They're there to help. It goes on all over the place. These people respect me, you see.'

So how does Rolf analyse his enormous appeal?

'Well, it's bloody simple, really. It's because I've been honest with people through all my career. I've never conned anybody. I've never done the Jeremy Beadle thing of chopping the tree down from under my people. I think people appreciate being treated as people. And like, with the Queen, when she pinned on my OBE, she discussed my career with me with such knowledge about what I was doing, it was *unbelievable*! She knew the whole history of my career. It was bloody amazing!'

So there we have it. The singin' scribbler tugs at his grizzled goatee, whether to remove all traces of bolognaise or to muse about matters of import is unclear. He removes his famous spectacles once more and gives them a deliberate polish. He has something more to say.

'You know,' he says very softly, 'I have this terrible need to be praised all the time. With everything I do. I need that praise. I'm always saying, What do you think of that? Hoping someone will say, That is good . . . I don't know.' Rolf sighs. 'I really don't bloody know. When my dad passed away, I had this awful feeling of, Who am I doing all this for, now? Who can I show all this great achievement to? It's an awful feeling.'

Once more Rolf Harris's eyes are brimming over . . .

Dennis Potter

Not content with having been crowned Arch Perv Of The Arts and Britain's Most Disgusting Voyeur, he is now a contender for the title of The World's Rudest Man.

WITH A DISEASED hand, the dramatist gestures towards the window, towards the BBC Television Centre premises outside. 'Look,' he says, in a voice almost cracking with elements of despair. 'Look! Fuckers. Fucking fuck them. Fuck off.' What, pray, is wrong with the dear old BBC? the interviewer enquires. But when you are Dennis Potter, the dramatist, you don't actually respond to questions of such a simple-minded nature as that. When you are Dennis Potter, you simply sigh and slowly shake your head and take another glug of your red wine and sigh again yet more slowly than before and go, 'Why do we bother? Why the fucking hell are you here doing this? You know, you're going to fucking die, right? So what's the point then? Why do we go through this fucking charade? Why don't we just sit down under a tree, cross our legs and wait for death? Because we know it's coming. We know we are going to decline. We know we are ill. So why do we bother?'

Yes, he's a cheerful cove, this playwright of some 58 summers, hurtling onward to dotage with a smile and a quip ever on his lips. A late afternoon's audience with the 'controversial' figure begins with merry greeting: 'I know what you're going to ask me and you know what I'm going to say, so why don't you just fuck off now? You see, the more interviews go on ... I mean, after the press showing of Blackeyes (Potter series universally condemned as the work of a voyeur, pervert and bore) this woman from the Sun came up and said, Do you have anything to say? And I said, Yes, fuck off. I mean, I wouldn't ask you into my house, I wouldn't permit you, I don't want to talk to you. So I'm an arrogant fucker. But I'm entitled to be, aren't I?'

It is not until he sees my packet of Marlboro, notices I share his enthusiastic smoking habit, that an inkling of acceptance crosses his clever mind. Before him, Potter has two packets of Rothmans and, like a nicotine evangelist, attempts to convert me to his brand. 'I used to smoke Marlboro,' he says, 'but if you look at the nicotine content of Rothmans, it's slightly higher. By point two of a milligram.'

And when I light my first cigarette of the interview using not a lighter but a trusty old Bryant & May matchstick, the grump actually deigns to smile. 'Oh! I love a man who lights a cigarette with a match! It takes me plunging back into my past . . .'

The past is all coal-mining kin and bullies in the schoolyard and codgers and their rustic dialects – 'How bist thou, butty?' – and black-faced blokes in caps lighting fags off the end of other fags or Swan Vestas, probably. The past is a place Potter returns to often in his writing and his conversation, too.

'I used to smoke roll-ups. Golden Virginia. But I can't do that now.'

The past, a trifle of misty-eyed nostalgia, a slice of ideological waywardness (smoking is bad), the predicament – as is well-known, he suffers from the crippling illness of the skin, psoriatic arthropathy – Dennis Potter all wrapped up in one brief statement. So that's alright, then. I think I will 'fuck off' now and leave the Q design team to fill up the space with artistic pictures of Gemma Craven with lipstick on her nipples in Pennies from Heaven or Joanne Whalley rubbing suggestive sticky all over Michael Gambon's private parts in The Singing Detective or Gina Bellman with clothes mysteriously falling off in Blackeyes or Gina Bellman with clothes falling off (again! encore! author!) in Secret Friends or Sting doing a rape thing in Brimstone and Treacle. But I don't 'fuck off'. Dennis Potter, the dramatist, has not quite finished with me yet.

'If you talk about my family, I will kill you,' he says.

'You little shit. The secret in life is not to trust anyone,' he says.

'I am not blessed with great patience. So fuck off,' he says.

Apart from the earlier question about the BBC, I haven't said anything yet. 'Words, words, words, what do they mean? As you can see, I had quite a lot of wine at lunch. I'm already on my way, slurring my words. You little shit,' he says.

Oh, don't worry about that, I pipe. Why, I myself had a pint of cider at lunchtime. This attempt at coaxing some semblance of jocularity from Mister Misery proves to be a pathetic failure. With a poorly hand, he hits the table and turns ferocious.

'Oh, shit! If there's one thing I hate, it's people who drink cider! Oh, for God's sake, why don't you just die?'

Excuse me, Mr Potter, I squeak with some indignation, but I don't think that's a very nice thing to say.

'Oh, you're so fucking polite,' rails my tormentor. 'You're like those polite people with bad teeth in a railway carriage . . . I'm not being hostile.'

Are you sure about this?

'Why don't you just tell me to fuck off?'

Right. Fuck off, Mr Potter. Sir.

'You see? I should have been a preacher, shouldn't I? God forbid. What do you think? Look, you're supposed to be interviewing me you little shit!'

I would much like to be interviewing Dennis Potter but he just will not allow me to begin.

'What do you fucking want to know? I think of God as a fat, black woman with a terribly amiable disposition under a tree. But what would be the point of proving the existence of God?' He sips gingerly from a beaker. 'And this wine is absolutely foul!'

What a crosspatch. What a surly old git. As a matter of fact, I think Dennis Potter is bloody great and that Lipstick On Your Collar, his latest small-screen experience – the office tedium, the clumsy sex, Roy Hudd's Dennis Potter-like spectacles and an Anthony Eden figure miming Carl Perkins's Blue Suede Shoes to a pair of blue suede shoes in the Houses of Parliament – is easily the best thing on the telly since GBH. But there is no point at all in saying things like that to Potter. He'll condemn you as an apologetic weed or suggest that you really do not understand the programme or swear at you or something like that.

'Never apologise. Never say "Sorry",' says Potter, as I (inefficiently, as it transpires) stub out a cigarette in his ashtray. 'Shit! If there's one thing I hate it's people like you who can't put out their cigarettes properly. You're fucking useless, really, aren't you?'

Oh, well. You can't blame Dennis Potter for his ill-temper, can you? It's not much fun being Dennis Potter. There's that disease and his wife Margaret has cancer. As a director, something he would like to be good at, he's been an utter flop (Blackeyes lambasted; Secret Friends ridiculed; hardly anybody watched either), and as a playwright, something he is good at, he's become Britain's Biggest Bête Noire, the Godfather-Of-All-Pervs. Heaving buttocks in the woods in The Singing Detective, heaving lingerie in Blackeyes. Salacious and corrupting, no? Mary Whitehouse and the ever-logical Sun and the kind of nincompoop who moans 'It's-disgusting-I-mean-kids-might-be-watching-and-it's-all-very-well-saying-you-can-always-turn-it-off-but-I'm-a-one-parent-family-blah-blah' in Right To Reply's 'Video Box' thought so. And now, inevitably, Lipstick On Your Collar – as gentle and tender and funny piece as Potter has ever conceived has been dragged into the boring debate about Britain's declining moral standards.

Dennis Potter sighs the sigh of the put-upon and drinks a little more foul wine.

'Oh, shit,' he says. 'Fuck. The alleged violence in Lipstick. There isn't a single blow that was struck against the woman in the first episode but it's so well done that these fucking critics thought they saw it. All you can say to those people is, Fuck off. To think that I would condone violence against women. It's almost as though I had killed that child in Liverpool. I can't put two fingers up (disease reference) but if I could, that is what I'd do to the critics. The "serious" critics – that's an oxymoron – think they understand me. Oh, Dennis Potter has got this disease, he was sexually assaulted as a child, so the sexual assault led to Blackeyes because my sexuality is warped or whatever and the disease led to The Singing Detective. But the only reason I used that disease in Singing Detective was because I am lazy. I didn't want to do research. I know about the disease and the drugs, I know about the Forest of Dean. So it makes people think about me . . . drama, drama, God drama, what a big pompous word. I've been around so long I'm just an easy target for the "serious" critics.'

He's an easy target for the non-'serious' critics, too. Oh, what fun the tabloids have had suggesting that Potter is nothing more than a revolting sex-fiend who's old enough to know better.

'Yes, the tabloids are still doing their stuff on me. The Sun's calling me Old Flaky, in reference partly to my skin and partly to my age. They used to call me Dirty Den but they've come up with another. And there was that piece in Time Out when Blackeyes came out that said, Dennis Potter is not only crippled in his body, he is crippled in his mind. I try to pretend to myself that those sorts of things don't hurt me, but I suppose they do, really. What can you do? What is the fucking point?'

Lipstick On Your Collar is the very last of Potter's lip-synching-wonky-old-songs affairs. There was Pennies From Heaven, the 1930s: The Singing Detective, the 1940s. Lipstick is the 1950s – Connie Francis and The Platters and not-very-good-artistes like that. There will be no more. Why? Because Dennis simply cannot abide the popular 'beat' music of the 1960s and beyond. To be frank, one is not entirely certain that he feels comfortable with those tinny, crappy sounds from the 1950s either. As a 'serious' critic in The Independent helpfully and pedantically pointed out, Potter's Lipstick On Your Collar is set in 1956 – Suez crisis and that palaver – but Connie Francis's exciting single of the same name wasn't released until 1959!

'That's a point, I suppose,' says Potter, contrite. 'But it's the kind of point that people make who don't get what the programme is about. People who make that kind of point just don't see. They are so canine, they are so huh-huh-huh (here Dennis is imitating the actions of a panting dog), they are so pissing-on-the-lamppost-like that they just don't see. I know that people don't necessarily get what I'm writing about, my use of music as metaphors – but really it doesn't matter whether they get it or not. What I really hate is these critics who can't take the idea that television is a serious form. It is. And it would break my heart to think it isn't. They can say what they fucking like about me but they shouldn't be pissing over the form, should they?'

Well, so what you are saying here is that you are not a major fan of the celebrated Italian-American songbird Ms Connie Francis after all?

'No. I'm not. Thank God. But that song is a perfect metaphor for what happened in Suez.'

Connie Francis has had a very dreadful life. She was a rape victim, you know, and . . .

'If you're just going to be silly and stupid there's no fucking point, is there? I'm just using a song that fits the time-frame but nobody seems to understand what I'm getting at . . .'

Criticism. Potter takes it like a man. The negative reaction to Blackeyes: 'I reacted to that with pain. Blackeyes was received with a mixture of hostility and incomprehension. The piece was about alienation but all I managed to do was alienate everybody in the land.' The negative reaction to Secret Friends (impenetrable nonsense all about a man, i.e. Alan Bates, who tries to eat a fish supper on a train but can't manage it because he keeps dreaming about this girl in underwear): 'I said that everyone was going to hate Secret Friends, so I was right, wasn't I? How to alienate everyone. The film was a disaster. Thank God. It was badly directed. And you're probably right to say it was impenetrable nonsense. But, you see, I just hate the way people in films talk to you about the audience; they say "bums on seats" and they say "punters" and I think, How dare you? and I go out and make a film that won't put any punters' bums on seats at all. That's my reaction. It comes from my childhood.'

Childhood. What would a doctor of the psyche make of the fact that England's most contentious writer (if you don't count Salman Rushdie) is forever dwelling upon youth and the past? Who cares? Potter was born of coal-mining stock in the Forest of Dean in 1935. He was a bright boy, reading at three though there were no books in the house, and he professes to feel his intelligence was a burden. Actually, he puts it more strongly than that:

'I was cursed. I had this incredibly high IQ. It wasn't my fault, it was a curse. I had the pressure of a very close-knit working-class coal-mining community and being different was a crime. I was correcting the teacher when I was six years old and when you do that, what happens in the playground? You get the shit knocked out of you. So I developed this technique of talking ironically, which has led me into huge amounts of trouble, even now. Being talented . . . I couldn't help it. It was given to me and it was something I had to deal with. So people say I am extraordinarily arrogant but I feel humble in the face of what I was given. I can be extraordinarily rude and offensive to people but I'm trying in here (he places a hand upon his heart, shakes his head in a display of despair), I'm trying in this fucking rathole of a heart to . . . (he becomes lost for words). It's very difficult for people to understand what I'm talking about.'

The gifted-yet-accursed one went to Oxford, where he read Politics, Philosophy and Economics, then to the BBC. In the early 1960s, he became a journalist. In 1964 he stood, unsuccessfully, as a Labour candidate in the General Election. By this time, disease was setting in. The flirtation with party politics was a ghastly experience.

'That's what I thought I wanted to be. A Labour MP. It was ghastly for me because I was already ill, but it was even worse for the fucking electors. My little act of grace was not to vote for myself.'

He turned to drama. There were two BBC plays about Nigel Barton (a miner's son who, er, stands for Parliament); there was Son of Man in 1969, Double Date in 1976, Brimstone And Treacle (banned by the BBC, filmed for the big screen with dashing Sting), Pennies From Heaven, a nation shocked by sheet-music salesman Arthur (Bob Hoskins) who confesses that he's so keen on sex that he'd even contemplate sexual congress with his own grandmother. Dennis Potter, TV Beelzebub, had arrived.

In 1981, Potter went to Hollywood because the Americans wanted to make a diluted version of Pennies From Heaven (starring Steve Martin) for 'theatrical release', as they say. Imagine the son of a coal-miner's surprise when one of the film's producers, concerned about the lack of dramatic impact in a key scene, attempted to gee-up the writer thus:

'He thought there was something lacking so he started searching around in the deep recesses of his sick mind for a description that would adequately convey what he meant and he plugged into his private life and said, What I want is, it's like you're about to come on a woman's face – and the phone rings! I didn't quite understand that because I'd never been in that situation and I probably never will, but there you go. In that unlikely event, I would carry on, presumably, spurting, but being in Hollywood, if the phone rings that's a climax in itself. I mean, oh shit, when I went to Hollywood, I met all of these Hollywood people and I was a) enchanted, b) astounded and c) disgusted.'

Potter disgusted by a perv? Can such things be when it is widely considered by the general mass that Potter is the Arch Perv Of The Arts himself? Dirty, Dirty Den. He's a disgrace.

'Oh, shit, I don't want to talk about sex,' he says in a tone that borders on whining crabbiness, 'I'm tired.'

And now, fuelled, perhaps, by red wine, he proceeds to go somewhat off his trolley. He lights a Rothmans. 'I started smoking in 1954 and I've only once tried to stop and that was in 1959 for 10 days. Whatever else happens to me, I'm not going to bother with that again because I remain sufficient of a Christian to know that to worry about your body is a tremendously complicated blasphemy.' He won't talk sex but is prepared to discuss religion, which to some quaint folk is the next best thing.

'Jesus – that witty, brave, noble, sometimes petulant, wonderful man – a man, yes a man, yes a man, a man, a man, a man, but a man who is a perfect mirror, reflecting back, down, up, sideways, whatever it is that we call grace. Jesus, that man . . . it's an interesting concept that we have grace at all. When we love somebody, what does that mean? What does it mean? Does it just mean that we just want to fuck them? What does love mean? What does music mean? What does pity mean? What does mercy mean? What are these words? They are abstractions. They are just other words for what we call God, surely? These words, they are not "things". How, how, how? Where are they? Are they in colours or shapes or what? Where are they? Tell me.'

I'm stumped. Afraid I'm a bit of an atheist regarding this one, I mutter, thus arousing the fellow's ire once more.

'An atheist, are you? That's a lazy option. You're just a lazy thinker. Have you ever been close to what it feels like to love God? You're not a theologian, are you? Alright, you may be wiser than St Paul because he didn't know about metaphysics but I think you're just lazy. But I'm tired and I don't want a theological discussion. Religion is not something you can talk about. It's like talking about sex.'

He stubs out his cigarette (improperly so, I might add) and moans, 'So we've done an interview, so why don't you just fuck off. Fuck off out of here, now.'

Oh, well. I rise to leave. But he hasn't finished with me quite yet.

'You're a snob, aren't you?'

I beg your pardon? What new tack of the loon is this? I don't think of myself as a snob, Mr Potter. In fact . . .

'Yes, you're a snob. You don't know it but you are.'

I've now given up being a polite person with bad teeth in a railway carriage and I ask, What the fuck are you talking about? – which only elicits a wry, mysterious sort of grin from this rude man.

'I can't explain it. It's something you have to work out for yourself. Think about it – it's good for your soul.'

I haven't got a soul!

'Oh, yes you have,' the rude man murmurs. Which is all totally exasperating. 'Now fuck off out of here, fuck off!' he roars. 'I'm fucking going,' I hiss. 'Fuck off!' Fuck off yourself, Dirty Den!

I open the door and Dennis Potter, glass in hand, clambers to his feet and the man who told me, 'Never apologise. Never say "Sorry" ', smiles a sheepish smile and goes, 'Oh shit, look, I'm sorry! You have to be charitable with me. I'm sorry.' And then he coughs and roars with laughter. What an exceedingly grouchy goat he is – possibly slightly mental too. Why is that one warms to him so?

David Mellor

Order! The Defrocked Minister for Fun is in the House with his foolish goggles, flared teeth and questionable football team loyalty. He'll bore you about art, tell the IRA to bog off and probably suck your toes as he does it.

THE BUNTERISH FIGURE of the Rt. Hon. David Mellor QC MP looms towards me bearing biscuits. Goggle-eyed, he stares down at the plate. 'Gosh! I haven't had a nice fig roll since I was in the school tuck shop!' he booms like some gorging goon. What a smile the disgraced Conservative ex-minister possesses, exposing the teeth that scared a nation in all their frightful glory. What a jovial cove he appears as he shows me the framed photographs resting on the window sill of his Savile Row office: there's Ron'n'Nancy – 'Ron and Nancy! Haw haw!' he guffaws with glee; there's Mellor beaming alongside Elizabeth Taylor – 'Liz! Haw!'; and there he is again with the hapless Princess of Wales – 'Di!'

A little earlier he had come at me with outstretched hand and an identifying cry of 'David Mellor! Jolly good, jolly good!' and had told me, 'I never want to be Prime Minister nor am I likely to be. I shall never storm the heights because I was never that driven. If I were driven and obsessive I couldn't really be talking to you the way I am now. One would deserve an Oscar, really, for the act, don't you think? So there you are!' His eyes went all a-twinkle behind his unsexy spectacles: if heights could be stormed on cheeriness alone . . .

There's nothing the Rt. Hon. David Mellor QC MP likes more than a jolly good old chinwag over a nice fig roll, it would seem. Since his fall from grace last summer at the hands and other parts of the unlovely 'actress' Antonia de Sancha, the ex-Minister for Fun has reinvented himself as a media figure: there's the phone-in show,

Six-O-Six, he hosts on Radio 5 – the amiable buffoon chats to the common herd about footer: 'And-now-Reg-from-Hammersmith-who's - a - Chelsea - supporter - Good - for - you - old - boy! - Haw-haw! - And-now-we'll-play-a-super-record-by-Michael-Jackson-before-talking-to-Ron-from-Leyton-about-the-damn-fool-backpass-rule-what?', that's his style ('I played Buddy Holly It's Raining In My Heart on Saturday,' he relates with some pride, 'and I was singing along like a good 'un. In fact, funnily enough, I took the kids along to see Buddy (ghastly West End musical) a couple of years ago and we thoroughly enjoyed the show!'); there's the weekly column in the Guardian, dreary stuff about opera and arts funding for the most part; he's been a judge of the Sony Radio Awards (he bemoans the present lack of 'great radio sit-coms'); he's hosted The Vintage Years (old recordings of classical music) on Radio 3; he's preparing a series of 'light classics' for Radio 2; he's on the telly quite a lot, which is quite surprising given his goofy specs, his useless haircut and those teeth. In his spare time he is a backbencher, the member for Putney. He makes more money today than he ever did as a mere Cabinet Minister (a figure not unadjacent to £350,000 per annum has been rumoured) but does he not miss the thrill of government, the power of it all? Oh no. Not a bit of it. He is, he claims, happy now.

'I'm certainly more relaxed,' he says, sipping from a nice china cup with tea in it. 'I have all the attractions, if you like, of being a politician and doing constituency work which I enjoy which is dealing with matters that you can actually solve. I mean, I'm not going to solve the crisis in Bosnia but I might be able to stop somebody building a sort of motorway through my constituency or flying too many jet aircraft overhead. Haw haw! So that's fine. I get invited on all the television programmes that I want to go on. And you know, it doesn't bother me to be sitting in a railway carriage with all manner of folk. So I'm perfectly, er, relaxed about it, really . . . Why don't you have a nice fig roll? You're awfully thin, haw, haw!'

What a fine fellow. What a decent chap. What a sport. Ah, but this man, media figure or no, is a Tory politician and therefore under suspicion. And just think what he did to his poor wife. Where is the sense of loyalty, decency, in a man who suddenly switches allegiance from Fulham FC to Chelsea football club (little Johnny Major's favourite team), or one who betrays his spouse in the bed of an unpleasant-to-look at and snotty-nosed 'actress' who has a horrid voice. 'One David Mellor! There's only one David Mellor!' chanted the Chelsea fans when he turned up at a game at the height of last year's scandal. But, actually, there are several David Mellors: the genial lark, the publicity-hungry hound, the rising-bright-spark-politico-that-is-no-more, the highbrow scribe, the goat on the wireless, the charming chap who chums up with everyone from John Major to Nigel Kennedy ('I took Nigel to a football match, a game between England and Brazil, and Maradona was there and I got Nigel introduced to Maradona and Nigel said, Proudest moment of my life . . . MONSTER! Haw haw!'). And who the hell do these David Mellors think they are?

Mellor was born in 1949, the son of a Dorset schoolmaster, and went to Swanage grammar school where he saw some nice fig rolls in the tuck shop. Mellor, the schoolboy, has been described as a 'precocious little swot'. He is somewhat affronted when I remind him of this. He puffs out his ample cheeks and says, 'Well, that could be said of anyone who achieved anything at school. I dare say there are other people who said of me, What a nice fellow, but then that's not very interesting, is it?'

For the benefit of Q, the politician once known as The Crab (after a succession of sideways moves in government), tries to remember the '60s, the pop music of that giddy decade.

'I couldn't live without music. I mean, if I'd gone deaf last summer, Christ, that would have been far worse than losing my job as a Cabinet Minister. God, I would have hated that. Music is a joy for life. I started off completely into pop. I used to sit around the old trannie – on Sunday afternoons, wasn't it? – for Alan Freeman, Pick Of The Pops. I used to record on my Grundig tape recorder all the great hits. I'm sure that was a thoroughly illegal thing to do, haw haw! And then I got into Jacques Loussier. I had very conventional taste: The Beatles, Rolling Stones, Four Seasons, Beach Boys. I was a sort of child of the '60s. OK, I think the Whitney Houston thing I Will Always Love You is quite good but so much of the pop material today is much more geared up for dancing than to actually have a tune which makes you say, Wow! the great thing about The Beatles and The Beach Boys is what wonderful tunes. Sgt Pepper – I can still see the psychedelic cover and all that stuff!'

Don't you like dancing, Mr Mellor? Don't you enjoy letting the old hair down and cutting a rug?

'Well, I wouldn't say I was a good dancer. I always think that politicians dancing are total prats. Was it David Steel dancing in that photo with the woman falling on top of him? Haw haw! Stupidest photo that's ever been. I admire those who dance well but it's not an art I have studied very much myself, I have to say.'

A 'child of the '60s', Mr Mellor? By this can we assume that you were once a pot-smoking hippy? He grins a gaping grin at the very thought of it.

'No, I think it would be fair to say I was not a pot-smoking hippy. I wasn't.'

Pity that.

'Er, my kids are heavily into rock. My son is into E.R.M. and stuff like that.'

E.R.M.? Isn't that something to do with European economics? Perhaps he means R.E.M.

'Oh, R.E.M. Yes. Shows how much I know about it. Haw haw!'

After school, Mellor read law at Christ's College, Cambridge. He was called to the bar in 1972 and entered Parliament in 1979, the Tory MP for Putney. In 1986 he was made a Minister of State at the Home Office and displayed the more flamboyant side of his character with a number of headline-grabbing visits to drug fields in South America and Pakistan. A year later he was moved to the Foreign Office but he was rather too liberal a chap for the venerable battleaxe Margaret Hilda Thatcher's liking (he argued with her over minesweepers sent to the Gulf; she said that Mellor would not have been up to being a Chancery barrister like herself and he was shunted sideways to the Department of Health). It was not until Thatcher was toppled and Mellor's old Chelsea-supporting mate John Major became Prime Minister that his star began to rise. In 1990 he was brought into the Cabinet for the first time as Chief Secretary to the Treasury and subsequently was asked to create the new Department of National Heritage, responsible for arts, sport and tourism.

The Minister for Fun – it was he who dreamt up this silly tag – was on his way . . .

Except he wasn't. For on July 19, 1992 the People 'sensationally' revealed his affair with Antonia de Sancha and what a hoot the nation had at his expense as we read tales of intrigue in Chelsea football togs ('MELLOR MADE LOVE IN CHELSEA STRIP! Night he scored four times with actress' squawked the soaraway

Sun) and of sucked toes and saucy sundries. On September 24 (following further revelations concerning a free holiday he and his family had accepted from Mona Bauwens, daughter of the Palestine Liberation Organisation's finance chief), Mellor resigned ('TOE JOB TO NO JOB' whooped the soaraway Sun).

He considers his fate.

'If one had been caught out murdering a child or something, one would have felt absolutely dreadful about it,' he says. 'But you know, if everybody who had an affair was hounded out of the job that they were doing, how many millions would we have on the dole? Haw haw! Politicians in the old days weren't exactly clean. I mean, Lloyd George and . . . er, so, you know, I was able to keep my self-respect despite the fact that undoubtedly I had been a bloody fool.'

Would he do it all over again?

'Oh, of course not. I was a bloody fool and I destroyed myself. I mean, I don't think I'm destroyed but I did it. I admit I was reckless in the conduct of my private life. But should President Mitterrand not have been President of France because they now think he had affairs with all these women? The answer is I don't think it matters tuppence. And indeed the French, they laugh. I went to lunch with some French journalists, lovely people, and they thought it was very amusing that the British could do this to someone like me. It is all so childish, the British obsession with other people's sex lives, isn't it?'

Indeed, but it's rather fun, too, isn't it? We all had a jolly good laugh at your expense. Cheered us up no end.

'Well, OK, there were many people who nipped along and bought their paper and were thoroughly amused by my goings-on as everyone is amused by other people's love lives, pratfalls, call it what you like. I had a relationship with a woman and . . . it's just part of life's rich pattern, really. More fool me. If you're stupid enough to have a relationship with someone who then goes off and talks to the press about it, you can't blame newspapers for printing it.'

Does Mellor feel that he is still a figure of fun, an object to be mocked?

'Well, you get the odd yob shouting after you in the street.'

Shouting what? How's the Chelsea strip, Dave?

'Yes, things like that. But the Chelsea strip was all the invention of this wretched man (Max Clifford, Antonia de Sancha's agent), as you probably know. All that stuff about the Chelsea strip was an invention as the newspapers knew full well. But more fool me. I shouldn't have got mixed up in the affair in the first place. But it's easy to be wise after the event. It doesn't do anyone any harm to fall flat on their face like I did and realise that, in the end, we're all human. Quite honestly, if no longer being a minister is the worst life ever does to me then OK God, thanks very much. I'm not proud of the bloody thing and it was pretty horrendous to go through but, you know, it's not as if some doctor had said to me, You've got cancer, you've got six months to live. So I'm not going through life complaining. I remember my esteemed colleague John Wakeham when he came back to the House of Commons after the Brighton bomb when his wife was killed and his legs were totally mashed up and he was lying in great pain on a sofa and he seemed very relaxed and I said to him, You know, John, I admire you for being completely free of bitterness. And he said, If I became bitter, they've won. So I'm not going through life full of bile and spleen. I'm not applying for sainthood but I'm not a hater.'

Doesn't he hate his Spitting Image puppet, that halitosis-ridden gargoyle?

'Haw haw! Well, they're very cruel about everybody, aren't they? Kenneth Baker's a great slug, isn't he? And John Major's some grey thing. Funnily enough, I've been accused of many things but I've never been accused of having bad breath. I do *not*, thank God, have bad breath. Haw haw!'

At this point, David Mellor spies something poking from out of my jacket pocket. It is a packet of Marlboro and this makes him rather excited.

'Ooh!' he says. 'Are you a Marlboro smoker? My God! Let me steal a cigarette off you. I haven't had one for days. I'm an occasional smoker . . . of other people's cigarettes, haw haw!' No Raffles man, he. Who'd have thought it?

The ex-minister puffs away contentedly. Was he actually any good as a top-flight politician? There were some who thought so: there was much anguish at his departure in the arts world as, unlike the common Tory philistine, this National Heritage leader seemed to care about the arts. Mellor was a politician who, at the very least, spoke his mind. Like the time in 1988 when, as Minister of State at the Foreign Office, he publicly upbraided an Israeli soldier on the Gaza Strip for not being very nice to Palestinians.

'I knew when that happened that I would make enemies for life

– and so it has transpired. A careerist would have slid in and out without anybody noticing but why be in politics just to be a time server? There are one or two politicians – no names, no pack drill – who I feel sorry for because they're just careerists, there to toe the party line. I do not count myself amongst them. I'm only in politics because I believe in certain things and I will use such abilities as I have to articulate them. Like the other day I spoke out about the IRA bombing of the City. You see, with the IRA, as well as having a stiff upper lip and saying business as usual, we've got to raise our game to match theirs. Because they're not just a lot of silly paddies. And as long as I am in politics, I will raise these issues.'

But since the mighty fall, the Right Honourable Member has been less 'issue-raiser', more media tartlet. He'll go on Any Questions? or any other silly programme, at the drop of a hat. 'I cannot deny that I have an ego. Rampant sometimes, haw haw!'

Did you know that going on radio as a phone-in presenter was a task far more terrifying to him than delivering his maiden speech in Parliament?

'I was petrified. Haw haw! Oh goodness, yes! Ah! God! I said to Terry Wogan when we went to a rugby match, I said to him, How do I sort this out? And he said, Relax, you'll soon find out whether you can do it or not. And I like to think I can do it. I like to think I'm not too pompous. You see football is a passion to me and football's not just about whether you're over the moon or sick as a parrot, football is . . .'

Here, Mellor bangs on about his sporting passion for some expanse of time and I interrupt and say, look here, you're a traitor because you used to support Fulham but switched allegiance to your friend John Major's favourite Chelsea, and he says no, he's not a traitor because he supported Chelsea first and then he went to Fulham and then he went back to supporting Chelsea so that makes it alright, doesn't it?

And then he remembers that, like it or not, he is still a politician so has to say things like this:

'You know, I'm not saying this to be pious, and you hopefully believe that I'm not an artificially pious person, but I have an enormous admiration for John Major and not just because he is a good friend of mine. One thing I regret about the events of last summer was causing John embarrassment and adding to his burdens at the wrong time. As I said in my resignation letter, I wanted to be a tower of strength and instead was a point of weakness. I do admire him. There's so much more to John Major than his detractors see.'

And before I can sneer, Yeah, like what, for instance? David Mellor is looking at his watch and saying, 'Er, I've got a small problem. I've got to get down to the House for this wretched Maastricht stuff.'

He bids me leave with such effusion that my hand practically drops off in the shake. 'So very, very nice to talk with you. Enjoyed it! Enjoyed it!' What a *frightfully* decent chap he is.

'I wouldn't like to think that I had shut the door on ever coming back into the Government,' he said, 'which is different from saying I wake up every morning thinking I must come back. We'll just have to see what happens.'

Bunter will be back. Probably.

George Best

You must not ask about the drink problem, the dolly birds, the gambling, the 'screwing', the prison sentence, the squandered thousands or the wasted·talent.

H<small>E'S ROUND ONE</small> man! He's round two! My goodness, what an incredible run . . . and, oh my word, look at that dummy, he's beaten three. This really is extraordinary! Classic skills and ooh, how about that? Remarkable he's *scored*! He's weaved his way, with silky feet, right up to the bar of a crowded public house in London and he's 'scored'. A bottle of champagne, that is. Well! Let's look at it again. What do you make of that, Trevor?

The bearded man they have called everything from the Greatest Footballer Who Ever Lived to Bevvied Bestie The Beastly Boozer stands in a West End pub called, somewhat fittingly, The Royal George, and raises a glass of the sparkling matter to his mouth. Dressed in an unpleasant Manchester United sweatshirt, well-filled by his sufficient stomach, his face plump and ruddy with the living of years as he stares vacantly at a television in the corner (upon which plays, soundlessly, the latest England cricketers' one-day disaster), he hardly looks the part of a celebrity to inspire awe. But it would seem that that's exactly what he is. A shell-suited woman, lank of hair, who I have never clapped eyes on in my life before, tugs my arm and hisses in my ear, in a state of unnatural excitement: 'That's George Best! That's George Best in this pub!'

She is absolutely right, of course, but I attempt to dissuade her from the notion. Oh, no, no, I whisper back, that's just some old bloke who sells The Big Issue. She looks daggers at me and scampers up to the Wayward Hero Of The Terraces. 'You're George Best!' she cries. George looks sad. Pestered again. Out comes some foul scrap of paper on which George Best must scribble his Best Wishes and his autograph. Ms Shell Suit squeaks in orgasmic delight and, as if in a trance, he performs his duty. George Best averts his eyes and turns once more to the TV screen. 'Ooh, do you like cricket then, George?' squawks some other unwanted admirer at the Legend. 'No,' is his curt reply . . .

He hasn't dribbled a ball for proper top professional money in something like 20 years, and yet 'Bestie' remains Britains most famous, most renowned, most loved footballer. Already, the upstart Paul Gascoigne is going out of favour for being a fat fool who can't play for toffee – Best, the boozer, the gambler, the great big 'shagger', is the idol of a nation for ever more. We forgive him anything and everything, don't we?

'I've always said that if there's one thing I could change in my life, it would be my face,' he had told me earlier. 'Most of the time, I just want to disappear and live a reasonably normal life and do normal things without being hassled by people. But as it is, I can't even walk into a pub without causing a stir and being hassled by people.'

How very true this is.

The circumstances of our meeting are these: Manchester United have won the First Division Championship (or 'the Premier League', to give it its new-fangled wizard title) for the first time in 26 years. A shoddy paperback book (peppered with misprints) has been rushed out. It's called The Story Of Manchester United's Winning Season: Champions: 26-Year Quest For Glory. And it's got a foreword by George Best. Not by Ryan Giggs or Bryan Robson or Mark Hughes or anybody else who actually plays for Manchester United but by George Best – the one who walked out on the team forever in 1974 – because he's the most well-known Manchester name of them all. And in a bookshop in the Charing Cross Road, this Roy of the Rovers (except Roy never had a drink problem or slept with masses of 'birds'), this hero of three dimensions is signing copies for an eager public. What's £9.99 for a duff book when it's got 'Best Wishes To Shirley. George Best' scrawled in the front?

Best arrives at the bookshop late. He is accompanied by a pair of PR blokes and his present leggy paramour Mary Shatila. (They've been together for three years; they're not married but she likes to call herself Mary Best.) Mary is a bossy number, a fussbudget of a woman. She doesn't seem too keen on her man, her charge, being interviewed at all. I am allotted a generous five minutes in the mythical presence. 'Now,' a PR bloke sternly warns me. 'There's to be no questions about alcohol, no questions about women. All you can talk about is the book and football.' I am led into a backroom of the bookstore and everybody sits down. The atmosphere could scarcely be described as comfortable. Oh no, we can't have Bestie saying anything untoward like 'I like screwing', as he did on the Wogan show three years ago, can we, now?

All I can talk about is the book and football. Oh. Alright, could you sign my book for me, please, George? Could you make it out to Peter? He's a friend of mine who quite likes Manchester United. I don't like Manchester United.

'Don't you? Neither do I,' says George Best, gruffly. Does one detect an undercurrent of bitterness in this remark? Mary and the PR bloke shift in their seats and chuckle at his quip less than convincingly.

He was born in Belfast in May 1946. He came to Manchester, shy and scared, to join a famous footer team in 1961. He scored his first goal in the Football League in 1964. And then his weaving hips and striking black mop-top turned him into the games's first pop-star-styled sex symbol. He had a fan club nearly as big as The Beatles' and shrieking girls would camp out on his lawn because he always played with his red shirt outside his shorts – ever so daring and groovy for the times. Soon, everybody in the game would have sideburns and a surfeit of hair (and later on they'd all go, rather disastrously, for the bubble perm). But it was George Best who invented all this, pioneered the excellent idea of Football As Fashion.

Those days at Manchester united were the happiest of his life, he says. He does not wax modest about his achievements – and why should he, for even to the untutored eye of the layman, it was obvious that as a player, George Best was a cut or two above the rest.

'Of course I was happy then,' he says. 'I went as a kid to a great club and in my first full season we won the Youth Cup, second full season we won the League, two years later we won the League again and we won the European Cup. I was European Player of the Year, British Player of the Year, First Division's leading goal goalscorer and Manchester United's leading goalscorer for six years in a row, so I couldn't have written a better script than that if I had planned it. To say that I was happy is an understatement. I was winning everything and getting very well paid for the privilege of doing it. If I was playing today, I'd be earning more than any of them, Gascoigne and everybody. If there's money to be made, you might as well hit it. It's a short life.'

So where did it all go wrong, George? He retired, effectively, from the sport in 1974 when he was just 27. There began a rampage of 'birds' – an array of Miss Worlds and third-rate actresses and Lynsey de Paul – and a committed assault upon the bottle. Tut, tut, went the sportswriters (reaching for their hip flasks); what a squandering of talent! In his 1990 autobiography, the supremely-titled The Good, The Bad And The Bubbly (alas, the title is the best thing about this wonky and predictable book), Best – or, rather, his co-writer, Ross Benson – relates a glorious tale: it's the early 1980s and George goes out on a gambling razzle with his floozy Mary Stavin, Miss World, 1979 ('one of my collection of Miss Worlds'), wins £15,000 and, back in his London hotel room, calls the night porter for a bottle of Dom Perignon champagne. 'When he delivered it, he saw £15,000 scattered across the bed and Mary prancing around, half naked and the other half falling out of her negligee. I opened the champagne and gave him a £50 tip. He started to walk out. He stopped. He turned around and said: Can I ask you something, Mr Best? I said: Sure, what do you want to ask? He looked at Mary. He looked at the £50 in his hand. He looked at the 15 grand on the bed. He said, Tell me, Mr Best – where did it all go wrong?' Boom, and furthermore, boom!

So tell me, George, where did it all go wrong? The latest Mary and the PR bloke are squirming and giving me nasty looks. This question is not in the script. This question isn't about football or 'the book'. Fortunately, Best is paying his minders no mind.

'You can analyse all you want but no-one will ever come up with an answer to what happened to my career. The only reason I threw it all away and retired too early is because I had an alcohol problem. It's as simple as that. You can dig as deep as you want and look for reasons but it was all down to one thing, quite simple: alcohol. I didn't actually get up one morning and say, Oh, I don't know what to do today, I think I'll become an alcoholic and throw my life down the toilet. It didn't quite work like that. I'm lucky because I've seen friends of mine who haven't been able to handle alcohol at all and have passed on. But I'm still around. I'm going to be around for a long time earning a good living, because I've learned how to handle it.'

He's tried all kinds of cures. They didn't work. So he handles the problem by, er, drinking if he feels like it.

He was such a star turn back then. He would slink and skitter past one outfoxed defender, past another, and another and then fail to pass the ball to Denis Law or someone who'd be waiting in the box.

'The reason that most of the time I didn't pass the ball to other players was that I knew I could do better than they could. It was my ball. It was my ball. It was always *my* ball . . .'

He was such a star that advertisers put him on the telly to urge the populace to eat millions of eggs at breakfast – 'E for B and Georgie Best', that was the catchphrase.

'I didn't mind that. I made £25,000 out of that.'

He was such a star that persons in the music 'biz' were forever trying to get Georgie into the recording studio for some novelty pop single experience.

'Over the years, many have tried to turn me into a pop star, but the only time I try things is if I can do them and I certainly can't sing, so it never interested me in the slightest.'

Kevin Keegan and Paul Gascoigne have made records, though, haven't they?

'Huh, yeah, well, if you can call them records,' he huffs dismissively. 'It's a rip-off, people trying to use their names to sell records when they know they can't sing. Anyway, I've always had enough problems without getting into the pop music business.'

Problems. Problems for Georgie Best started with the fame.

'I have never felt comfortable with fame and I never will. I've been through it all. I've seen it all and I've done it all and I've heard it all and you just don't realise what a monster it is being in the public eye. I found out the hard way. I lived in a goldfish bowl, under constant pressure and all the hype. I couldn't handle it.'

Problems. In keeping with that old cliché of the newly-moneyed sportsperson, George opened some nightclubs. 'I was just interested in getting people in there to have a drink. I would just run the bar side of things.' He allows himself a faint chuckle. 'After all, the bar – that's where my expertise was . . .'

Problems. Off the pitch, never to return, he hit the bottle more and more. The problem became public. He turned up on Wogan sozzled to the gills. He said 'I like screwing'. He said, 'Shit'. He accused the oily Leprechaun of having 'messed himself'. Bevvied Bestie The Beastly Boozer, on target to outdo Oliver Reed as the King Of The Showman Drunkards? 'Shocked viewer Alan Crouch, 74, a retired electrical engineer of Ashtead, Surrey, said: 'I have never heard and seen such atrocious and disgusting behaviour in my life!' reported the Daily Express on September 20, 1990. Well, what a sad and sheltered existence Mr Crouch must have led. For here was just another tabloid storm in a champagne flute.

'The BBC didn't seem to be bothered whether I drank or not, which can be dangerous if you've got someone like me in the studio a couple of hours before going on air,' he tells me as the minders twitch in discomfiture. 'There was always a possibility that I might have too much to drink – and that's unfortunately what happened. It was good from a marketing point of view, all the publicity I got out of it. But I went back and apologised. I'm always man enough to stand up and say when I've made a mistake.'

(Part of the marketable publicity was gained due to Q magazine. For on the Wogan thing, Best made certain disparaging remarks about Paul Gascoigne – and interviewed in Q shortly after, 'Gazza', rather eloquently, had this to say; 'Yur, and you see the fat man's got jealous of me. George Best, the drunken fat man is jealous. He absolutely slaughtered us for a bit of cash and that's a scum bastard.' The Mirror and the Sun picked up – nicked – this fine piece of reporting. How we roared at the GASCOIGNE CALLS BEST SCUM B*****D headlines.)

The chairs squeak anxiously again. From the corner of my eye I see George's Mary and publicity man twisting in discomfort. This short interview not to their liking at all.

'You see, the thing about me is I have experienced everything,' George carries on regardless.

Yes, he has. He's experienced prison – three months for drunk driving. He's experienced a lot of women.

'Women are a lot of fun. I just couldn't resist them, but . . .'

This is the last straw. Mary has got to her feet and the PR man is making desperate signals – an index finger slashing across his throat. Cut! Cut! This interview is terminated forthwith.

'It is only because you are nice and George likes you that we allowed you to talk so long,' says Mary, a hint of menace in the voice. Eight minutes. The soccer supremo must simply *adore* me.

The queue for George Best's signature in a cramped bookshop stretches out into the street. Disaffected youths in garish neo-psychedelic Manchester United away strips, old buffers who can remember pre-Munich days, ladies with hairdos and spotty girls a-giggling as if they were on the point of meeting the most fabulous member of East 17. Best carries out the chores in morose fashion. 'Oh God, you're great, George. Always wanted to shake you by the hand. Can you make it out to Jimmy and Lucky and Pod and Ren from Arbroath? Cor, cheers mate. It's an honour.'

'George, you should make a video what like with all your goals on it and you could call it The Best Of Best. That'd be good, wouldn't it? The Best Of Best!'

George nods wearily. 'Can I have yer picture, George? Ooh, and can I have yer picture with me in it as well? Oh no, me flash ain't workin'!'

For one who dislikes fame so, he does little to shy away from it.

'Can you make it out to me, George?' 'Sure. What's your name?' 'Oh, well, it's a bit difficult to spell, see.' 'How do you spell it?' 'Oh, well, er, I better write it out for you because it's a bit difficult to spell. Have you got a pen? A bit of paper?'

It goes on for an hour, this signature business, and George Best looks entirely miserable throughout. They say he's a master of the one-liner – he's had a stage show with Rodney (Rod-er-neee) Marsh and it is reported that, when asked by a member of the audience whether he got more excitement 'scoring' at Old Trafford or with Miss World, he replied, quick as a flash, 'Well, the goal lasted longer.' Boom boom and ho ho. But there is no evidence of this rapier-like wit on offer today.

'I've lost probably half a dozen close friends through drink and drugs,' he had said, so wistfully, earlier, 'so I am the lucky one. I'm still here, earning a good living. I'm enjoying my life. I have nothing to complain about.'

But there was a distance, a certain sadness in the eyes as he said this.

It was only once the signing session was through and he softly enquired of the big boss Mary, 'Are we going up the road for a, er, a drink?' and she nodded, that the former maestro of ball-control showed much interest in anything at all.

Chris Eubank

Whenever he speaks, people hit the canvas laughing. Super-middleweight pugilist by trade, featherweight philosopher by accident, he has now met the toughest opponent of his career.

CHRIS EUBANK, WEARING this day a designer jacket that cost several million pounds, no doubt, but which resembles nothing more than an ill-fitting blazer of a minor public school, has just told me something rather astonishing about music, something I never knew before.

'Bob Marley,' the notorious cocksure pugilist has just said, 'Bob Marley, he sung of Essex!'

Essex? Are you absolutely sure about this, oh golden-gloved one? Marley sung of Trenchtown, Jamaica, yes, but Essex?

Eubank is quite irritated at my stupidity – and reasonably so: the little-loved prizefighter has the most pronounced showbiz lisp since that of Ms Toyah Willcox and it's this that has caused our minor misunderstanding.

'Not Essex, *ethics*!' he says, all sibilant, though these two words sound identical in Eubank parlance. 'Ethics. Bob Marley sung of moral conduct. He spoke of even though one is living a life of poverty, that one should still be optimistic. Even though people are oppressing, even if there is no food, listen to the music and let the music feed you. No matter what the tribulation is around you, rise, *rise* above it and be joyful. Be of good spirit. This is what Bob Marley taught me. This is what the Bible teaches me. This is what God's doctrine teaches me. The music what's in my stomach is rock steady music, not ska, not reggae, rock steady. That's the chronological order of it. Rock steady comes just after ska. But outside of the stomach I have only three heroes. Bob Marley. Mike

Tyson. God. They teach me. And in my way in this world with the time I've got in this boxing world, I'm trying to speak out against things which are wrong. In my boxing, I am trying to say that people should live together and live good together . . .'

Some say that he's just an average boxing person but Chris Eubank came to salve the world.

It is not to the morally-improving strains of Bob Marley's reggae that Chris Eubank struts and swaggers through packed halls and baying crowds towards bowing rings, however. No. The theme tune used as the lights go flash and the TV commentators scale the cliché mountain is a rather annoying rock 'anthem' by Tina Turner. 'Simply the best,' it goes. 'Better than all the rest.' It's Eubank's boast, a self-aggrandising message. But is it true? The best?

'I'm a paragon, a demi-God,' Eubank has bragged.

'Hero – look it up in the dictionary and you'll see a picture of me,' Eubank has blustered.

Parp, parp and parp again goes the trumpet of the World Boxing Association's super-middleweight champion – but who does Mister Simply-The-Best ever actually exchange buffets and blows with upon the canvas top? Mexican taxi-drivers and sacks of particularly old potatoes, that's who. Or so the boxing experts tell us.

Poor Chris Eubank. Nobody seems to love him, apart, perhaps, from wife Karron ('Love ya bad, Karron. Be home soon') and their two sons – and the staff of the Park Lane hotel where he sits today eating salt beef sandwiches and greeting attendants by their Christian names.

For the general public, Eubank is just too arrogant, too full of swank. Muhammad Ali was haughty and lippy, too, but he was an American so it didn't count. Americans are supposed to be over the top. In Britain, we want our boxers to be gentle giants, splashing themselves all over with Brut like Henry 'Our 'Enery' Cooper, or playing the role of gormless minstrel 'nigger' like Frank Bruno. Eubank just doesn't fit the stereotype of the Black British Boxer at all. He poses around in pricey designer togs (white American racists once referred to such behaviour as 'acting proud as Cuffy'), he calls himself great and uses words that are sometimes quite long ('hierarchy' springs to mind). He doesn't do panto. Oh, why can't he be all nice and dim, another 'Where's 'Arry?' type, like he's expected to be?

For the boxing fraternity, Eubank is a thorn in the liniment because he talks too much. He has called the sport barbaric (which, of course, it is but you're not supposed to say so – even though you've damaged the brain of an opponent, Michael Watson, and put him in hospital for a very long time). 'If I can fight dead people for money, I will,' he has said: this is very much not the required phoney gladiatorial spirit.

'I am Jekyll and Hyde,' he tells me, lifting a tea cup to his lips with a hand festooned with extravagant jewellery. 'Sometimes I am going to tock.' (Chris Eubank is something of an expert at the delivery of quite baffling – gnostic? – statements.) 'There is a message in life to be learned from Chris Eubank. There is Chris Eubank who is the fighter and there is Chris Eubank who is talking to you now who is a far different personality. He is a personality which is true, which is real and above all he is good. He's got so much to offer youngsters. He speaks to youngsters and gets them away from the detrimental things of life, the drugs, the crime. Chris Eubank is a good man and what he says is get away from that badness. No badness. You see, reality is messed up. Reality is like a square (he gestures with his hands to form a reality-shaped square) but it's tilting from an angle, a 40 or 55 degree angle. Do you understand what I'm saying?'

Um, not entirely. Rather than pursue this line of argument, I change the subject, ask the unsmiling philosopher about the barbarism of boxing. Does he really detest his craft?

'Of course! Of course I hate it. I say it is barbaric because Chris Eubank tells the truth. Why should I not upset the boxing establishment. Chris Eubank is not playing their game. I am playing my game and my game is just living the truth. I want everyone to live good. Should I be a liar? If I were to like boxing, if I were to like what I do, I would not be stable and I am stable. There's a desperateness that takes place in boxing. Your pride is on the line. Your self-esteem is on the line. Your manhood is on the line. People are questioning your manhood!' Heaven forfend! 'This is not enjoyable. I am of stable mind. I am not professionally deformed. If I was professionally deformed, then I would say, Well, I do like this, I do like hurting people, and I do like taking pain. The crowds, they all want scar tissue and they want blood and perhaps they want death. It's ugly. It's ugly. It is barbaric, is it not? They want to see me get beaten up – but they'll be waiting a long time. I win. I'm sorry I make it look so easy sometimes but that is the tick and sometimes I tock. It's a natural law. I work for money. There is nothing wrong with this. Money is the key for your freedom. Boxing is chains and money brings the escape . . .'

And Chris Eubank rails against the indignities of his chosen profession (for which he gets paid between £100,000 and £500,000 per fight) for quite some time.

He was born in Peckham, South London. He was, he has said, 'born bad'. Expelled from school some 15 times, apparently.

'I wasn't expelled 15 times,' he protests. 'I got expelled from school two times. I got suspended from school a lot of times: 18 times in one school and four or five in another. And do you want to know why? I had fights. I was not wrong. Some other kids were being wrong with bullying and I was trying to put them right. I was fighting to correct. As I am doing now. I have so much to offer youngsters out there. I must keep on living. I must keep on trying.'

The early heroes of this playground scrapper for justice were not boxers but Bob Marley instead.

'It's not Bob Marley *was* my hero, it's Bob Marley *is* my hero,' he corrects me. And God is my hero. And Mike Tyson is now one of my heroes. Good man. Wronged by the system. It's disgusting.'

Is he intimating here that there was racism afoot in the Mike Tyson rape trial? Mike Tyson was a black man; Mike Tyson went to gaol.

'I choose not to talk about the colour black,' Eubank replies with a hint of anger. 'I choose not to talk about the colour white or any colour. If you want to speak to me about colour, speak to me about the colour of this mustard tin.' He jabs an index finger at the condiment container before him (which is more of a 'pot' than a 'tin', but why be pedantic when there's a bruiser sitting next to you?). 'The mustard tin is yellow. What does that tell you about the mustard tin? Does the mustard tin think of its colour? No! So I refuse to surrender, to even discuss the word "colour" between people. There is no colour. We are all equals. We are all one. Let us look in our hearts and work and live together. I will not reduce my dignity by talking of "colour". That is what I am saying. The mustard tin means nothing.'

The mustard tin is looking somewhat cowed and contrite by this point. Eubank returns his concentration to Bob Marley, he who sung of Essex, and I interrupt his laudatory flow by pointing out that Bob Marley was well-known for puffing profusely away at the ganja, something of which Eubank, would-be role model for the young, might, presumably, disapprove. No? No. Not a bit of it.

'I do not disapprove. I understand marijuana. I understand it completely. The Rasta, and the doctor for that matter, does not see marijuana as a drug, he sees it as a herb. This herb, it makes you relax, it makes you withdraw, it makes you considerate, makes you love. I would say to you that if everyone in the world smoked marijuana, there would be no greed and there would be pure love in the world.'

Gracious, it almost sounds as if this pugilistic gentleman has actually tried the stuff, does it not?

'I have. I come from the inner city. I smoked weed from . . . I smoked marijuana from ages 13 to 16 . . . or from 12 to 16. Or perhaps I was smoking marijuana from a younger age group. I drunk alcohol from when I was a kid until I was 16. I smoked cigarettes from age six to 16. I bought my first packet when I was nine or 10. Ten Embassy. Good stuff. I don't think they do 10 Embassy any more only 20s. So I've lived it. I've been there. I've shoplifted. I've gone out there. I've done the boisterous things, drugs and petty crime. They are not evil things. They are bad things. Marijuana can bring you joy but alcohol and stealing they are bad things and they can't drag me back into such behaviour. I had an ambition to be something better and bigger, so when I got the chance to go to the United States, I went and I stopped drinking.'

Eubank's mother had left home when he was still a child. At the age of 16 he went to live with her in the Bronx where he began to box.

'Against all the laws, I stopped drinking and I stopped smoking in the Bronx. I didn't keep any friends. All I did was trained, learned to box, studied, went to school. I didn't keep any company. I had nothing. No girlfriends. Nothing. I got determination. All I did was pray and quit that drinking, I quit stealing, quit that shoplifting and I haven't looked back. People can't drag me back into those bad things because I know what it is. That's how I see so clearly to speak on these subjects. I want people to be humane. I want alcohol to be known as a very bad evil. I am very frustrated because I have so much to offer people but the media have made this misconception of me where I am a bad person. They like to make me out to be a bad person because it sells their newspapers. But then we know that democracy is a form of slavery.'

Chris Eubank is a Bad Person because he hurt Michael Watson in the ring and, shortly after, a motorway construction worker was killed when the boxer's Range Rover swerved off the A23. He doesn't care to discuss such things. Anyway, most journalists are 'jealous' and even 'evil', so they make 'mountains out of ant's nests'.

Chris Eubank is a Bad Person because he makes ideologically unsound statements about a woman's place being in the kitchen.

'I'm an old-fashioned man,' he explains to me, 'so my wife she cooks and she looks after the children and that's the only way you can live in my household. But I hold the woman sacred. I love the woman. I love the female. I respect the female. I saw a film called Scent Of A Woman with Al Pacino and he makes a statement that women are the very essence of life. That is a fact. But I understand old-fashioned ways. The woman should sustain while the man pursues and he hunts and the woman she is water for the man, she puts the fire out in the man, she calms and soothes the man.'

Chris Eubank is a Bad Person because, the sportswriters tell us, he doesn't fight boxers, he fights creaky wheezers and tubs of lard.

The man fumes agin the accusation: 'Was Nigel Benn in 1990 a weak opponent? No, he wasn't! Neither was Michael Watson. He beat me to a pulp but unfortunately I landed a punch that's left him, er . . . (he pauses here, and sadly shakes his head) . . . But let's say for argument's sake that you are correct, that I only want to fight people who can't hurt me. Well, would you blame me? No!'

Above all Chris Eubank is a Bad Person because, well, simply because he is decidedly not Frank Bruno, that celebrated panto-mime horse. Chris Eubank, bless him, does not want to be Frank Bruno.

'Frank Bruno fits the stereotype of a boxer. I fight against the stereotype. Period. Frank Bruno is conventional. I don't want to be conventional. I want to be, er . . .' Unconventional? 'Yes! Unconventional. That is Chris Eubank.'

Chris Eubank wouldn't dream of trotting up in daft costume as a panto turn even if he were asked, he assures me.

'Never! I would never do pantomime. It's not in my nature. I won't degrade myself. I'm not that type. That very tall guy, that Matthew Kelly who has that television programme You Bet! (idiotic game show featuring pointless stunts with steamrollers and custard), he says, Come and do the show, you'd love the show, so he doesn't understand me at all. That show, You Bet!, is not acceptable. I am not a Celebrity Squares sort of person at all. I am a tryer. I am a risk-taker and I have so much courage and I have all the things that are needed to be a champion: determination, good will, diligent work, a sound mind, a body which is tough, discipline, good conduct. I am not a person to go beneath my dignity with a show like You Bet!'

Nevertheless, Chris Eubank would not be averse to doing commercials on the telly.

'I would love to do that but people won't use me because they are afraid of me.'

And, perhaps surprisingly for one so steeped in ... gravitas if you will, he is quite delighted with his Spitting Image puppet, the impish thing with the lithp.

'I like the character of that puppet because he's not thick, he is not stupid, he is not stereotypical. If they made my puppet going around talking like that (he feigns the accent of a dim-wit; sounds remarkably like Bruno) with my eyes all droopy and being punch-drunk, then that would be bad. But the puppet character is sprightly. He is jolly. He is like how I am.'

'Jolly' is scarcely the word I would have chosen to describe this unusual boxer whose line of conversation runs more to utterances such as 'I talk as a radical but it is not accepted by the people. I've often thought of going back to school so maybe I will hire a retired don from Cambridge or Oxford and study three hours a day, five days a week because I want this world changed to be a better place' than to anything remotely resembling levity. But let it pass. Let us talk about Chris Eubank, Man of Style. The garments this master of braggadocio chooses to parade in do not come cheap. By no means.

'I am a Versace man,' Eubank announces with a pride normally reserved for a first round knockout. Eubank, unbeaten in his 36-bout career, is pleased to be dressed by pompous Italians.

'I am a Versace man but I am the type of Versace man which is subtle. I am discreet, not loud. I have got very good dress sense.'

Do you spend a lot of money on underpants, I ask? He remains totally unflustered at the question.

'I bought a pair of underpants the other day by Versace for £90, believe it or not,' he says loudly, seemingly assuming that I will be struck dumb by awe at the announcement. 'Mike Tyson wears Versace. This jacket I am wearing, it is Fujiwara. It is casual wear.

It is very nice, as well. And Comme des Garçons. I've got about three pieces of Comme des Garçons.'

He now proceeds to rattle off an impressively lengthy list of favoured designers whose names I fail to catch (and would be unble to spell even if I did). You're not into grunge, then, Mr Eubank?

'Grunge?' he says, appalled. 'I have never heard of it. I choose not to think of grunge. I'm into looking decent. Not loud, not outrageous, just decent.'

Chris Eubank, rich and somewhat infamous, rides a Harley Davidson motorbike (often, it is rumoured, without due care and attention). He pays particular scrutiny to his raiment when he is aboard his 'hog', he reveals.

'When I ride my Harley Davidson, I wear riding attire – jodhpurs, riding boots, tie, waistcoat, flying jacket, sometimes polo boots. That is me. It's horse-riding attire, not motorbike attire. But then I consider my bike to be a horse.'

What a dash the swaggerer must cut as he roars along the byways, eh?

'I've got a profile like you would not believe!' he goes, once more in boastful mode. 'I pose. I strut. That is the Mister Hyde of me. But I have so much to offer the world – more than you could possibly believe!'

Chris Eubank. When it comes to the art of self-confidence, he is, as croaky little Tina Turner puts it every time, 'simply the best'. There again, he thinks his motorbike is a horse. He 'ticks', he 'tocks', and as I take my leave, the philosophical one has a final pearl of wisdom to impart.

'What you must always remember is this. I will tell you. Boxing is not the same as embroidery.'

Freddie Starr

Here he comes, the truly alternative comedian with his stories about cold beans and John Lennon, his half-eaten rodent roll, and his all-too-accurate impression of cocaine abuse. And all the time you're wondering if he's wearing the Hitler knickers.

'YEAH, ER, YEAH . . .' The somewhat plump man in the dressing room on the pier at Great Yarmouth, the Blackpool of the East Coast, is struggling to make a cup of tea and to respond to a journalist's question, both at the same time. This is too much for him. He is a teetotaller, we hear, he has won his long and valiant battle with drugs (cocaine, valium). He is back on his feet. But still he doesn't understand that you have to plug in a kettle if you wish it to boil. I point this out to him. 'Ooh, who's a clever boy then?' goes the comedian, flipping a limpy wrist and puckering his lips (so old-fashioned, he still believes a 'homo' 'joke' to be amusing beyond belief). 'How many sugars did you say, sweetie?' I have already told him several times that I do not require a cup of tea. Can we get back to the matter in hand?

The corpulent comic attempts to pull himself together. His words remain blurred, his thought processes apparently slurred. We were talking about rock music . . .

'Er, yeah, well, you see, I went to see John Lennon when he was alive. I mean, up to his house, knock on the door, he came with a kaftan on and said, Stay for lunch and I said, Yeah. So he opened me a can of beans and a fork and we sat on the floor and ate them. Cold. Bizarre. That was John Lennon. Other people that I've met, the great people like Tommy Cooper and he was just joking all the time and you never knew anything.'

Such are the reminiscences of Freddie Starr, the variety maestro

who has, so often, reduced Des O'Connor to tears of laughter on
the Des O'Connor sofa.

There's an all-pervading smell of burgers and onions, of candy-
floss and badly-behaved children as the chill winds whip across
the seafront of a bleak Great Yarmouth. You want to play bingo
for really crap prizes made in the Far East? Do so. You want to
watch Gerry And The Pacemakers or Keith Harris And Orville
(the duck) or Linda Lusardi or any number of 'as-seen-on-TV'
hypnotists/magicians and has-beens performing here this summer
season for the short-tempered holiday crowd? Do so. My Dad
Went To Great Yarmouth And All He Bought Me Was This Lousy
T-Shirt. £7.99. The smart money, however, is upon Freddie Starr,
whose merriment show upon the pier is all but sold out. Who is
Freddie Starr? Oh, come, now, you must remember . . .

Mafeking Relieved. King Abdicates. Hitler Dead. Churchill Dead.
Elvis Dead. Lots of 'Argies' dead. (GOTCHA!) Headlines such as
these pale into insignificance when compared to the most famous
headline of them all: FREDDIE STARR ATE MY HAMSTER.
There it was on the front cover of the soaraway Sun on Thursday,
March 13, 1986. ('Comic put a live pet in sandwich, says beauty')
A masterstroke of British newspaper publishing; a five-word statement to be reproduced on T-shirts around the land; a fabulous yarn
to be debated around dinner tables from Hampstead to Halifax. At
that time, the nation, or most of it, had all but forgotten who
Freddie Starr actually was: there were dim recollections of this
bloke dressed up like Adolf Hitler in Wellington boots, shouting
nonsense and falling over a lot on the box but nothing more. He
hadn't been on the telly for ages (he was just too wild and anarchic
for the TV powers to take; well, that's his story; possibly no-one
actually found him very funny anymore.) But then he ate 'model'
Lea La Salle's hamster – 'I saw him take a bite. Then I saw part
of my hamster Supersonic sticking out from between the bread!
He killed my pet' (did no such thing, of course: a tabloid fantasy)
– and thus was a name and a career revitalised.

'Oh, Freddie Starr ate my hamster,' groans Freddie Starr who
never ate a hamster. 'That's so boring. That, more than anything
I've ever done in my whole career or has ever been printed about
me, has made me famous, like, er, people still say to me, Did you
eat the hamster? They actually ask me that sort of question and I

say, No. Fuck off. You get people shouting out to you all the time, Hamster! They're all dickheads, really.'

Seven years after the invention, the domestic animal non-incident, the hectic clown is back on our screens, cavorting with busty modoms and pulling outrageous faces just like Benny Hill used to do before his sad demise (Starr even does a 'Fred Scuttle' in his new TV show). And seven years after, I am stretched out on the Great Yarmouth dressing room floor of the one they always call wacky and zany and madcap, the one whose trousers have actually been known to fall off on stage such is the subtle nature of his humour. I don't want to be stretched out here on this carpet, you understand, but I am: all because 'our' Freddie, the Scouse git, seems more intent on impressing me with his karate skills than answering any of my enquiries. 'Here, pull my hair,' he instructs me. 'Go on. Pull it. Harder!' I do as I'm bid and – golly! – he's toppled me deftly upon my back. 'And they say I'm just a fat bastard!' he cackles victorious. Ooh, that is most impressive, sir, so could we continue with our chat now? We were discussing rock music.

'U2. I like U2,' he confides, 'and UB40. But it's not like it used to be, like Eddie Cochrane, Little Richard, Presley, people like that, you know. Jerry Lee Lewis. I did a show with Jerry Lee. Him and The Beatles. Did a show with Little Richard once. He wanted to take me back to America with him.'

At this Starr grins widely and winks (Little Richard is rather a 'poof', you see). 'Little Richard (wink) wanted to take me back to America and un, and um . . . teach me how to play the piano!' Boom boom!

The glittering career of Freddie Starr (né Frederick Fowell), 49 or thereabouts, began in Liverpool in the early 1960s where he wanted to be a pop star just like everybody else. He sang with Howie Casey And The Seniors and with his own Freddie Starr And The Midnighters (three awful flop singles on Decca produced by the legendary Joe Meek); according to Pete Frames's 'family tree', Liverpool 1963: Cavern Kids 1: 'Witnesses say that in his heyday he was one of the best rock singers in Liverpool but imitation and parody eclipsed any original style.'

'I toured with Howie Casey And The Seniors, toured Germany for about three years,' says the comic, pondering upon the mysteries of the electric kettle. 'Played with Gerry And The Pacemakers,

Kingsize Taylor And The Dominoes, people like that. The Beatles. Tony Sheridan, who John Lennon pinched his dance off. I shared a place with him (John Lennon) for about two weeks because I got thrown out of my place for being a naughty boy.'

Naughty boy? What is this? Drugs? Women? Starr just affects a silly smile and winks at me. 'John was a nice guy. He was a naughty boy, too. He was a bit mad like me, a comedian.' So how did Starr transform himself from failed pop singer to top funnyman, one wonders?

'The comedian in me was always there. I've never looked at life that seriously or taken showbiz as Tinseltown, as people call it. I'm not a showbiz person. I don't particularly like showbiz people. I don't play golf with anybody. I keep well away from them, the little cliques of show business who play golf. (A dig at dear, old 'Tarby' here, possibly?) I mix with my own sort of people.'

And who exactly are your 'sort of people', Mr Starr? Sometimes, often, it is clear that Freddie Starr is not listening or paying much attention to one's questions. He answers this one thus:

'Yeah, you're right. You see, I've always gone against the establishment. Like you mustn't do that, you mustn't smoke – so I smoke. (With unsteady hand he lights up a Benson & Hedges to prove the point, to show the rebel in him.) Or you mustn't park on double yellow lines – so I park on double yellow lines. Why not? I mean, can prostitutes have babies? Yeah, that's how they make traffic wardens!'

He looks at me with a look that tells me I am supposed to now laugh at this rib-tickler. I fail singularly to do so and he seems a little displeased. 'What's your wife look like? Mine looks like Gandhi . . . Goosey Goosey Gandhi, that is!' Hur hur. (Actually, he's separated from his wife and the point of this quip at this juncture is . . . God only knows). And he still hasn't told us how he switched from pop to comedy. Please tell us. We are dying to know.

'It just happened,' he sighs as if this were the most boring and obvious question ever posed. Finally, having, for some reason, accused me of concealing all the dressing room teaspoons in my pockets and given me another swift karate briefing, he elaborates.

'What happened was I just laid back and be'd what I want to be. It was singing songs, like serious ballads. I just could not do that and not laugh, you know, seeing the expressions on some of the girls' faces in the audience. I'd say, and I still say it to this day,

Do you want to play with my willy, darling? Do you want to play with it, baby? I was doing that years ago. I was writing sort of Monty Python things years before Monty Python came out. What I do is just what the average guy in the street wants to see and it's better what I do than most of these pisspots and prima donnas.'

Freddie Starr does not care particularly for what was once called alternative comedy.

'There's so many of them, the Rik Mayalls and that lot. Oh, they shag. They say the word "shag" and "fuck" and things like that, which I say on my adult shows. They talk about "shag" and masturbation and all that. I don't compete with them because I am the alternative comedian. No-one can analyse what I do, my humour. I defy them to. You get someone who's never been on the fucking stage in their life and they sit there with a pen and pad and they try to write down the psychology of my comedy! Fuck them.'

The bare-faced cheek of it!

'Yeah, and nobody can psychoanalyse me! What is it? You can never psychoanalyse what makes people laugh. When you see a fella fall over a tray of fucking food and break his back, it makes you laugh doesn't it?'

Er, not really, no.

'Yeah. See? It's like cartoons. And me, I'm unpredictable. It's like there's a boxing ring and there's Mike Tyson and after the last bell's gone, I'll jump in. What I am is . . . er . . . unpredictable.'

What Freddie Starr is is . . . well, in his 'adult' shows he tells jokes like this: 'I had a Lebanese last night. I woke up with the Shiites,' which is quite sophisticated, really. He will say to a woman in the audience, 'You've got big tits, haven't you?' He will use the word 'clit' and he'll hold 'farting competitions' and he'll do some pedestrian rock'n'roll, like Buddy Holly's Rave On.

'What's wrong with that? I don't like songs that go "I jumped overboard and fell through a glass house where I found Jesus but it was Frank Bruno". I do songs like Rave On and The Great Pretender that reflect on parts of my life. I could sing any song that was ever written better than most people could, you know, but sometimes I have to play to the middle of the road and do songs for them.'

F. Starr does not like to give offence. Not to his adoring public. That's why he humiliates them so. They love it. 'Feel my cucumber, darlin'.'

'I don't like any racial sort of gags at all,' he says, going strangely sincere on me, 'because look there.' He points to a table in the corner of the dressing room upon which one can spy a copy of the Bible. 'That there is a book called the Holy Bible. That book's killed more people than any atomic bomb. So I think that religion is a very personal thing and it's no business of anybody else. So I don't like racism at all.'

Does he not realise that his Adolf Hitler-in-Swastika-festooned-undergarments has given offence to Jews in the past? His answer? 'Pavarotti in the Park. What a cunt. The longer you know a person, the shorter his name gets. I call him "Pav". He calls me "Ffff". I'm doing a concert with him but I'll have a wet suit on.' This is a display of the famed unpredictability of Freddie Starr, one supposes. Very droll. We were talking about Hitler?

'Well, the thing about Adolf Hitler is that he was a complete twat,' says Freddie, and he seems to mean this from the heart. He becomes aglow with sincerity once more as he fumbles for another fag.

'I would dearly, dearly, have loved to have put a bullet through Hitler's head. And Eva. The double act. I would dearly love to have burnt them both and opened the doors of the concentration camps and let every Jewish person out. So I don't do Adolf Hitler as a . . . er, I come on in shorts and wellies and it's done in a way that the man is saying we shall reign for a thousand years as the Third Reich. Well, he didn't last long, so I take the piss out of Adolf Hitler . . . It's like . . . it's like . . . you know, it's like.'

Freddie Starr has worked himself up into a state of indignation about the horror of Hitler and all that and he has something further to say. If he could only work out what it was.

'It's like . . . you know . . . have you got a teaspoon in your pocket, or are you just glad to see me? Hur . . . no . . . you know, what I mean is . . . rapists!'

Pardon?

'Rapists! It's the criminal element. It's just getting out of hand, you know. They just get a smack on the wrist and they don't care. That's the attitude. If I shoot somebody, I'll probably get 10 years and I'll be out after three. I don't think that's a good system to scare anybody away. If you got a rapist and you cut his testicles off and his penis and stuck his penis to his head, right there on the top so he could never wear a cap, then I think that would scare them off. And I would volunteer to do the operations, actually. I would. With a Black & Decker.'

Freddie Starr, at this particular point, is not joking. Often Freddie Starr resembles somebody who's suffering from a slight drug problem. As, of course, he once was. Addicted to cocaine, addicted to valium, or so the tabloid press took great relish in informing us. I attempt to alter the subject to that of 'Freddie's Drug Misery' and, with a knowing smirk, Starr mimes the operation of a person snorting a mammoth line of coke. He does it again, so make that two mammoth lines of coke. And then his features take on an expression of great piety.

'No,' he says, 'I just think people should behave themselves a bit more, you know. Like, if you have a drink that's OK. If you start drinking three bottles of whisky a day, you're in trouble. I didn't know valium was so addictive but I kept taking them and I was taking them to an extent, lots and lots of them, where I couldn't keep a tight rein on them and I wasn't controlling them, they were controlling me and . . .'

Starr shifts in his seat, stands and moves to the window, stares out at the beach and the cold, grey sea. He turns around and glares at me. He seems annoyed. He has just twigged something: I have asked him a personal question. Freddie Starr doesn't care for personal questions from members of the press.

'What is your right as a journalist sitting down speaking to me and asking me a personal question?' he barks, stubbing out a cigarette with some fury. 'You've got as much right as a fellow walking down that beach to come up and ask me a personal question. If somebody on that beach came up and asked you a personal question, what would you say to them? You'd say, Fuck off, go away!'

I gather that the slapstick supremo is telling me to fuck off. And go away.

'The press. They're all hypocrites. They can go out fucking, they can go out and get pissed every night. But nobody else can, so they're hypocrites. They get away with murder. They've got their hit lists. If it's not me, it's Ian Botham. And then there's the guys they won't write about, like Cliff Richard. Hur hur!'

A man of mood swings, a man of wonky attention span, Freddie has now forgotten all animosity toward me and launches into a surreal joke about Cliff and teaspoons and Pavarotti which I confess I do not understand at all. He mimics the partaking of cocaine again. He lunges at me in a further karate demonstration. You're mad, aren't you? I go. This, evidently, is not a personal question. His reply is hyperactive.

'Of course I am. Of course I am. We're all mad. I sat next to Michael Jackson at an awards thing once. I didn't know I was sitting next to Michael Jackson because it don't interest me, that kind of star thing. We're all human beings. I don't believe in the word "star". Never have done. Just put bums on seats and I'm only Freddie Starr when the band strikes up and the curtain goes up and I go on stage and it's like breaking out of prison. When's the wheel going to fall off? When's the people not going to want to see me no more? I'm not that bothered, really. I know it's going to happen. It's like death. I know that's going to hapen. So fuck it, eh?'

Absolutely. So you have no regrets, then, Freddie Starr?'

'Regrets?' Freddie ponders the point. Gravitas or wisecrackery: which tactic will he adopt this time? 'Yeah, I'd like to be white.' He wheezes at the jocular riposte. 'I'd like to be white, yeah. Er, what would I like to be? I'd like to be a model, a female model that was beautiful and pretty and could slip into famous people's wallets and get married to them and take them for a ride and get all their money.

'If I had my time over again, if there was such a thing as that – what's it? – er, reincarnation, I'd be a hooker. I'd be a female groupie hooker. Yeah, and probably have a child. I would like to have been a woman. That's fair enough, isn't it? Come and examine my bollocks.'

Oh, the hilarity of it all. But this moment of high jocularity is followed by a further abrupt change of tone. Serious. Starr's voice goes all grave and pianissimo.

'But, listen. Jesus tried to please everybody. And look what happened to him. Am I right? Am I right? Am I right?'

William Roache

He is one of this country's biggest television stars and something of a sex symbol. He's stalked Coronation Street for more than thirty years, proved in court that he's not boring and is not a Druid. Fame, he says, is a strange animal.

THE MAN with the sensible shoes, the homely cardigan and the retrospective haircut strolls up to the bar. 'Half a bitter, please, Bet,' he says in his drear yet amiable drawl as he clinks coins in the palm of his hand and the peroxide siren with the earrings from Hell obliges. 'One for yourself!' 'Ta, chuck.' This is the ritual known to millions of British television viewers as Ken-Barlow-dropping-in-at-The-Rovers-for-a-swift-one. Sometimes said ritual ends in loss of tempers and fisticuffs – 'Right, that's it, Baldwin!' More often it's a thing of badinage and platitudes – 'So, how are the pigeons, Jack?' 'Well, you shouldn't put so much pressure on Tracy, Deirdre, after all she's a young woman now, with her own life to lead ... now, now, Deirdre, I'm only trying to help.' But always it starts with a half of bitter (Newton & Ridley's) and it has been going on now for 32 years.

William Roache *is* Ken Barlow. He protests that he's just an actor – a professional actor dedicated to his craft – playing a part, but he has a tendency to turn into Ken – Boring Barlow – before one's very eyes. We are strolling together down Coronation Street, the most famous street in England (far better known than, say, Downing Street), past The Kabin where Rita and Mavis sell huge quantities of The Weatherfield Gazette, past Alf's Mini Mart (where a fat man with a heart problem does a roaring trade in convenience foods and sausages and cigars for the evil dwarf Baldwin), and we come to the door of Number 2. William Roache touches the door – strokes it, almost – and says, with a seeming regret. 'This is the door that Deirdre has slammed in my face so many times.' Deirdre is Ken Barlow's estranged wife. And if you've never seen Coronation Street, you won't know what on earth he is talking about. Coronation Street is fiction and we can't drop in at the Rover's Return, right there next to Number 2, for a half of bitter because the pub doesn't actually exist. Nonetheless, William Roache *is* Ken Barlow. People come up to him in the street (as opposed to the Street) and ask, he tells me, 'When are you going to get back with Deirdre, then, Ken?' But, you see, the people do this with so much love. 'Oh,' says William Roache, actor, 61, 'people have so much affection for me . . . er, for Ken, because Ken is a very gentle character. And if people confuse me with the character I play, there's no harm done. It's a compliment, actually. It shows I'm doing my job.'

There are two discernible minor differences between Roache and his school-teaching on-screen character, however. Firstly, the shoes: Ken's are ever so polished and nicely turned out while William, this day, is sporting a pair of Pat Boone-styled loafers that were all the rage 30 years ago. Secondly, William – 'Bill' to friends and Granada TV security staff – is 'feeling really rough'; William has a slight hangover – too much wine at the lunch party for his autobiography Ken and Me last night. Ken (if you don't count that stormy patch he went through a couple of years ago when he lost his job and his extra-marital affair with Wendy Crozier fell to pieces and he hit the bottle and the pills) never has a hangover: it's 'Half a bitter, please, Bet' and that's the limit. Ken and his real-life alter ego have, famously, been called 'boring' in the public prints. Well, there's no smoke without you know what, or is there?

It was on December 9, 1960 when the 28-year-old actor appeared in black and white, tinkering with a bicycle and talking in an accent from oop North. Ken Barlow – Lancastrian youth (he was supposed to be 18) with ideas above his station (he wanted to go to university!) – was born. Ken's accent has evolved over the years into an unidentifiable middle-class thing. Ken and William Roache sound exactly the same. As I sit down in Roache's cramped dressing room, where snapshots of Ken amongst assembled cast and newspaper clippings saying how great Coronation Street is are pinned up upon the wall, I tell the soapmeister that I'm very worried about little Tracy. (Explanation for non-aficionados: Tracy is Deirdre's daughter and Ken Barlow's adopted daughter and, well, it's a long and unlikely story but what's happened, to cut it short, is Tracy's gone all sulky of late episodes and is living with a bloke called Craig who's got long hair! What a muddle!!)

'Oh, we're all very worried about Tracy,' he goes. 'I'm very worried about her boyfriend as well. That scene I had with the boy, when I went to see him . . . it was infuriating, it was frustrating. My daughter, who only yesterday was a little girl playing with her doll at home, is suddenly shacking up with him. And, really, all you want to do is drag them out and bang their heads together, but you've got to walk on eggshells. This boy was so arrogant!'

The actor is getting quite steamed up and emotional about the Tracy-leaving-home situation. Should I remind him that it's only a story? You sound just like Ken, I say. Do you ever dream that you're Ken?

'Oh, no,' he replies, 'But I don't get all uppity and shout "I'm William Roache" when people come up and call me "Ken". I don't. I know who I am.'

But as he has been Ken for more than half of his life, a certain amount of confusion could be understandable – especially as Ken Barlow was a sort of public figure (of England's dreaming) almost from the start. Coronation Street was an instant success. Within moments there were celebrities – The Beatles, Tom Jones, the Queen and her lovely husband – paying visits to the Granada lot to meet the folk of back-street fiction. Ken Barlow was famous, so William Roache thought he was, too. In the 1960s, the jobbing thesp of the small screen became a bit of a lad. Yes, in real life he did the thing that soap men do on a daily basis: he betrayed his wife.

'Yes,' he said, a contrite expression settling upon his crumpling features. 'Fame is a strange animal,' he murmurs. 'Well, no, it's not in my nature to be a, er, "bit of a lad" but what happened was that I was married and the wife and family were in London and I was up here in Manchester Monday to Friday and I . . . misbehaved. I've never hell-raised or anything in the sense of going out and drinking late at night and all that but, yes, I had some affairs. You can say that what I did was horrible or you can say that I was a Jack-the-lad but it was neither. I didn't like the goings-on that I got myself into but it happened. And I think I learned a lot. It makes me value the family and things now.'

Did William Roache ever smoke pot, we'd like to know? His reply is awesomely Kennish:

'No, I was too scared in my own skin to go into the drug scene.

You see, I have a slight hearing problem that happened in the army (he did National Service in the early '50s: there was a bit of a muck up with a live mortar that blasted his ear drum). And that means that in background noise I can't hear at all, so I can't join in on noisy pub scenes or nightclub scenes. So I could never inspect the drug scene. Also, I've never particularly liked big social groups. I prefer one to one or going out to dinner or something.'

He looks rather a misery as he makes this dull confession. He has already told me, 'I'm the tragedian of the Street. I am a one-man Greek tragedy.' Time, I think, to jolt him from out of the gloom by posing a jolly question. Such as: so tell me, Mr Roache, are you and Ken really boring?

In 1991, a Sun journalist, Ken Irwin, wrote a piece which claimed that William Roache was smug and arrogant and boring and went on to direct other unkind accusations at the fellow. Roache sued. And won £50,000.

'I didn't go into litigation because he called me boring,' says Roache, somewhat annoyed. 'No, no, this is a good point because everybody thinks I did. I take on the nose any criticism that anybody wants to make – I've had 32 years of it. You get people that don't like you – fortunately mostly they do. But if someone says that in his opinion I am boring, then fine. I don't like it but I accept that. But the litigation was over something that I've never had happen to me before. This guy, Ken Irwin, came out and said that I'd been up for the sack more than any actor in the Street, that I couldn't do my job, that I was a joke with the writers and that I was hated by the cast. Now he couldn't back up one of those statements. He couldn't bring forward a single witness to justify it. It was a direct attack on my professional standing. It was nothing to do with being smug and arrogant and boring. I would not dare go to court to prove that I'm not boring. Boring is a funny thing. I've never been voted the most boring man on television. Ever. But that whole article was demeaning and denigrating and was a knife aimed straight at the heart of my professional ability. And no-one had ever said that before. They'd always said that I am a good actor. You don't get awards, you don't keep your job for 32 years, you don't have the strong scenes written for you if you're not a good actor!'

Roache becomes quite heated as he waits there before the dressing room mirror defending his honour. There's simply no stopping him:

'Truth! That's why I went to litigation. The truth is the basic thing. And the tabloid papers who continually commit libel should have their licence revoked, something that hurts them. So apart from Ken Irwin hitting me professionally. I also had this fierce missionary zeal that the tabloids were getting dreadful, worse than dreadful, and I wanted somehow to put a stop to them. That's why I did it. It was not a pleasant experience.'

So William Roache is not boring.

'About 10 or 12 years ago there was a phase when I . . . when Ken was moving from being a juvenile into middle age and the script writers got him a bit lost. That's when all the boring thing came in. He was meant to be boring to give Deirdre a reason for going off with Mike. It was Ken who said to Deirdre. You think I'm boring! He shouted it. (*Roache shouts it*). YOU THINK I'M BORING! So the press pick up on it. Boring Barlow is an alliteration, it sticks. I get very annoyed at the way the press just knock and they shove these adjectives in. Boring. Or everybody's "Raunchy", Raunchy Mavis. They just put these unthinking, reactionary adjectives in.' He pauses, tempers his indignation, adds as a *non-sequitur* 'But you see, when we're handling things like marital problems in the Street, a lot of people write in and say that it has helped them.'

So William Roache believes his talents as an actor to be ample. But it must be a right old doddle, surely, playing the same slipper-loving character decade after decade.

'Well, last night someone said that. "Oh, 32 years, you just bowl up and sort of ad-lib your way through it." People like that, they just do not know! It's demanding. It's tough. In the theatre you have time to work, to create, to build, but I have to get into the work and do it instantly. It takes great personal discipline. We are top-line actors and very professional and anyone who thinks otherwise just ought to come in and watch us working. The people who come in and watch are quite staggered at the pressure and the speed of the work and the adrenalin and the nerves. That is acting. Acting is a craft that has to be learned. There's not many can do it.'

William Roache goes on to provide examples of his craft at its best.

'The hardest bits of acting ever were all my weeping and wailing over the Deirdre business and really getting furious and slamming her against her door. No, actually slamming Deirdre against the door was quite satisfying. I enjoyed that. The hardest thing to portray was my pill-taking. I did talk to someone who had done that, taken pills, and they said there was this feeling of unreality. You slip into a sort of staring or glazed state . . .' Who'd have thought it? 'When you act out scenes of anger, you really have to release anger. The adrenalin pumps through your system. I don't know whether that's good or bad for you. I don't know what a psychologist would say.'

A charge that has been levelled often in recent times against Coronation Street is that the series is stuck in a land that time forgot, fails to show England as it is today, fails to portray black folk or anything 'controversial', is cosy, a televisual comfort blanket. Roach sighs. He's heard it all before.

'What people forget is that Coronation Street is an entertainment – and the fact that it's still there after 32 years and top of the ratings shows that it is good entertainment. If people say, You've got to put a black in, alright perhaps we'll put a black in but then the Chinese will want to be in, the Asians will want to be in, you've got to have your gay, your lesbian, your right and left wing politicians and all your religions and handicapped people. Where do you stop? It's like saying that Children's Ward (*kiddies' telly series all about little people with bandages on their heads*) hasn't got enough grown-ups in it. It's not a fair criticism. We are not supposed to be a documentary showing the social structure of Britain. We're a little street, a little community, perhaps slightly out of date, slightly nostalgic. What's wrong with that?'

Our tabloid newspaper have contrived to play it both ways with the famous William Roache/Ken Barlow. One minute he is Mister Boring and there are cartoons of people snoozing in front of their tellies as Roache delivers his post-Sun trial speech. He plays golf with Tarbie and Brucie and Eddie Large. The next he is not boring at all but instead an amazingly and astonishingly fascinating figure because . . . he is some kind of religioso/spiritual nutcase, the David Icke of the soaps. In the 1970s, he would turn up at Stonehenge dressed in sandals and crisp white sheets, a member of the Druid Order. Recently, he popped up on Dr Anthony Clare's psyche-quest of a radio programme and expounded upon his belief in reincarnation. So he is not boring, he is bonkers, it's as simple as that. Tell me, Mr Roache, are you a loony or what?

'Oh, no. Look. I'm not a sanctimonious person, I'm just a normal guy with a family falling way behind the ideals that I have, but I do explore. I have explored and searched for truth. It's not pious, it's actually quite unbelievable, frightening, awe-inspiring when you get into this because you begin to know with a capital "K". There is ridicule, of course: Charles gets it (that's Prince Charles to you). Charles knows with a capital "K". But there are things he can't talk about because the materialistic people don't want to know and they tend to ridicule because it's an area that makes them feel uncomfortable.'

I don't think I feel particularly uncomfortable. I just rather wish I knew what he was going on about.

'I often get rung up by people in television saying, We've got a late night show on witchcraft, will you come along? Will you wear your Druid's outfit? No, I will not. I am not a Druid. It was part of my studies. I was with them for a few years and their philosophy, basically, is look for the truth. But I only talk about my beliefs to people who are interested.'

Which rather rules me out. I suppose. Perhaps not . . .

'People who are searching know that somewhere there are these people, there are gurus, there are men of God, men of heightened consciousness, heightened awareness, they are around. But you will only find one when you deserve one.'

Is Ken Barlow a guru, one wonders?

'I have been fortunate enough to meet a Master. But this is something that only happens when you're ready.'

He warms to his theme (whatever it is).

'There are good, spiritual people searching and the Church isn't giving them the information. I get very cross with the Church. The Church should be teaching about life after death, teaching about the progressive reincarnation that the human spirit goes through which is (*here he clenches his fists and hisses*) the only thing that makes sense! The responsibility is in your own hands for your next life! The minute you truly understand that we are spirits incarnated in physical bodies and we are drawn to the one that is of the same vibrational set-up that we are – it's like gravity – everything makes sense! This is the truth. This is the TRUTH!! If anybody should get this truth over (*he begins to slap his fist into his palm, the better to emphasise the 'truth'*) problems in Ireland (*slap*), South Africa (*slap*), Yugoslavia (*slap*), war (*slap*) would disappear over-night (*mighty slap*)! You don't need to be spooky, walk around in funny robes or anything to find the truth. Anyone can explore the truth and find it. This is why I think Charles is a super guy. I'm really upset about the girls who hit the Royal Family and give an excuse for the anti-Royalists. Once you understand reincarnation, you know that Charles is not just an accident of birth. He hasn't got there for no reason. In his progressive reincarnations, he has earned his position!'

Which hardly goes very far to explaining Prince Andrew, does it? But I do not murmur this, for as the non-boring one says, it's so very easy to ridicule. Nonetheless, what would Bet Gilroy think if Ken Barlow sauntered up to the bar of the Rovers and started spouting forth in this manner? She'd probably give him a funny look and softly say, 'Now, now, chuck, don't be soft. We don't want to upset my regulars, do we?' And then she'd put the kettle on.

Mr Blobby

How it tickles us, this seven-foot piece of pink rubber, this preposterous bow-tied blancmange with luxuriant lashes and an acute standing up problem. How we hoot when he utters his restricted catchphrase and tumbles, once again, to the ground.

WITH HINDSIGHT, one could argue that it was all horribly inevitable. With the self-same hindsight, one could argue that it was the end of English civilisation as we knew it. What was it about the English that, fast approaching those old *fin-de-siècle* blues, they became so obsessed with, so adoring of, only fat fools? Cyril Smith. He had once passed himself off as a politician. Ended his career as a clown-star of vulgarian television commercials. There was Paul Gascoigne. 'Gazza' to the nation. It wasn't his silky footballing skills we loved him for, was it? No. It was the fact that he blubbed at the World Cup, wore fake bosoms, acted the goat and was fat and dumb. There was Frank Bruno. It wasn't his inspirational pugilistic endeavours we worshipped him for, was it? No. It was the fact that he was a loser with an idiotic catchphrase ('Know what I mean, 'Arry?'), did panto ('what a sport!'), acted the goat and was, if not fat *per se*, large – and very dumb.

And then came the fattest, the dumbest of them all, 'someone' whose only talent was looking quite ridiculous, whose powers of 'language' were restricted to the one word 'Blobby'. It is fair to say that, at the time of going to press, Mr Blobby, buffoon creation of idiot television, is the most famous 'person' in the land. Beats the Princess of Wales (who may not be fat but is certainly stupid) at a canter.

Observe. The Q photographer takes the pink and yellow entity out into the street for some amusing snaps. Instantly windows are opened and there are office girls gazing out in wonderment and shouting hallelujahs at the superstar who responds to these attentions in the only way he knows how – by falling over. Falling over is the only thing that Mr Blobby is any good at, the fat fool. How we love him. Oh, Mr Blobby, titter titter, go the office girls. Blobby takes a bow. Yes, wherever our plump pal appears, there is a joyous lifting of hearts. Smiles break out, a light comes into the eyes of old and young, there is a murmur of pure pleasure, the clouds roll back, the sun-beams dance and everyone begins to count their blessings again. PS We are all mad.

He was born just over a year ago, this preposterous blancmange, this simpleton star. He was conceived as a joke for the popular BBC programme Noel's House Party. The wheeze was that celebrities would be fooled into taking part in a (fictitious) kiddies' show called Mr Blobby where, with the aid of the show's wobbly host, they would educate children about their specialist subject. And Blobby would do his best to annoy them. So we got Valerie Singleton, she of The Money Programme fame, teaching Mr Blobby about money – he fell over a sheep and Val looked perplexed. We had camp gourmet team Hudson and Halls teaching Mr Blobby the secrets of cuisine – he dropped all the food and assaulted a trifle and the telly chefs became rather irate. We had Will Carling on rugger (collapse of goalposts), Garth Crooks on soccer (ditto) and Wayne Sleep on dance (much slipshod leg movement and falling over). Best of all, there was the bronzed plater-spinner 'Whoo!' Gary Davies telling the rotund buffoon how to be a useful disc jockey; the portly pretend thing (betwixt bouts of falling over) scratched records to buggery and Davies was singularly unamused by the antics. (Interesting Fact: Most of the aforementioned japes crop up on the best-selling video – 'It's the Blobbumentary of the Century – Mr Blobby': but the Gary Davies interlude is strangely absent. One wonders why.)

The original Blobby joke was, it must be said, quite funny, but in recent months, since Noel's House Party returned for another season, the joke has changed entirely and isn't comical anymore. The role of the bow-tied jackass is no longer to make fools of minor celebrities but to be a celebrity in his own right instead. Mr Blobby has made a single. It went to Number 1 despite the fact that Radio One wouldn't play it on the thoroughly reasonable grounds that it was simply ghastly. *'Blobby, oh Mr Blobby/ You're the guy who puts the 'do' in 'do or die'/Blobby, oh Mr Blobby/*

Your deeds are guaranteed to stupefy' chirruped a lot of children to a tune that made Lily the Pink seem sophisticated (and evidently unaware that the word 'stupefy' doesn't mean, as is commonly believed, 'amaze', it means makes stupid or torpid, deprive of sensation). Mr Blobby. He's great at toppling over. Thus he became a brainless icon for the modern age.

'*Blobby, Mr Blobby/You're the one who bears the pink and yellow crest.*' He bears no such thing, actually, but '*crest*' rhymes with the bit that's coming up next. '*Blobby, Mr Blobby/You'll always prove that Blobby is the BEST.*' And here in the stout creature's PR offices, I sit next to him conducting a so-called interview. This is utterly ridiculous.

Q: 'Do you think that Mr Blobby represents the Zeitgeist, if you will, of modern Britain?'

Mr. Blobby: Silence. Followed by unseemly farting sound.

Q: 'Are you proud of your pop record?'

MB: 'Blobby, blobby, blobby!'

Mr Blobby's publicist: 'Are you going to be writing stuff about the actual record, how it has done, in your piece for Q? Because sales of today are now 540,000.'

MB: 'Blobby, blobby, blobby!'

Q: 'Christ, and it's a bloody awful record, isn't it?'

MB: Pushes me off the end of the sofa. 'Blobby!'

What larks.

You know something has become a phenomenon when the quality newspapers start printing lengthy and tedious think pieces about it. Mr Blobby was obviously going to be taken up by the tabloids. They'd have him in rib-tickling photographic situations. They would compare our tubby Hush-Puppied Chancellor Mr Kenneth Clarke to Mr Blobby ('Mr Blobby's Budget' headlines all over the shop). They'd conduct polls asking, 'Who should be the next manager of the England football team?' and Mr Blobby would come out on top. There'd be cartoons in the Sun and the Star in which it was side-achingly revealed that Mr Blobby was, in fact, Prince Charles in crafty disguise. (NB Mr Blobby has been a blessing and a gift to cartoonists throughout the land: even I could draw him if I felt like it.) But then, in early December, the intelligentsia, the literary, bounded up aboard the good ship Blobby, too, and things were out of hand.

The Blobby syndrome was discussed by Dominic Lawson, editor of The Spectator and chess buff (close personal friend of another national goon-superstar, Nigel Short) in the (fittingly) pink pages of The Financial Times. 'A couple of weeks ago, he (cartoon editor of The Spectator, Michael Heath) began filling the paper with cartoons of a strange figure, who bore a passing resemblance to the Michelin man,' wrote Lawson. "Who is that?" I asked. "Who is that?" said my cartoon editor. "You're like the judge who had never heard of The Beatles. That is Mr Blobby." "Who is Mr Blobby?" I persisted. "It doesn't matter," sighed my cultural adviser, "but he's massive. He's huge. He's taking over the country." And he was right.' (Spectator Blobby cartoon included Blobby with Her Maj. the Queen saying, 'Oh, Charles! Do pull yourself together!', and someone in the National Portrait Gallery observing a portrait of . . . Mr Blobby. Ho ho.)

In The Independent, arts person John Lyttle wrote an open letter to the gargantuan clot, 'You're the furthest evolution yet of that peculiarly British phenomenon "a good laugh", a term invariably prologued by the weasel words "It's just . . ." You are, in short, a great dumb joke, just what these tired, shallow times deserve. When you speak, you speak with the clear, authentic voice of the people . . . What's that you say? Speak up! "Blobby, Blobby, Blobby".'

In the Mail on Sunday's Night and Day section, Brian Appleyard, a man with a very large brain indeed, considered the tomfoolery. 'Mr Blobby is the eternal, well-intentioned wrecker. He is the comic bottom line – that which is always funny simply because it is so utterly stupid. He means nothing and he looks dreadful. He is devoid of significance.' (Come again? 'Devoid of significance'? Well, why are you, Mr Appleyard, and three million other eggheads analysing 'him' to death? Eh?)

And in the Sunday Times of December 12, Cosmo Landesman (husband of Julie Burchill) went totally bonkers on the Blobsome subject. 'Defining the zeitgeistian meaning of Mr Blobby is a game everybody can play. For those of the Camille Paglia persuasion, Mr Blobby represents the return of Dionysian paganism which our Christian culture has repressed for centuries . . . For the Jean Baudrillard brigade, it's more a case of hyperreality. For them, Mr Blobby is the first truly post-modern pop star, a simulacrum of stardom created to conceal the fact that there is no such thing as a real star anymore. As for the Neil Lyndon School of Male Paranoia, Mr Blobby is obviously a feminist plot to make the phallus look funny.'

Mr Blobby, you are a post-modern penis. It has been written.

Q: 'How do you feel, Mr Blobby, about these jolly serious, scholarly, pieces that have been written about you of late?'

MB: Long silence. Followed by immense farting commotion. And our fat friend tumbles off the sofa.

The trouble with interviewing Mr Blobby is that he does not have much to say for himself. Fart-wise sounds and exclamations of 'Blobby', blobby, blobby!' are his absolute limit. The publicists provide you with a 'Mr Blobby Fact File', a supposedly amusing Q&A.

Favourite pop star/band?

Mott the Hoople. (Don't get that.)

Favourite movie?

Straw Dogs. (Don't get that either. A very violent film featuring prolonged rape sequence with Susan George. Blobby is supposed to be a gentle innocent, is he not?)

Q: 'Why is Straw Dogs your favourite film?'

MB: 'Blobby, blobby, blobby!

Things are desperate here as I sit on this settee alongside the rubber-foam contraption. I must break it to you gently, readers, Mr Blobby does not actually exist. There is a man inside the oversized costume, a human being making the generous hand gestures and going 'Blobby!' It's a man that does all the falling over. A man called Barry. Barry Killerby. Sometimes Barry is a Shakespearian actor but right now he is Blobby. Barry has been quoted (in the soaraway Sun) as saying, 'I take Mr Blobby just as seriously as Shakespeare. In fact, I think it's harder to do Mr Blobby than Shakespeare.'

Alas, I am not permitted to converse with the man inside that pink and yellow finery. The BBC ('Mr Blobby is a trademark and copyright of the British Broadcasting Corporation 1992. Licensed by BBC Enterprises Limited') forbids it. Why, if I were to talk to Barry, thus unleashing the awful truth that Mr Blobby is a total fabrication and not a genuine article at all, it would be like telling the children of the world that Santa doesn't come down the chimer-nee of a Christmas Eve or that God is something entirely made up by lunatics, wouldn't it?' We can't have that.

Oh, but we can. Barry Killerby, who turns out to be a sensitive and somewhat serious soul, is as fed up with this phoney interview as I am. He is growing just a bit tired of saying 'Blobby, blobby, blobby!' and falling over. So bugger the BBC. Barry – the innards of the Blobmeister – wants to speak.

He is wearing shorts, is Barry. Unlike his alter ego, he is short and lithe. 'Mr Blobby,' he says, 'er, at the end of the day, it's only a bit of fun, isn't it?' Weasel words: 'It's only'.

'There are all these people waxing lyrical about the phenomenon of Mr Blobby. Like, apparently, you know, if the human eye sees yellow on a pink background it sends a message to the brain which tells the brain that it's found something funny and the brain instructs the relevant muscles to laugh. Oh dear. That was on the Today programme on Radio Four with Brian Redhead the other day. Talk about killing a gag! I thought, Give us a break! Oh dear. But while there's all that scholarly thought behind Mr Blobby, I was at the Royal Marsden cancer unit yesterday and I was crying inside that costume. Crying about the cruelty and condition of the patients and also about the joy that Mr Blobby was creating. The children and also the nurses – Mr Blobby gave everybody a lift. So people can criticise Blobby all they want but if you can bring a smile to children's faces, what's the harm in that? Mr Blobby is a bit of an unsung hero, actually, because most of the stuff that we've been doing is for charity. Like the Starlight Foundation for terminally sick children. They get three wishes, they can go to Disneyworld or fly on Concorde or anything like that, and one little boy said, I just want Mr Blobby to come to my fifth birthday party, so of course I went, and it was the most brilliant experience of my life. He was the most courageous person I've ever met, really. He died two weeks after that and his parents sent me a letter saying, Mr Blobby gave our son the best day of his life.'

Is this a lump I feel in my throat? I strongly suspect it is.

How long, I enquire, can Mr Blobby live on for?'

'Well, Mickey Mouse has just celebrated his 65th birthday and Mr Blobby is a lot funnier than him, so if it's handled properly, I don't see why he can't be around in 65 years. But with all this hype, all this press, all these people like you wanting to write about him, people could easily get bored.'

They could.

'People are knocking the record but it's the only one you can bounce around to these days, isn't it? What's wrong with that? I remember, Rolf Harris's Two Little Boys was the first record I ever bought. What's wrong with that? What's wrong with Mr Blobby? He just lifts people's spirits. I mean, we've had such bad news this year what with the recession going on for evermore, all that awful stuff in Liverpool with those children and all that kind of stuff, you know people just need a break, don't they? And I'm sorry that some people don't find that a good enough reason to enjoy something like Mr Blobby. I know that critics like you have to cover a piece of paper, but in a sense Mr Blobby has the last laugh because he's only a seven-foot piece of pink rubber and here you are wasting time and energy trying to analyse him. The joke is that he's a joke. He's a pastiche of every children's character that's ever been invented.'

From Pinky & Perky, from Titch & Quackers, from the Wombles to here. The path to madness this way, what? Have you ever met Bungle (recently replaced man in a daft bear's costume on TV's popular kiddiwinks experience Rainbow)?

'No, but I've met the man who played Basil Brush. Mr Blobby is much the same as Basil Brush because whatever the psychology of it is, whether you're 3 or 63, he appeals to the full range of people. Children love Blobby because he does things that they're not allowed to do (Barry makes a farting sound) and parents love him because he is anti-establishment.'

What, as an act-*or*, is your motivation, Blobbywise, Barry?'

'Er, well, no actor has ever had the licence that Mr Blobby allows. His conversation is a bit limited but the essence of Mr Blobby is that he has no brain but a very, very big heart.'

You thought you despised Mr Blobby. I trust that, having read the thoughts of Barry, you feel suitably chastened. So go out and buy all the Blobby nick-nacks you can. Blobby mugs. Blobby boxer shorts. Blobby cakes. Blobby togs and toys. Blobby computer games, bedroom furnishings and Mr Blobby's Make and Do Book. Go and fill the coffers of the BBC. And come this time next year, when Blobbymania has abated, a long-forgotten craze, take all that junk to the nearest car boot sale.

What *is* it about the English? What *is* Mr Blobby – just a gormless colossus or something of far grander import? I don't know. As someone said on the wireless just the other day, 'It's just far too big to get your intellectual hands around.'

John Lydon

He's not the Anti-Christ, he's just a very naughty boy. He used to puke in airports and fling filth at our pop kids. But now what does he do? He moans about being misrepresented, whinges about everything else and is professionally BORED.

THE INTERVIEW, Q vs Lydon, should have taken place several months ago but when I turned up on his Fulham doorstep and rang his bell, he failed to invite me into his lovely home. 'Go away!' the unmistakable voice came whining from the entry-phone. 'I'm fucked up. Go away!' I went away. Fortunately, all this time later, the singer now has 'fresh product' to promote, his punk rocker memoirs, Rotten: No Irish, No Blacks, No Dogs and so, in a First Class carriage of an Intercity train bound for Manchester (where he is to sign copies of the book for his adoring public), he is holding court. Ever the arch exhibitionist, he is showing off again. The trademark toxic glare is very much in evidence, the baggy, ballooning suit can only be described as comical, the voice swoops wildly, his every word an upper case italic, as he moans about how extremely *BORED* he is just sitting there on platform 15 and why can't the train just *GO*? (Well, possibly because this is the three o'clock train and it's not quite 10 to . . .) 'Doesn't the driver know *I'M* aboard?' he wheezes, swivelling those piercing eyes like a man possessed. 'Could he not feel the waft of arrogance as I walked down the platform? I'm *HERE* now, driver. We can *GO*!' A high-pitched snigger (another Rotten trademark: 'Heh, heh, cough, splutter, heh,' it goes) serves as the full stop to the comedic interlude.

Yes, Lydon, the boy who was Rotten, is arrogant alright. In Rotten: No Irish . . . the co-author (he had more than a little help from his friends) admits as much with glee. No one is safe from his scathing insults – Malcolm McLaren and Glen Matlock and The Clash and Cliff and Elton ('a fat buffoon') and the teacher who expelled him from school (Johnny later pissed on Mr Prentiss's grave) and poor old Bill Grundy, scorned and savaged all – except for himself. He invented punk rock all by himself, and his withering sarcasm and his ability to annoy are marks of a genius. And the Johnny Rotten persona was a brilliant creation of Lydon's making, believe it or not. 'Johnny Rotten' was based on Laurence Olivier in Richard III. Pardon? 'Having seen it aeons ago,' he writes, 'I took influences from Olivier's performance. I had never seen a pop singer present himself quite that way. It wasn't the norm. You're supposed to be a nice pretty boy, sing lovely songs and coo at the girlies. Richard III would have none of that. He got the girls in other ways.' But he says, 'Oh, you shouldn't believe everything you read, dear boy!' How Johnny loves to contradict himself. 'Arrogance is something I have aspired to and something that didn't come naturally. It's been perfected. It's a skill that I had to learn. I did a crash course through the Pistols.'

Lydon claims he's given up beer – 'I've had a spot of the Botticellis' – but when the PR woman from the publishing company goes to the buffet, it is beer Lydon calls for. This is a relief: John without beer and belching just wouldn't be John, somehow.

It's nearly 20 years now since this swaggering figure shocked the world by throwing up in airports, by throwing 'filth' at our 'pop kids', by throwing abuse at our own, dear Queen. In the book, he appears to claim . . . 'What do I appear to claim in the book? I haven't read it yet, heh heh heh . . .' In the book, he appears to claim that God Save The Queen was some kind of act of revolution, that he single-handedly paved the way for the monarchy's present travails and parlous condition.

'Yeah, it's just bog standard conversation now, isn't it, being rude about the royals? But that's the way life is. Somebody does it first, gets their head chopped off for it, and then it's alright. The only thing I feel sorry about is that Fergie did it ever so much better than me, heh heh heh, which is a real pisser. It makes me really like her, her whole attitude from start to finish was wonderful; milk it for all it's worth and then leave the sinking ship. I don't mind Fergie wanting to keep the curtains in her new luxurious manor. Why not? Much better than going out and buying a new set of Laura Ashley prints, isn't it?'

It's nearly 20 years since the boy brought a chapter of musical history to a close at San Francisco's Winterland, crouching on the stage and grumbling, 'Ever get the feeling you've been cheated?', The Sex Pistols' famous last words. What a terrible racket the group made that night; one has always imagined that the words were directed at the audience, but no. As Lydon tells it, he was asking himself the question – because The Sex Pistols had been a 'disaster' from start to finish.

'Ever get the feeling you've been cheated? Yeah. I was talking about myself and the band and everybody really all round. It's not a bad observation to have made. It's just fact, you know. It was just the whole sorry sourness of it all. The Sex Pistols just became a publicity fiasco rather than something with actual content and purpose. All that was thrown by the wayside and we ended up as some sorry rock'n'roll sad, sad thing that I didn't want to be a part of.'

In the beginning it was three blokes who couldn't play (well, Glen Matlock could, a bit) and one bloke who couldn't sing, in a rehearsal room, loathing one another. 'I still can't sing,' Lydon says with evident pride. 'My voice is an instrument of torture and that's good enough for me. I'm an expressionist.' A Situationist? 'Ooh, no, no, certainly not that. No poncey Left Bank politics from Paris for me.' Steve Jones and Paul Cook, the wideboys, wanted the band to be like The Faces. Johnny Rotten, the arty one, very much did not. Glen Matlock dug The Beatles: Johnny didn't. Why did he persevere with this seemingly hopeless project?

'Because what else was there to do? It never occurred to me to be in a band and to make music. They tried to get me to sing Maggie May! It was impossible. It should never have worked. Every day it just seemed to get worse – pitfalls, booby traps and mines. You must understand that when I joined The Sex Pistols, I had no prospects whatsoever and this was my last chance to do something and I tried to use it to the best of my ability, without being a cliché. I gave myself some weird disciplines and rigid morality codes to try to work things out in. I made it work.'

Yes, in the end it did work, didn't it? They swore on the telly and then they made some of the most exciting records ever and then they broke up.

'We could have been the weediest band ever. But it couldn't have worked without Steve being as structurally limited as he was. I found it absolutely thrilling to be next to him on a stage, the power that would come out of that poxy little amp with usually three strings, because that's all he could remember to hit at one point . . . But Glen's tunes I never came to terms with very well – too many memories and Beatles influences in there that I found completely unrefreshing. They would always remind me of my mum and dad's record collection, everything Glen ever did. He'd turn out some crappy old Beatles thing on a Dansette. Not very nice.

'I think what I learned in the Pistols was that I never wanted to write a love song in my entire life: it was a daily battle in rehearsal rooms because that's what they insisted I should be doing. They always wanted me to write love songs. Always. Seriously, Malcolm wanted some kind of, like, naughty version of The Bay City Rollers and that's what Glen wanted with his Soho poof's ideas. I had no training, no nothing, so I had no fears. My subject matters would be not based on anything previous at all. That's the best way to be. Ignorance leaves you without fear. It is a wonderful tool.'

John Lydon downs a can of beer, opens another, belches a satisfyingly loud belch, much to the consternation of fellow First Class 'customers'.

The Sex Pistols' encounter with Bill Grundy on the telly, the episode that prompted some daft bugger to kick his TV set in and worked the tabloid newspapers up into a froth of gleeful indignation, was shown again on Channel 4 the other night. And looking back on it, one is hard-pressed to recall what the fuss was all about. It was so tame. And that Johnny Rotten fellow appeared to be so timid.

'Yeah, but I'm sure that Kenneth Tynan (first person to use the F-word on the box) would look timid now, too. That's the point, small steps. But, yes, it is staggering to look back on all that and to see how pale it all was. When you look back on that, you really feel embarrassed. People should really feel sorry for me. A lot of what The Sex Pistols did was so tame, but you have to look at it in terms of history. There's no point in shocking people these days, there's no gain in it. It's trivial. I've got other emotions to tamper with.'

Are Nirvana 'shocking'? Are they The Sex Pistols of the 1990s?

I ask the punk philosopher, knowing full well with what scorn the enquiry will be greeted.

'Huh!' he goes and rolls his eyes. 'Huh! Well, that's Rory Gallagher, isn't it? That's the Rory Gallagher fan club. You take one look at those shirts and that's it. Those shirts just put me off. I'm sorry, Nirvana should lay off the Black Sabbath albums. Although I can see the good in everything – except for Guns N'Roses, for some peculiar reason. Actually, I was going to work with him, Kurt (Cobain), at some point last year. Kurt and me were going to meet but he would only meet me if I would take him to the zoo, him and his kid. It was just bizarre, I wasn't walking around a bloody zoo with him and his brat!'

In the autobiography, Lydon makes the astonishing revelation that Paul McCartney once expressed a desire to work with the spikey-topped star, too.

'Yeah, but I think he only wanted to do that to amuse his kids. Jesus! Things like that are just daft. They are embarrassing to remember. And I handled that all very badly because I just shied away without confronting it, locked myself in a room rather than cope with it, because it just made me feel so middle-aged all of a sudden. It was so hurtful. It was the industry getting back at me in the worst way possible. Oh, John, Paul would *lurve* to make a record with you. Oh my God! What have I done wrong? Has it come to this? You can't do that kind of thing. You just turn into Johnny Showbiz. You might as well call yourself Matt Monroe or Des O'Connor and pack up your troubles. That's when you're looking for the pension and you end up doing these dreadful charities, singing along with all the old farts, a big jam session at the end with 100,000 people thinking it's splendid. It's not. It's horrible. It's misery. Live Aid would have been spectacular and great if only three people had turned up . . .'

John rants on, spilling bile on charity concerts and Free Nelson Mandela, for several centuries. Charity concerts really get John's goat. But then so does almost everything. Glen Matlock (fed with a spunk sandwich at one point in the book)?

'No, I don't hate Glen,' he corrects. 'It's just his lifestyle to me is deeply silly. He was frightened of God Save The Queen because his mummy wouldn't like it and he thought the song was about fascism which it certainly was not. It's funny that the only person in the country who came to that conclusion was Glen Matlock –

and he was the bass player. But there again, before I formed Public Image, I don't think anybody ever listened to bass players.'

The Clash?

'Joe Strummer's never been over-endowed with wisdom, has he? I never liked that band. I always thought they were far too serious and far too childish. It was sloganeering. Pick up a copy of Karl Marx, underline a few sentences and call that "attitude". It's just daft.'

The Sex Pistols after John had quit the band?

'That Frigging In the Rigging, everything that went on after I left, was just awful. They shouldn't have carried on that way. It ruined it, completely shattered it. We should have ended with a full stop in San Francisco but they kept on and on at it and it's been to their detriment ever since. Going to Brazil to see bloody Ronnie Biggs – I found all that embarrassing and childish and stupid. I'm very bitter about that element of it, I don't applaud liars and cheats and thieves. There was nothing clever about that. People that hurt people to steal other people's money: where's the fun in that? Disgraceful.'

Malcolm McLaren, the self-styled Svengali of Pop (or something)?

'Malcolm was scared of me. I wasn't the stupid little gobshite that he originally perceived me to be, so he did his best to wreck the American tour. Him and Vivienne (Westwood) are manipulators; they like to manipulate the gullible. I took them on at their own game so they tried to write me out and pretend I'd never existed after I'd written some of those songs that put them on the map. That was annoying and very hurtful.'

Nancy Spungen, Sid Vicious's idiotic American girlfriend (deceased)?

'No, I think Nancy could have been a decent person. It's impossible for me to imagine, but . . . I could go on for years about Nancy. It would make a stunning play. Or Nancy: The Musical. Imagine that. Opening scene on some toilet, a massive shooting party going on. No, Nancy was dreadful. I don't feel bad about speaking ill of the dead, not at all. I mean, I'm hardly nice to the living, am I, now I come to think of it?'

Sid himself? Does Lydon feel any guilt about Sid's death? Does he feel he could have done more to keep his oft preposterous friend away from all those frightful drugs?

'Yes, well, that is, unfortunately, getting into hindsight, which is a thing I don't like. I don't know what I could have done to save Sidney. What could I do – hide his Lou Reed albums? I suppose that would have been a good start, because he did believe all that drugs and rock'n'roll nonsense to be something marvellous. He just did not see the humour in Lou Reed at all. He missed that completely. And then he had Nancy telling him that he was the real star of The Sex Pistols and Malcolm was doing that too and he believed it. And through the years, Sid had been mythologised to the point where he's seen as some kind of superhero when, I'm sorry, but the reality is very different. He was just stupid, bent on a slow suicide which should not be seen as something graceful or skilful or smart. It's just sad and stupid.'

The beers are slipping down a treat. Lydon talks of his glittering career as a Hollywood ac-tor (10 years ago he appeared in the not-very-good Order of Death alongside Harvey Keitel). 'Harvey's really famous now, isn't he? I like to think I helped him along the way, heh heh heh. I still get offered parts in films but the offers are so appalling, you just don't want to know. I don't like doing films. The endless takes, you just get *BORED*. Good actors have to be incredibly dull people because if you've got any kind of personality at all, it's just not going to work. But I heard I got a bit in In The Name Of The Father. Apparently, I'm on a poster in the prison. It makes the film, dear boy. I should get an Oscar for that.'

He talks of Chrissie Hynde, who Lydon once agreed to marry (immigration reasons) in exchange for two quid, then chickened out and sent Sid Vicious along as groom substitute (but, of course, Sid was too blotto to make it to the altar). 'Why didn't I marry Chrissie? Need you ask? Listen to any of her albums. No, to my mind you don't make commitments like that lightly because it would have been a lifelong commitment. I could definitely feel that there was a clinging going on with Chrissie which I didn't want none of, thank you. I have a fear of being mothered, I suppose. Women just want to mother me and smother me in marriage.'

Does Nora (Mrs Lydon) mother and smother you?

'No. Not at all, not at all. She won't let me get away with anything.'

Are you frightened of your wife?

'Yes, very much so.'

Is she the only person in the world you are frightened of?

'I think so. Oh, yes. Well, apart from my father, actually, because I can't fool him, not at all, not about anything.'

What did your father make of the Sex Pistols 'outrage', the airport puking and like unsavoury antics?

'(*Adopts Irish accent*) Oh, Jaysus. John, you're a fockin' disgrace! He thought we were throwing our lives away, which I must admit I felt we were doing many a time. It did all seem rather useless. Life is so disappointing and mediocre. That's why I want more of it, heh heh heh . . .'

Finally, he slumps back in the First Class seat, yawns, belches, and, for no evident reason, turns his attention to the subject of baldness. 'Howard Devoto (one-time singer with The Buzzcocks and Magazine) just gave up, didn't he? He went bald. It's very difficult when you're bald. People tend not to take you seriously. It's the end of your life. Coming back and promoting this book and dealing with this Sex Pistols stuff all again. I'm amazed just how many people from that period are now bald. It amazes me. I always had very, very thin hair, but Clairol and all the hair bleaches I've used over the decades have done wonders for me . . .'

The queue at Waterstone's book shop in Manchester that patiently awaits the appearance of the punk rock star of yesteryear, here to scribble his exciting signature for the public delight, contains many a bald or balding person. There are men in shellsuits with their Manchester United-shirted sons. There are what can only be described as grizzled hippies in overcoats of distressed condition. There is a matron of middle years who bears an extraordinary resemblance to Elizabeth Taylor (bloated version). There is not a spiky-top or safety-pin to be seen. And a strange dearth of leather. Where are you, punkers of yore? And when John sits at the book-stacked table to carry out his promotional chores, he is politeness itself, pressing the flesh, chatting to Peter 'Hooky' Hook out of New Order and saying 'Thanks for coming' to all and sundry in non-sarcastic tones. There's no gobbing, no larks with vomit, not even a lusty belch, this evening. Ever get the feeling you've been cheated? It is, as the saying goes, like a punk never happened.